Robert Renwick

Charters and Other Documents

Relating to the Royal Burgh of Stirling

Robert Renwick

Charters and Other Documents
Relating to the Royal Burgh of Stirling

ISBN/EAN: 9783337161392

Printed in Europe, USA, Canada, Australia, Japan

Cover: Foto ©Andreas Hilbeck / pixelio.de

More available books at **www.hansebooks.com**

₍CHARTERS

AND

OTHER DOCUMENTS

RELATING TO

THE ROYAL BURGH OF STIRLING.

A.D. 1124-1705.

GLASGOW:

PRINTED FOR THE PROVOST, MAGISTRATES, AND COUNCIL OF THE
BURGH OF STIRLING.

MDCCCLXXXIV.

FAC-SIMILE OF CHARTER (No. XIII.) BY KING DAVID

KING ALEXANDER II. TO THE BURGH

(*Stirling Charters*

PREFACE.

It was at one time anticipated that the publication of selections from the Charters and Records of the Burgh of Stirling would, after the issue of the forthcoming volume of Glasgow Charters, be the next undertaking of the Scottish Burgh Records Society. Preparations for the volume had been in progress for some time, but, with the announcement that the work of the Society would in all probability be shortly brought to a close, it became necessary to consider the expediency of devising some other way of accomplishing the object in view. The Corporation of Stirling were not inclined to abandon altogether the proposed publication, and eventually they gave instructions for having at least the principal Charters printed, reserving for after consideration the question as to whether or not these should be followed by selections from the Council Records.

In compliance with the instructions thus given, the present volume has been compiled. In addition to a number of miscellaneous documents, it embraces all the Royal Charters granted to the Burgh, the originals of which have been found, as well as others transcribed from the Great Seal Register where the originals were not available.

The great bulk of the matter contained in the book has not been previously printed; but, to add to the completeness of the collection, especially in the earlier period, a few charters have been taken from some of the published chartularies and registers of religious houses issued by the Bannatyne and Grampian Clubs, and other publications have also been resorted to. In the Table of Contents will be found a reference to the source from which each document is taken.

The earliest royal charter known to have been granted to the Burgh of Stirling is that of King Alexander the Second, dated 18th August, 1226; but it is well known that Stirling had a municipal existence for at least a century before that time. The Charter of 1226 is granted to "our burgesses of Strivelyn," implying a previous burghal organization, while the charters of King David the First (1124-53) and King William the Lion (1165-1214), reprinted in this volume, refer to "my burgh" of Stirling as an existing institution. In the words of the warrant for the charter by King Charles the First, Stirling was "ane of the maist ancient burghes of this his Hienes kingdom of Scotland, being erectet *before* the days of umquhile King Alexander."

As accounting, so far, for the lateness in date of the first direct grant from the crown, it may be mentioned that it was not till the reign of Alexander's immediate predecessor that burghs appear to have begun to ask and obtain charters from the King. Alexander's charter to Stirling is somewhat similar to those granted to some other Royal Burghs in his and the preceding reign, and is partly made up of provisions imported from the old laws relating to burghs and made applicable to the special circumstances of Stirling. The original has not been preserved, but it has fortunately been engrossed at full length in a confirmatory charter by King David II., which is still in existence, and is in a good state of preservation. A *facsimile* of it, produced by photo-lithography, is prefixed to the volume.

There is also given the photo-lithograph of another charter, about which a word may be said. Originally each burgess, as a crown vassal, paid a yearly rent to the King for his property in the burgh. These rents, with the small customs, fines of the burgh court, &c., in course of time came to be collected by the bailies of the burgh, who, at intervals of usually a year or more, accounted for their intromissions to the Great Chamberlain, and had their accounts audited in exchequer. Afterwards the system crept in of burghs obtaining yearly tacks of their revenues, and eventually feu charters came to be given, whereby, in consideration of a fixed yearly payment, the community of a burgh obtained a renewed grant with a perpetual right to collect and apply to its own uses the

rents, customs, and dues formerly levied by the Crown. Stirling obtained
such a charter from King Robert the Second on 13th July, 1386, the
annual feu-duty being fixed at £13.

When making a selection from the old charters and documents, such
of them as were not considered to be of sufficient importance to be printed
in full were arranged and inventoried, and of those abstracts of the more
interesting are given in Appendix No. I. The remainder, about a hundred
in number, are largely composed of titles to individual properties, and are
not of much public interest.

The regular series of the records of the Town Council as now existing
commence in 1597; but in searching amongst the old papers there were
discovered some fragments of the earlier records embracing portions of the
years 1561-3 and 1594-7. Extracts from these are printed in Appendix III.
In Appendix II. are given abstracts of some of the documents contained
in fragments of protocol books, (1473-80), which were also found in the
course of the search.

In the frontispiece is given a representation of the old common seal
of the Burgh. It is thus described in Mr. Henry Laing's "Descriptive
Catalogue of Impressions from Ancient Scottish Seals":—

"Stirling, No. 1138.—A fine large seal, in excellent preservation, and of a re-
markable design. A bridge of seven arches; from the centre one rises a large cross,
with the Saviour extended. Above, on the dexter, a star, and on the sinister a
crescent. On the dexter side of the cross are three soldiers armed with bows and
arrows, the foremost one discharging his arrow towards three soldiers on the sinister
side of the cross, who are armed with spears, the foremost one in the act of charging. *Hic Armis Bruti Scoti Stant Hic Cruce Tuti.*"

"No. 1189.—Counter Seal.—The front of a castle; at each side are branches of
foliage, and scattered round the top and sides are five stars and two roses. *Con-
tinet Hoc In Se Nemus Et Castrum Strivelinse.*"

The old seal—the original matrix of which is still kept at Stirling—
was the one appended to such of the documents printed in this volume as

required to be attested in that way; but, as none of the seals so affixed
are in a perfect condition, the plate has been drawn from a new cast
taken for the purpose. The seal, also an ancient one, which is now
generally used is the one of which an illustration is given on the title
page.

Of late years materials, invaluable for a proper and authentic history
of the ancient Burgh of Stirling, have been accumulating. The several
club books, and the rapidly-increasing series of historical works issuing from
the General Register House in Edinburgh, are full of deeply-interesting
matter suitable, but hitherto almost entirely unused, for that purpose. It
is hoped that the contents of this volume will tend still further to elucidate
the history of the burgh, and possibly encourage the Corporation to enter-
tain with favour the publication of a selection from their early records.

With the aid of the Table of Contents and the Index, in which, for
convenience in genealogical research, every name is inserted, it is believed
that there will be little difficulty in finding anything in the volume which
may be wanted.

R. RENWICK.

GLASGOW, *December*. 1884.

TABLE OF CONTENTS.

TABLE OF CONTENTS.

. . . .

c

APPENDIX.

d

CHARTERS AND DOCUMENTS

RELATING TO

THE BURGH OF STIRLING.

CHARTERS AND DOCUMENTS

THE BURGH OF STIRLING.

I.

CHARTER by King David the First to the Church of the Holy Trinity of Dunfermline of, *inter alia*, a dwelling place in his Burgh of Stirling. Dunfermline, *circa* 1124-7.

DAUID, Dei gratia, Rex Scottorum: Roberto, electo Sancti Andree, et omnibus comitibus et baronibus et omnibus fidelibus suis, salutem. Sciatis me concessisse et dedisse in perpetuum in elemosina, pro anima patris et matris mee et fratrum et antecessorum meorum, ecclesie Sancte Trinitatis de Dunfermlin omnem decimationem de omnibus dominiis meis de Dunfermlin nisi de illis que ad alias ecclesias pertinent. Et unam mansuram in burgo meo de

DAVID, by the grace of God, King of Scots: To Robert, elect of St. Andrew's, and to all earls and barons, and all his faithful, greeting. Know ye that I have granted and given for ever in alms, for the soul of my father and of my mother and of my brothers and ancestors, to the Church of the Holy Trinity of Dunfermlin, all the tithe of all my lordships of Dunfermlin, except of those pertaining to other churches. Also one dwelling place in my burgh of Dunfermlin, free and quiet, and

Dunfermlin, liberam et quietam, et aliam in burgo meo iu Striuelin et aliam in burgo meo de Perth, et aliam in burgo meo de Edenesburg. Testibus: Roberto, electo Sancti Andree, et Herberto, cancellario. Apud Dunfermlin.

another in my burgh [of] Strivelin, and another in my burgh of Perth and another in my burgh of Edenesburg. Witnesses: Robert, elect of St. Andrews, and Herbert, chancellor. At Dunfermlin.

II.

EXCERPT from Charter by King David the First, granting and confirming to the Church of the Holy Trinity of Dunfermline, *inter alia*, a dwelling place, two churches, and other property in the Burgh of Stirling. *Circa* 1129-30.

IN NOMINE Sancte Trinitatis, ego Dauid, Dei gratia, Rex Scottorum, auctoritate regia ac potestate, Henrici filii mei assensu et Matildis Regine, uxoris mee, episcoporum, comitum baronumque regni mei confirmacione et testimonio, clero etiam adquiescenteque populo, ecclesie Sancte Trinitatis Dunfermeline, predecessorum meorum pietatis studio et largitionis initiate, omnia subscripta concedo et pace perpetua confirmo . . . Preterea do eidem ecclesie vnam mansuram in Berwich, aliam in Rokesburc, aliam in burgo de Hadingtun, aliam in Edenburg, aliam in Linlitheu, aliam in burgo de Striuelin, et in endem villa duas ecclesias et vnam carucatam terre que adiacet ipsi ecclesie

IN THE NAME of the Holy Trinity, I David, by the grace of God, King of Scots, by royal authority and power, with consent of Henry my son and Queen Matilda my wife, with the confirmation and testimony of the bishops, earls and barons of my kingdom, the clergy also and the people acquiescing, grant and in perpetual peace confirm all the underwritten to the church of the Holy Trinity of Dunfermline, founded through the zeal for religion and liberality of my predecessors, . . . Moreover I give to the said church a dwelling place in Berwick, another in Roxburgh, another in the burgh of Hadington, another in Edinburgh, another in Linlithgow, another in the burgh of Strivelin, and in the same town two churches and a carucate of land which lies contiguous to the said churches . . .

. . Et medietatem coriorum et seporum et sagiminis omnium bestiarum que occidentur ad festinitates tenendas in Striuelin et inter Forth et Tay . . . Preter ista supradicta dono et concedo abbati et monachis ut habeant singulis annis v mercas argenti ad uestimenta eorum de primis nauibus que ueuient ad Striuelin uel ad Perth.

Also the half of the hides, fat and tallow of all beasts killed at the feasts held in Strivelin and between the Forth and Tay . . . Besides those above mentioned, I give and grant to the abbot and monks that they may have in every year five merks of silver for their vestments from the first ships arriving at Stirling or at Perth. . .

III.

CHARTER by King David the First to the abbot of Dunfermline of the tithe of his rent of Stirling. Stirling, *circa* 1124-53.

DAUID, Rex Scottorum: Vicecomitibus et prepositis de Striuelin, salutem. Sciatis me concessisse Deo et abbati de Dunfermlyn decimam denariorum de censu meo de Strivelin. Quare uolo et firmiter precipio ut sine omni disturbacione faciatis ei eam habere sicut denarij ueuient. Testibus: Roberto de Bruus et Hugo de Moreuilla. Apud Striuelin.

DAVID, King of Scots: To the sheriffs and bailies of Striuelyn, greeting. Know ye that I have granted to God and the abbot of Dunfermlyn the tithe of the pennies of my maill of Strivelin. Wherefore I will and firmly command that ye cause him to have the same without any trouble as the pennies shall accrue. Witnesses: Robert of Bruus and Hugh of Moreville. At Striuelin.

IV.

EXCERPT from Charter by King David the First to the Abbey of Holyrood of Edinburgh, containing grant from the King's rent of Stirling, a toft there, and the draught of a net for fishing. *Circa* 1143-7.

IN NOMINE Domini nostri Jhesu Christi, et in honore Sancte Crucis, et Sancte

IN THE NAME of our Lord Jesus Christ, and in honour of the Holy Rood, and of

Marie Uirginis, omniumque sanctorum, ego Dauid Dei gratia Rex Scottorum, regali auctoritate, assensu Henrici filii mei, et episcoporum regni mei, comitum quoque baronumque confirmatione et testimonio, clero etiam aquiescente et populo, diuino instinctu, omnia subscripta concedo ecclesie Sancte Crucis Edwinesburgensi, et pace perpetua confirmo . . . Et redditum centum solidorum singulis annis ad indumenta canonicorum de cano meo de Pert et hoc de primis nauibus que negotiationis causa uenient ad Pert; et si forte non uenerint concedo prefate ecclesie de meo redditu de Edwines- burg quadraginta solidos et de Striueline uiginti solidos et de Pert quadraginta solidos.   Et unum toftum in Striueline, et tractum unius retis ad piscandum   . .

Saint Mary the Virgin, and of all saints, I, David, by the grace of God, King of Scots, of my royal authority, with the assent of Henry my son, and with the confirmation and testimony of the bishops of my kingdom, of the earls also and barons, the clergy and the people also assenting, of divine prompting, grant and in perpetual peace confirm all the things underwritten to the church of the Holy Rood of Edinburgh. .   . And a rent of a hundred shillings yearly for the clothing of the canons, from my cane of Perth, and this from the first ships that come to Perth for the sake of trade; and if perchance it happen that they do not come I grant to the aforesaid Church from my rent of Edinburgh forty shillings, and from Stirling twenty shillings, and from Perth forty shillings. And one toft in Stirling, and the draught of one net for fishing.

V.

CHARTER by King David the First to the Church of St. Mary of Stirling (Abbey of Cambuskenneth), containing grants to that church from the revenues of Stirling. *Circa* 1147.

IN NOMINE Patris et Filii et Spiritus Sancti, amen.   Ego Dauid, Dei gracia, Rex Scotorum, assensu Henrici filii mei et episcoporum regni mei comitumque et baronum confirmatione et testimonio, concedo ecclesie Sancte Marie de

IN THE NAME of the Father and of the Son and of the Holy Spirit, amen.   I, David, by the grace of God King of Scots, with consent of Henry, my son, and with the confirmation and testimony of the bishops of my kingdom and of the earls and

Striueling et canonicis in ea regulariter viuentibus ea que subscripta sunt et
pace perpetua confirmo. Hec itaque sunt que prefate ecclesie concedo : terram
de Cambuskynneth et piscaturam inter eandem terram et Pollemase et vnum
rethe in aqua ; terram quoque de Colling cum nemore et suis rectis diuisis ;
terram eciam de Tulibodeuin que est inter aquam ciusdem terre et terram
de Lochin ; quadraginta quoque solidos de redditu meo de Striueling et
canum vnius nauis, et vnam salinam et todidem terre quot habet vna de
salinis meis, et decimam firme de dominiis meis de Striueling ; et oblationes
que in predicta ecclesia oblate fuerint ; et insulam que est inter Pollemase
et Tulibodeuin, et viginti cudermis de caseis redditus mei de Striueling.
Eandem quoque libertatem et consuetudinem quam ceteris ecclesiis terre mee
concessi et confirmaui eidem ecclesie concedo et confirmo. Volo itaque vt
quecunque predicta ecclesia in presenti possidet vel in futuro possessura est,
ita quiete et libere sicut ego prefatas terras possideo, possideat. Salua
defensione regni et justicia regali si prelatus aliquo impulsu a justicia
exorbitauerit. Hujus confirmationis testes sunt Comes Henricus, filius
Regis ; [etc.].

barons, grant and confirm in perpetual peace to the church of St. Mary of Striveling
and to the canons living under rule in the same, the things underwritten. These,
therefore, are what I give to the foresaid church : the land of Cambuskynneth and
the fishing between the said land and Pollemase and one net in the water ; also the
land of Colling with the wood and its just marches ; also the land of Tulibodevin
which is between the water of the said land and the land of Lochin ; also forty
shillings from my rent of Striveling and the cane of one ship and one salt pit, and
as much land as pertains to one of my salt pits, and the tithe of the farm of my
lordships of Striveling ; and the offerings which shall be made in the foresaid church ;
and the island which is between Pollemase and Tulibodevin, and twenty "cudermis"
of cheese of my rent of Striveling. I grant and confirm also to the said church the
same liberty and custom which I have granted and confirmed to other churches of
my land. I will therefore that whatsoever the foresaid church at present possesses,
or shall in the future possess, it may possess as quietly and freely as I possess
the foresaid lands. Saving the defence of the kingdom and royal justice, if the
judge by any impulse swerve from justice. The witnesses of this confirmation are
Earl Henry, son of the King ; [etc.].

VI.

CHARTER by King William the Lion granting to the Bishop of Glasgow a toft in the Burgh of Stirling. Stirling, *circa* 1188-99.

WILLELMUS, Dei gracia, Rex Scottorum: Omnibus probis hominibus tocius terre sue, clericis et laicis, salutem. Sciant presentes et futuri me dedisse et concessisse et hac carta mea confirmasse Deo et Sancto Kentigerno et Jocelino, episcopo Glasguensi, omnibusque eius successoribus vnum plenarium toftum in burgo meo de Strinelin. Tenendum in liberam et quietam et perpetuam elemosinam, ita libere, quiete, plenarie et honorifice sicut aliquis episcopus in toto regno meo aliquod toftum in aliquo burgorum meorum, liberius, quietius, plenarius et honorificentius, tenet et possidet. Testibus: Comite Dauid, fratre meo; [etc.].

WILLIAM, by the grace of God, King of Scots: To all good men of his whole land, clerics and laics, greeting. Know ye, present and to come, that I have given and granted and by this my charter have confirmed to God and St. Kentigern and to Joceline, bishop of Glasgow, and to all his successors, one full toft in my burgh of Strivelin. To be held in free and quiet and perpetual alms; as freely, quietly, fully and honorably, as any bishop in my whole kingdom holds and possesses any toft in any of my burghs most freely, quietly, fully and honorably. Witnesses: Earl David, my brother; [etc.]

VII.

CHARTER by King Alexander the Second granting to his Burgesses of Stirling a Weekly Market, a Merchant Guild, and other Privileges. Kyncardin, 18th August, 1226.

ALEXANDER, Dei gratia, Rex Scottorum: Episcopis, abbatibus, comitibus, baronibus, iusticiariis, vicecomitibus, prepositis, ministris et omnibus probis hominibus tocius terre sue, clericis et laicis, salutem. Sciant presentes et

ALEXANDER, by the grace of God, King of Scots: To bishops, abbots, earls, barons, justiciars, sheriffs, provosts, officers, and all good men of his whole land, clerics and laics, greeting. Be it known to those present and to come that we have granted and

futuri nos concessisse et carta nostra confirmasse burgensibus nostris de
Striuelyn diem fori in burgo nostro de Striuelyn, scilicet diem Sabbati in
qualibet ebdomoda; nostramque firmam pacem iuste dedisse omnibus qui
ad forum illud venient; et prohibemus firmiter ne quis illis qui ad predictum
forum nostrum venient in veniendo vel in redeundo iniuriam vel molestiam
aut grauamen aliquod iniuste inferat, super nostram plenariam forisfacturam.
Prohibemus etiam firmiter ne quis mercator extraneus infra vicecomitatum
de Striuelyn extra burgum nostrum de Striuelyn aliquid emat vel vendat
super nostram defensionem, sed extranei mercatores deferant mercaturas suas
ad burgum nostrum de Striuelyn et ibi eas vendant et denarios suos implicent.
Siquis vero mercator extraneus super hanc defensionem nostram inuentus
fuerit in vicecomitatu de Striuelyn aliquid emens vel vendens capiatur et
detineatur donec voluntatem nostram de eo precepimus.   Prohibemus etiam
firmiter ne quis mercator extraneus secet pannum suum ad vendendum in
burgo nostro de Striuelyn nisi a die ascensionis Domini vsque ad vincula
Sancti Petri, infra quos terminos volumus vt ipsi pannos suos secent ad
vendendum in foro de Striuelyn et ibi vendant et emant pannum et alias
mercaturas communiter cum burgensibus nostris sicut dominici burgenses

by our charter confirmed to our burgesses of Strivelyn a market day in our burgh of
Strivelyn, that is to say Saturday in every week ; and we have rightly given
our firm peace to all who may come to that market : and we strictly forbid any one
wrongously to cause injury or molestation or any trouble to those who shall attend
our foresaid market, in coming or returning, upon our full forfeiture.   We also
strictly forbid any stranger merchant within the sheriffdom of Strivelyn to buy
or sell anything outwith our burgh of Strivelyn, on pain of our interdict, but stranger
merchants shall bring their merchandise to our burgh of Strivelyn and there sell the
same and interchange their pennies.   Also, if any stranger merchant, upon this our
prohibition, shall be found buying or selling anything in the sheriffdom of Strivelyn
he shall be apprehended and detained until we have declared our pleasure concerning
him.   We also strictly forbid any stranger merchant to cut his cloth to be sold
within our burgh of Strivelyn except from the day of the ascension of our Lord till
the feast of St. Peter *ad vincula* (Lammas) within which terms we will that they
cut their cloth to be sold in the market of Strivelyn, and there sell and buy cloth
and other merchandise in common with our burgesses in the same manner as our

nostri, saluis rectitudinibus nostris. Precipimus etiam vt omnes qui manent
in burgo nostro de Striuelyn, et cum burgensibus nostris, ad forum communicare
voluerint, communicent cum illis ad auxilia nostra reddenda cuiuscumque
homines sint. Prohibemus etiam ne aliqua taberna habeatur in aliqua villa
in vicecomitatu de Striuelyn nisi vbi miles sit dominus ville et in ea manens,
et ibi non habeatur nisi vna sola taberna. Concedimus etiam eisdem burgensibus nostris de Striuelyn vt habeant gildam suam mercatorialem, exceptis
fullonibus et telariis. Prohibemus etiam firmiter ne quis manens extra
burgum nostrum de Striuelyn in vicecomitatu de Striuelyn faciat pannum
tinctum vel tonsum infra vicecomitatum de Striuelyn nec facere faciat, preter
burgenses nostros de Striuelyn qui sint de gilda mercatoria et qui communi-
cant ad auxilia nostra soluenda cum burgensibus nostris de Striuelyn exceptis
illis qui de hac libertate cartas suas[1] hucusque habuerunt. Quare prohibemus
firmiter ne quis in vicecomitatu de Striuelyn facere presumat pannum, tinctum vel tonsum super nostram plenariam forisfacturam. Si vero aliquis
pannus tinctus vel tonsus inuentus fuerit factus super hanc defensionem
nostram precipimus vicecomiti nostro quatenus capiat ipsum pannum et inde
faciat secundum quod consuetudo fuit tempore Regis Dauid. Has autem

proper burgesses, saving our rights. We command, also, that all who dwell in
our burgh of Strivelyn, and who wish to take part with our burgesses at the market,
shall take part with them in contributing to our aids, whose men soever they be.
We forbid also that any tavern shall be kept in any town in the sheriffdom of
Strivelyn, unless where a knight is lord of the town and dwells therein, and there
shall not be kept more than one single tavern. We grant also to our said burgesses
of Strivelyn that they shall have a merchant guild, except the waulkers and
weavers. We strictly forbid, likewise, that any one dwelling outside our burgh of
Strivelyn in the sheriffdom thereof make or cause to be made cloth dyed or shorn
within the sheriffdom of Strivelyn other than our burgesses of Strivelyn who are of
the merchant guild, and who take part in paying our aids with our burgesses of
Strivelyn, except those who have had their charters with this liberty heretofore.
Wherefore we strictly forbid any one in the sheriffdom of Strivelyn to presume to
make cloth dyed or shorn, upon our full forfeiture. And if any cloth dyed or shorn
shall be found made upon this our prohibition, we command our sheriff to seize
the said cloth and do thereupon as was the custom in the time of King David.

[1] See Foot-note 15, p. 18.

omnes consuetudines et libertates predictas predictis burgensibus nostris de
Striuelyn concedimus et hac carta nostra confirmamus.   Testibus: Thoma
de Striuelyn, cancellario; Henrico de Balliolo, camerario; Waltero Comyn;
Henrico de Striuelyn, filio comitis Dauid; Willelmo de Burgo, Radulpho de
Champayngis, Hugo de Cambrun, Willelmo de Lyndesey, Johanne de
Vallibus, Waltero Byset.   Apud Kyncardyn, decimo octauo die Augusti anno
regni nostri duodecimo.

And all these customs and liberties foresaid we grant and by this our charter confirm
to our foresaid burgesses of Strivelyn.   Witnesses: Thomas of Strivelyn, chancellor;
Henry of Balliol, chamberlain; Walter Comyn; Henry of Strivelyn, son of Earl
David; William of Burgh, Radulph of Champayn, Hugh of Cambrun, William of
Lyndesey, John de Vaux, Walter Byset.   At Kyncardyn on the eighteenth day of
August in the twelfth year of our reign.

VIII.

CHARTER by King Alexander the Second granting to his Burgesses of
Stirling Freedom from Toll and Custom on their Goods throughout the
whole Kingdom.   Edinburgh, 20th July, 1227.

ALEXANDER, Dei gratia, Rex Scottorum: Omnibus probis hominibus
tocius terre sue, salutem.   Sciatis quod concessimus burgensibus nostris de
Striuelyn qui in eodem burgo erunt manentes vt quieti sint inperpetuum
de tolneio et consuetudine de dominicis catallis suis per totum regnum
nostrum.   Quare firmiter prohibemus ne quis eos contra hanc concessionem
nostram iniuste vexare presumat exigendo ab eis tolneium vel consuetudinem
de dominicis catallis suis.   Testibus: Magistro Matheo, cancellario; Johanne
comite de Huntyngtoun; Henrico de Balliolo, camerario; Henrico de

ALEXANDER, by the grace of God, King of Scots: To all good men of his whole land,
greeting.   Know ye that we have granted to our burgesses of Strivelyn who are
dwelling in the said burgh, that they may be for ever quit of toll and custom of
their proper goods throughout our whole kingdom.   Wherefore we firmly
forbid that any one, contrary this our grant, presume unjustly to trouble them in
exacting from them toll or custom of their proper goods.   Witnesses: Master
Matthew, chancellor; John, Earl of Huntyngtoun; Henry of Balliol, chamberlain;

Striuelyn, filio comitis Dauid; Petro de Valoniis; Waltero Comyn; Alexandro de Striuelyn; Reginaldo de Crauford, vicecomite de Are. Apud Edinburgh, vicesimo die Julij, anno regni nostri terciodecimo.

Henry of Strivelyn, son of Earl David; Peter de Valine, Walter Comyn, Alexander of Strivelyn, Reginald of Crauford, sheriff of Are. At Edinburgh, on the twentieth day of July, in the thirteenth year of our reign.

IX.

CHARTER by King Alexander the Third to the Church of St. Mary of Stirling (Abbey of Cambuskenneth) of twenty merks from the ferm of his burgh of Stirling. Stirling, 30th April, 1265.

ALEXANDER, Dei gracia, Rex Scotorum: Omnibus probis hominibus totius terre sue, clericis et laicis, salutem. Sciant presentes et futuri nos dedisse et concassisse et hac carta nostra confirmasse Deo et beate Marie de Striueling et canonicis ibidem Deo seruientibus et imperpetuum scruituris, in excambium molendini nostri de Clacmannan, viginti marcas singulis annis percipiendas de firma burgi nostri de Striueling, scilicet, medietatem ad Penthecosten et aliam medietatem ad festum Sancti Martini. Quare volumus vt predicti canonici predictas viginti marcas ad predictos terminos habeant et teneant de firma predicti burgi nostri de Striueling, in liberam, puram et perpetuam elemosinam, adeo libere et quiete, plenarie et honorifice, sicut aliqua elemosina in tota terra nostra, liberius et quietius, plenius et honorificentius tenetur et

ALEXANDER, by the grace of God, King of Scots: To all good men of his whole land, clerics and laics, greeting. Be it known to all men, present and to come, that we have given and granted and by this our charter confirmed to God and St. Mary of Scriveling and the canons there serving God, and to serve for ever, in excambion of our mill of Clacmannan, twenty merks every year payable from the ferme of our burgh of Striveling, namely, one half at Whitsunday and the other half at the feast of St. Martin. Wherefore we will that at the foresaid terms the foresaid canons have and hold the foresaid twenty merks, of the ferme of our foresaid burgh of Striveling, in free, pure, and perpetual alms, as freely and quietly, fully and honorably as any alms in our whole land is most freely and quietly, fully and honor-

possidetur.   Prohibemus eciam firmiter ne preposti nostri de Striueling
predictis canonicis sepedictas viginti marcas vltra terminos eis statutos detin-
cant super nostram plenariam forisfacturam.   Volumus eciam vt dicti canonici,
preter dictas viginti marcas, percipiant de firma eiusdem burgi nostri de
Striueling tres marcas annuas quas percipere consuerunt ex dono antecessorum
nostrorum.   Testibus: Magistro Matheo, cancellario, Henrico de Bailliolo,
Johanne de Makkiswell, Barnardo Fraser, Waltero Cumyn, Dauid Marschell,
Johanne de Haya, Waltero Bysset, Alexandro de Striueling.   Apud Striueling
vltimo die Aprilis, anno regni domini regis sexdecimo.

ably, held and possessed.   We also strictly forbid our provosts of Stirling to withhold
the foresaid twenty merks from the foresaid canons beyond the terms appointed to
them, upon our full forfeiture.   We will also that, besides the said twenty merks,
the said canons shall uplift from the ferme of our said burgh of Strineling the three
merks yearly which they were wont to uplift by gift of our predecessors.   Witnesses:
Master Matthew, chancellor; Henry of Bailliol, John of Makkiswell, Barnard Fraser,
Walter Cumyn, David Marschell, John of Hay, Walter Bysett, Alexander of
Striveling.   At Striveling, on the last day of April, in the sixteenth year of the reign
of our Lord the King.

X.

CHARTER by the Abbot and Convent of Arbroath to Richard Cristinson of
all their lands in the Burgh of Stirling.   A.D. 1299.

NOTUM SIT omnibus fidelibus presens scriptum visuris vel audituris, quod nos,
frater Nycholaus, permissione diuina abbas de Aberbrothoc, et eiusdem loci conuentus, de expresso consensu tocius capituli nostri, damus concedimus et presenti
carta nostra confirmamus Ricardo, filio Cristini, filij Lochlani, et heredibus
suis, omnes terras nostras quas habemus in burgo de Strewelin, iacentes

BE IT KNOWN to all the faithful who may see or hear the present writing, that we,
brother Nycholas, by divine permission abbot of Aberbrothoc, and the convent of the
same place, with the express consent of the whole of our chapter, give, grant, and by
our present charter confirm to Richard, son of Cristine, son of Lachlan, and his heirs,
all our lands which we have in the burgh of Strivelin, lying between the land of

inter terram religiosorum virorum abbatis et conuentus de Culros ex parte
australi, ex parte vna, et terram Sancte Marie de Strevelin quam idem Ricardus
tenet ad firmam ex parte boreali, ex parte altera, quas Johannes de Drilaw
de nobis iure tenuit hereditario et quas Willelmus, filius et heres eiusdem
quondam Johannis, pro defectu seruicij nobis inde debiti per fustum et
baculum, in pleno capitulo nostro apud Aberbrothoc, sursum reddidit ac
pro se et heredibus suis resignauit inperpetuum.   Tenendas et habendas dicto
Ricardo et heredibus suis in liberum burgagium, de nobis et successoribus
nostris, cum omnibus commoditatibus, aisiamentis et iustis pertinencijs suis,
salua nobis iusticia regalitatis et alijs placitis nostris in dictis terris cum
voluerimus tenendis.   Reddendo inde, nobis et successoribus nostris dictus
Ricardus et heredes sui, quatuor solidos et sex denarios argenti ad duos
anni terminos, medietatem videlicet ad festum Penthecostes et aliam
medietatem ad festum Sancti Martini, in hyeme; et inueniendo abbati
de Aberbrothoc qui pro tempore fuerit et eius monachis et conuersis
et clericis, balliuis et attornatis eorundem, venientibus pro negocijs et causis
monasterij. quociens aduenerint, singulis secundum statum suum, cum familia
sua, honestum hospicium; aulam in qua honeste poterunt comedere, cum

religious men, the abbot and convent of Culros, on the south side, on the one part,
and the land of Saint Marie of Strevelin which the said Robert holds in farm, on
the north side, on the other part, which John of Drilaw held of us by heritable
right, and which William, son and heir of the said deceased John, for default of
service due to us therefrom, in our full chapter held at Aberbrothoc gave up, and for
him and his heirs resigned for ever.   To hold and to have to the said Richard and
his heirs in free burgage of us and our successors, with all commodities, easements and
their just pertinents, reserving to us the right of holding courts of regality and our
other pleas in the said lands when we will.   Paying therefor, the said Richard and
his heirs, to us and our successors, four shillings and sixpence of silver at two terms in
the year, namely, one half at Whitsunday and the other half at Martinmas, in winter;
and providing honest lodging for the abbot of Aberbrothoc, who shall be for the time,
and for his monks, lay brethren and clerks, their bailies and attornies, coming for the
business and causes of the monastery, as often as they shall arrive, each according
to his station, with their attendants; a hall in which they may becomingly eat, with
tables and trestles and other furniture, a spence with a buttery, a chamber or

mensis et trestulis et alijs apparatibus, spensam cum butellario, cameram seu cameras vbi honeste recubare poterunt, coquinam honestam et stabulum pro equis ad numerum triginta equorum et infra.   Inuenient eciam in aduentibus predictis personis sufficienter focale, tam in aula et in camera quam in coquina, albas candelas de sepo quo wlgariter nuncupantur *candele de Peris*, lecterium stramentum in aula et camera et sal pro mensis.   Sed si abbas vel monachi sui, clerici aut attornati sui predicti, vltra tres noctes continue hospitati fuerint, dictus Ricardus aut heredes sui non tenebuntur pro illa vice ad focale et albas candelas, sed omnia alia onera subibunt pro mora personarum predictarum et eorum familia.   Preterea, cum nuncij vel cursores abbatis interuenerint ad hospitandum sine contradictione admittentur, ad sumptus tamen pro cibarijs suis idem Ricardus et heredes sui non tenebuntur.   Volumus etiam quod dictus Ricardus et heredes sui leuent firmam nobis debitam de duabus peciis terre quas Thomas Sanser et Willelmus de Kyrcaudi, clericus, tenent infra terras nostras predictas, vna cum proparte seruicij nobis debiti de eisdem racione hostilagij, et nobis de ipsa firma et hostilagio respondeant sicut de firmis et hostilagijs nobis debitis pro alijs terris nostris quas de nobis tenent vt supradictum est.   Dictus vero Ricardus seu heredes sui nullo modo

chambers where they may comfortably sleep, a decent kitchen, and a stable for their horses to the number of thirty horses and under. They shall provide also on the coming of the foresaid persons sufficient fuel, as well in the hall and chamber as in the kitchen, white candles of tallow, which are commonly called *candles of Paris*, bedding and straw in the hall and chamber, and salt for the table. But if the abbot or his monks, his clerks or attorneys foresaid, shall continue in the lodging beyond three nights, the said Richard or his heirs shall not be held liable in that case for fuel and white candles, but they shall undertake all other charges during the stay of the foresaid persons and their attendants. Moreover, when the messengers or runners of the abbot shall come to the lodging they shall be admitted without gainsaying, but the said Richard and his heirs shall not be liable for the cost of their food. We will also that the said Richard and his heirs uplift the maill owing to us for two pieces of land which Thomas Sanser and William of Kyrcaudi, clerk, hold within our foresaid lands, together with a proportion of the service owing to us from the same, on account of the hostilage, and they shall account to us for the said maill and hostilage as for the maills and hostilages owing to us for our

terras et hostilagia predicta vendent, impignorabunt seu alienabunt vel ad firmam dimittent, alicui persone, nisi de consensu predictorum abbatis et conuentus qui pro tempore fuerint. In cuius rei testimonium presenti carte commune sigillum capituli nostri concorditer fecimus apponi. Teste eodem capitulo.

other lands which they hold of us as is aforesaid. Also the said Richard or his heirs shall in no wise sell, impledge, or alienate or let to any person the foresaid lands and hostilages, except with the consent of the foresaid abbot and convent who shall be for the time. In witness whereof we have with one consent caused the common seal of our chapter to be affixed to this present charter. Witness the same chapter.

XI.

CHARTER by King Robert the First confirming to the Burgesses of Stirling the right of Pasturage for their Horses in the Forests between the Waters of Forth and Carron, and of Digging Peats in the Peat Moss of Skewok. Stirling, 4th April, 1317.

Sciatis quod quarto die Aprilis, anno Domini millesimo tricentesimo [decimo] septimo, coram consilio nostro apud Striveling, per bonam et fidelem et assisam fidedignorum . . . . compertum et declaratum est quod burgenses nostri de Striveling, habere solebant tempore predecessorum nostrorum, regum Scocie, et de jure et consuetudine habere debent [communem pasturam equorum] . . . bosco in forestis nostris inter aquas de Forth et Carroue; solvendo pro quolibet equo per singulas septimanas forestariis nostris ibidem qui pro tempore fuerint . Et quod iidem burgenses

Be it known that on the fourth day of April, in the year of our Lord one thousand three hundred and seventeen, in presence of our council at Striveling, it is found and declared by a good and faithful assize of trustworthy men that our burgesses of Striveling, in the time of our predecessors, kings of Scotland, were wont to have, and by law and custom ought to have, a common pasturage for their horses in the . . . . wood in our forests between the waters of Forth and Carron; paying to our foresters who shall be there for the time . . every week for each horse,

nostri fuerunt temporibus predictis in plena possessione fodiendi petas in petaria de Skewok ; solvendo pro qualibet wanga. . . . . annum unum denarium tantum. Quare, volumus et concedimus burgensibus nostris, et hac presenti carta confirmamus eisdem ut ipsi et eorum successores . . . in omnibus habeant, teneant et possideant, imperpetuum; vnde mandamus et firmiter percipimus vicecomiti nostro de Strivelin, et ballivis suis qui pro tempore fuerint, predictos burgenses . . . . et eorum successores in eadem libertate in omnibus custodiant manuteneant et defendant

And that our said burgesses have been in the times foresaid in the full enjoyment of digging peats in the peat moss of Skewok, paying for each . . . one penny yearly only. Wherefore, we will and grant to our burgesses, and by this present charter for ever confirm to them that they and their successors may have, hold and possess, [the said common pasturage and right of digging peats] in all . . . wherefore we command and firmly charge our sheriff of Striveling, and his bailies who shall be for the time, to keep, maintain, and defend our foresaid burgesses and their successors in the said liberty in all things.

XII.

ACCOUNTS of the Burgh of Stirling. audited in Exchequer. Dumbarton, 25th January, 1327-8.

(1). ACCOUNT OF THE MAGISTRATES.

COMPOTUM Mauricii Hunter et Fynlai Sutoris, prepositorum burgi de Striuelyn, redditum apud Dunbretan xxv° die Januarii, anno gracie supradicto, de firmis dicti burgi de duobus terminis huius compoti. Iidem onerant se de xxxvj li., receptis per firmas dicti burgi de anno huius compoti. De quibus, pro superexpensis suis factis in compoto suo precedenti xl s. j d. et ob.

Account of Maurice Hunter and Fynlay Sutor, bailies of the burgh of Strivelyn, given up at Dunbretan on the twenty-fifth day of January, in the year of grace [one thousand three hundred and twenty-seven], of the fermes of the said burgh for the two terms of this account.   They charge themselves with £36 received on account of the fermes of the said burgh for the year of their account.   Whereof, for their superexpenses made in their preceding account 40s. 1d. halfpenny.   And in duties

Et in feodis abbatuin de Cambuskyneth et Dunfermelyn, hospitalis de
Striuelyn et hospitalis de Torphichin, per tempus compoti, xxiij li. v s. iiij d.
Et Fratribus Predicatoribus de Striuelyn, ex elemosina regis annua, x li.   Et
pro constructione cuiusdam domus pro coquina ad opus regis, liij s. iiij d.   Et
in diuersis cariagiis per tempus compoti, xxvj s. et viij d.   Summa huius
expense, xxxix li. v s. v d. et ob.   Et sic superexpendunt lxv s. v d. et ob.
Iidem petunt allocacionem de xl s. pro multura de Cragorth subtracta de
molendino de Striuelyn, que est in manu Reginaldi More, super quo con-
sulatur rex, qui sibi postmodum allocantur.   Et sic superexpendunt cv s. v d.
et ob.   De quibus, sibi soluuntur per allocacionem sibi factam in compoto
custumariorum de Striuelin, de alia parte rotuli, l s. et v d.   Et sic superexpendunt de claro lv s. et ob.

to the abbot of Cambuskyneth and Dunfermelyn, the hospital of Strivelyn and the
hospital of Torphichen, during the time of the account, £23 5s. 4d.   And to the
Friars Preachers of Strivelyn of the yearly alms of the king, £10.   And for the
building of a certain house for a kitchen for the use of the king, 53s. 4d.   And in
sundry carriages during the time of the account, 26s. 8d.   Sum of this outlay,
£39 5s. 5d. and a halfpenny.   And thus they superexpended 65s. 5d. and a halfpenny.   They ask also allowance of 40s. for the multures of Cragorth abstracted
from the mill of Stirling, which is in the hand of Reginald More, on which let the
king be consulted, which is afterwards allowed to them.   And thus they superexpended 105s. 5d. and a halfpenny.   Whereof, paid to them by allowance made
to them in the account of the custumars of Strivelin on the other side of the roll
50s. and 5d.   And thus obviously they superexpended 55s. and a halfpenny.

(2). ACCOUNT OF THE CUSTUMARS.

COMPOTUM custumariorum burgi de Striuelyn, redditum apud Dunbretan
xxv° die Januarii, anno gracie supradicto, de receptis et expensis dicte custume
[i.e., noue custume], ab vltimo die Februarii anno gracie xxvi vsque in diem
presentis compoti.   Iidem onerant se de lj s. et viij d. receptis per custumam

ACCOUNT of the custumars of the burgh of Strivelyn, given up at Dunbretan on the
twenty-fifth day of January, in the year of grace above mentioned, of the receipts
and outlays of the said custom [i.e., new custom], from the last day of February, in
the year of grace [1326] till the day of the present account.   They charge them-

sex saccorum et quinque petrarum lane, et nouem dacrarum coriorum, per tempus compoti. De quibus, in seruicio collectorum, xv d. Et debent 1 s. v d. qui assignantur prepositis burgi de Striuelyn et alia parte rotuli, in partem superexpensarum suarum. Et sic eque hic.

selves with 51s. 8d. received for the custom of six sacks and five stones of wool and nine dacres of hides during the time of the account. Whereof, for service of the collectors, 15d. And they owe 50s. and 5d., which are assigned to the bailies of the burgh of Strivelyn on the other side of the roll in part of their superexpenses. And thus this is equal.

XIII.

CHARTER by David the Second confirming the Charter by Alexander the Second of a Weekly Market, etc. [No. VII. hereof]. Scone, 26th October, 1360.[1]

DAUID, Dei gracia, Rex Scottorum: Omnibus probis hominibus tocius terre sue, clericis et laicis, salutem. Sciatis nos quamdam cartam, recolende memorie, domini[2] Alexandri, Dei gracia Regis Scotie, predecessoris nostri burgensibus burgi nostri de Striuelyn confectam,[2] non cancellatam, nec[3] abolitam, aut[4] in aliqua sui parte vitiatam, veraciter inspexisse, in hec verba:—ALEXANDER, [etc., ut supra, No. vii., p. 6]. Quas quidem consuetudines et libertates, omnes et singulas, nos predictis burgensibus nostris de Striuelyn et suis successoribus, in omnibus et per omnia prout superius est contentum, ratificamus, approbamus, et hac presenti carta nostra confirmamus; volumusque et firmiter precipimus pro nobis et nostris heredibus quod premissa omnia et singula premissorum[5] perpetui

DAVID, by the grace of God, King of Scots: To all good men of his whole land, clerics and laics, greeting. Know ye that we have truly inspected a certain charter of the lord Alexander, by the grace of God, King of Scotland, our predecessor, of good memory, not cancelled, not abolished, nor vitiated in any part, in these words:— ALEXANDER, [etc., as above, No. vii., p. 6.]. Which customs and privileges, all and sundry, we ratify, approve, and by this our present charter confirm to our foresaid burgesses of Strivelyn and their successors in and by all things as is above contained; and we, for us and our heirs, will and strictly command that all and

[1] Another charter to the same effect is dated at Scone, 27th October, same year. The only variations are the fol- lowing: — [2] "domini" and from "pre- decessores" to "confectam" omitted: [3] "non;" [4] "nec;" [5] "eorundum;"

roboris optineant firmitatem. In cuius rei testimonium presenti carte confirmacionis[6] nostre sigillum nostrum precepimus apponi. Testibus: Venerabilibus in Christo patribus, Willelmo[7] episcopo Sancti Audree et Patricio[8] episcopo Brechinensis, cancellario nostro; Johanne abbate de Dunfermelyn;[9] Roberto, senescallo nostro Scotie, comite de Strathern, nepote nostro;[10] Willelmo comite de Douglas;[11] Willelmo de Keth, mariscallo nostro Scotie; Willelmo de Leuyngston, Roberto de Erskyn[12] et Johanne de Danyelston, militibus. Apud Scon, in parliamento nostro tento ibidem,[13] vicesimo sexto die[14] Octobris anno regni nostri tricesimo primo.

sundry the premises remain valid and of perpetual force. In testimony whereof we have commanded our seal to be appended to our present charter of confirmation. Witnesses: The venerable fathers in Christ, William, bishop of St. Andrews; and Patrick, bishop of Brechin, our chancellor; John, abbot of Dunfermelyn; Robert, our steward of Scotland, earl of Strathern, our nephew; William, earl of Douglas; William of Keth, our marischal of Scotland; William of Levyngston, Robert of Erskyn, and John of Danyelston, knights. At Scon, in our parliament held there, on the twenty-sixth day of October, in the thirty-first year of our reign.

XIV.

CHARTER by King David the Second confirming to the Burgesses of the Burgh of Stirling the Charter by Alexander the Second of Freedom from Tolls and Customs [No. VIII. hereof]. Scone, 27th October, 1360.[1]

DAUID, Dei gracia, Rex Scottorum: Omnibus probis hominibus tocius terre

DAVID, by the grace of God, King of Scots: To all good men of his whole

---

[6] "confirmacionis" omitted; [7] " Dei gracia " inserted here; [8] "eadem gracia" inserted here; [9] this name omitted; [10] "Thoma comite de Marr" inserted here; [11] "consanguineis nostris" inserted here; [12] "Hugo de Eglynton" inserted here; [13] "in parliamento" omitted;

[14] "vicesimo septimo die mensis." [15] In the confirmed charter the words "cartas suas" are substituted in the confirmation dated 27th October for the words "cartam suam" in the one dated 26th October. [Antea, No. vii., p. 8, line 13.]

[1] Another charter to the same effect is dated at Scone, 26th October, same year. The only

suc,[2] salutem. Sciatis nos quamdam cartam, recolende memorie, domini[3] Alexandri, Dei gracia, Regis Scotie, predecessoris nostri, non cancellatam, non abolitam, nec in aliqua parte sui[4] vitiatam, veraciter inspexisse, in hec verba:— ALEXANDER, [etc., ut supra, No. viii., p. 9.] Quamquidem libertatem, per omnia et in omnibus,[5] prout superius est expressum,[6] nos pro nobis et nostris heredibus,[7] burgensibus dicti burgi nostri de Striuelyn et eorum successoribus, ratificamus, approbamus et per presentem cartam nostram[8] confirmamus. In cuius rei testimonium presenti carte confirmationis nostre sigillum nostrum precepimus apponi. Hiis[9] testibus: Venerabilibus in Christo patribus, Willelmo episcopo Sancti Andree et Patricio episcopo Brechinensis, cancellario nostro; Roberto, senescallo nostro Scotie, comite de Strathern, nepote nostro; Thoma comite de Marr, Willelmo comite de Douglas, consanguineis nostris;[10] Willelmo de Leuyngston, Roberto de Erskyn et Johanne de Danyelston,[11] militibus. Apud Sconam, in parliamento nostro tento ibidem,[12] vicesimo septimo die Octobris anno regni nostri tricesimo primo.

land, greeting. Know ye that we have truly inspected a charter of the lord Alexander, by the grace of God, King of Scotland, our predecessor, of good memory, not cancelled, not abolished, nor in any part vitiated, in these words:—ALEXANDER [etc., as above, No. viii., p. 9.] Which liberty, by all and in all, so far as is above expressed, we for us and our heirs ratify, approve, and by our present charter confirm to the burgesses of our said burgh of Strivelyn. In testimony whereof we have commanded that our seal be appended to our present charter of confirmation. Witnesses: The venerable fathers in Christ, William, bishop of St. Andrews, and Patrick, bishop of Brechin, our chancellor; Robert, our steward of Scotland, earl of Strathearn, our nephew; Thomas earl of Marr, William earl of Douglas, our cousins; William of Levyngstone, Robert of Erskyn, and John of Danyelston, knights. At Scone, in our parliament held there, on the twenty-seventh day of October in the thirty-first year of our reign.

variations are the following:—[2] "clericis et laicis" inserted here; [3] "domini" omitted; [4] "sui parte;" [5] "in omnibus et per omnia;" [6] "contentum ;" [7] "heredibus nostris;" [8] "in- perpetuum" inserted here; [9] "Hiis" omitted; [10] "consanguineis nostris" omitted; [11] this name omitted and "Hugo de Eglynton" inserted; [12] "in parliamento nostro tento ibidem" omitted.

XV.

PRECEPT by King David the Second to the Sheriffs and Bailies of Stirling as to damage caused by certain burgesses of Stirling to the cruives and fishings of the abbot and convent of Cambuskenneth. Scone, 27th July, 1366.

DAVID, Dei gracia, Rex Scotorum: Vicecomitibus et balliuis suis de Striueling, salutem. Quia per decretum consilij nostri in pleno parliamento nostro, tento apud Sconam vicesimo septimo die mensis Julij, compertum fuit et determinatum quod burgenses de Striueling, videlicet, Hugo Vrry et complices[1] sui, cum armis, violenter et iniuste inuaserunt et fregerunt crouas et piscarias religiosorum virorum, abbatis et conuentus monasterij de Cambuskynneth, in nostre regie maiestatis offensam et dampnum dicti monasterij non modicum et grauamen, vobis firmiter precipimus et mandamus quatenus dictos burgenses ex parte nostra moneatis et districte compellatis quod, infra quadraginta dies a data presentium numerando, predictas crouas et piscaturas

DAVID, by the grace of God, King of Scots: To the sheriffs and their bailies of Striveling, greeting. Whereas by decreet of our council in our full parliament held at Scone on the twenty-seventh day of the month of July, it was found and determined that burgesses of Striveling, namely, Hugh Urry and his accomplices, with arms, violently and unlawfully assailed and broke the cruives and fishings of religious men, the abbot and convent of the monastery of Cambuskynneth, to the offence of our royal majesty and no little loss and damage of the said monastery, we strictly command and charge you that on our part ye warn and strictly compel the said burgesses within forty days counting from the date of these presents to re-erect and

[1]The following are given as the names of the burgesses who attacked the cruives and fishings:—Hugh Vrry, Robert Raa, Richard Tector, Adam Sissor, Robert Foster, William Ker, William Vemys, John of Erskin, Roger Merchant and Henry Merchant, his brother; Gilbert Faber, Thomas Potator, John Gollane, John Skinner, Thomas of Ireland, Robert Harrow, John Brune, Adam Gamilsone, John Witste, Thomas of Brigerakis, Patrick Merchant, Robert the executioner, Thomas the brazier; also, the fishers, viz., John, son of Hugh; John of Callenter; John, son of Michael; John Tennand and Philip his son; Mure of Corntone and William his brother; John, son of Heruot; and many others. (Register of Cambuskenneth, No. 55, p. 76, and Supplement to Acts of Parliaments of Scotland, p. 14.)

FAC-SIMILE OF CHARTER (No. XVI.)

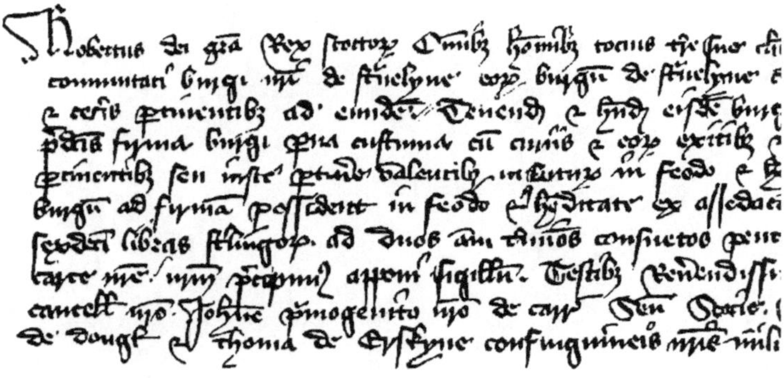

TO THE BURGH OF STIRLING, dated 13th July 1386.

pp. 21, 22.)

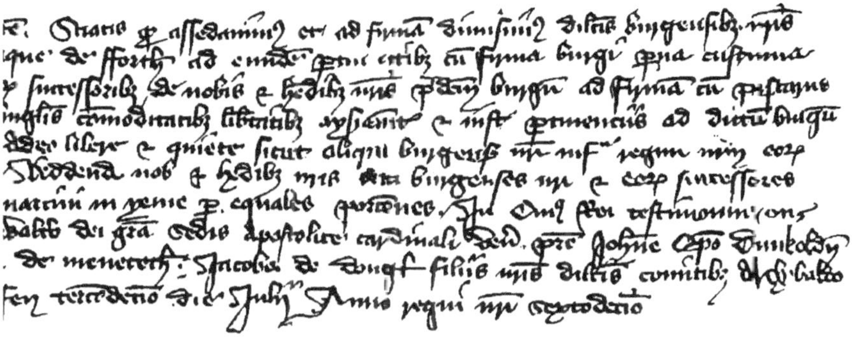

re-edificent et construant competenter prout antea fuerant, et quod plene
satisfaciant de dampnis expensis et iacturis que et quas dicti religiosi ex
huiusmodi maleficijs sustinuerunt, secundum decretum consilij nostri et
ordinationem, super nostram plenariam forisfacturam. Et hoc nullo modo
omittatis nec omittant sicut nostram indignationem volueritis et volucrint
euitare. In cuius rei testimonium presentibus sigillum nostrum penes
predictos religiosos mansuris et vobis ostendendis precepimus apponj. Apud
Sconam, vicesimo septimo die Julij anno regni nostri trigesimo septimo.

competently construct the foresaid cruives and fishings as they were previously, and
fully make satisfaction for the damages, expenses, and losses which the said religious
men have suffered by such mischiefs, in terms of the decreet and ordinance of our
council, on pain of our full forfeiture. And this ye and they in no way omit as ye
and they will avoid our displeasure. In witness whereof we have commanded our
seal to be affixed to these presents to remain with the foresaid religious men and to
be shown to you. At Scone, on the twenty-seventh day of July in the thirty-seventh
year of our reign.

XVI.

CHARTER by King Robert the Second granting the Burgh of Stirling to
the Burgesses thereof, with the Fishings in the Water of Forth and the
Small Customs and others pertaining to the Burgh. Methven, 13th
July, 1386.

ROBERTUS, Dei gratia, Rex Scottorum : Omnibus hominibus tocius terre
sue, clericis et laycis, salutem. Sciatis quod assedauimus et ad firmam
dimisimus dilectis burgensibus nostris communitati burgi nostri de Strinelyne
eorum Burgum de Striuelyne; cum piscariis nostris aque de Forth ad eundem
pertinentibus; cum firma burgi, parua custuma, et ceteris pertinentibus ad

ROBERT, by the grace of God, King of Scots: To all men of his whole land, clerics
and laics, greeting. Know ye that we have set and in ferme let to our beloved
burgesses, the community of our burgh of Strivelyne, their burgh of Strivelyne;
with our fishings of the water of Forth pertaining to the same; with the ferme of
the burgh, small custom, and others pertaining to the same. To hold and to have

eundem. Tenendum et habendum eisdem burgensibus nostris et eorum
successoribus, de nobis et heredibus nostris, predictum burgum ad firmam,
cum piscariis predictis, firma burgi, parua custuma, cum curiis et eorum
exitibus, et cum omnibus et singulis commoditatibus, libertatibus, aysiamentis
et iustis pertinenciis ad dictum burgum pertinentibus seu iuste pertinere
valentibus in futurum, in feodo et hereditate inperpetuum, adeo libere et
quiete sicut aliqui burgenses nostri infra regnum nostrum eorum burgum ad
firmam possident in feodo et hereditate ex assedacione Regis eis facta.
Reddendo nobis et heredibus nostris, dicti burgenses nostri et eorum successores, sexdecim libras sterlingorum, ad duos anni terminos consuetos, Pentecostes,
videlicet, et Sancti Martini in yeme, per equales portiones. In cuius rei
testimonium presente carte nostre nostrum precepimus apponi sigillum.
Testibus: Reuerendissimo in Christo patre Waltero, Dei gratia, sedis apostolice
cardinali; venerabile patre Johanne episcopo Dunkeldensis, cancellario nostro;
Johanne primogenito nostro de Carrick, senescallo Scotie; Roberto de Fyf et
de Meneteth, Jacobo de Douglas, filiis nostris dilectis, comitibus; Archibaldo de Douglas et Thoma de Erskyne, consanguineis nostris, militibus.
Apud Methfen, tertio decimo die Julij anno regni nostri sexto decimo.

to our said burgesses and their successors, of us and our heirs, the foresaid burgh in
ferme, with the foresaid fishings, the ferme of the burgh, small custom, with the
courts and their issues, and with all and sundry commodities, liberties, easements,
and just pertinents belonging or that may justly belong to the said burgh in future, in
fee and heritage for ever, as freely and quietly as any others our burgesses within
our kingdom possess their burgh in ferme, granted to them in fee and heritage by
the gift of the King. Paying, our said burgesses and their successors, to us and our
heirs, sixteen pounds sterling, at the two usual terms in the year, to wit Whitsunday
and Martinmas in winter, by equal portions. In witness whereof we have ordered
our seal to be appended to our present charter. Witnesses: The most reverend father
in Christ, Walter by the grace of God cardinal of the apostolic see; the venerable
father John bishop of Dunkeld our chancellor; John earl of Carrick, our eldest son,
steward of Scotland; Robert earl of Fife and of Meneteth, James earl of Douglas,
our beloved sons; Archibald of Douglas and Thomas of Erksine, our cousins, knights.
At Methfen, on the thirteenth day of July in the sixteenth year of our reign.

XVII.

CHARTER by King Robert the Second confirming the Gifts which King David the Second and others made to the Altar of St. Laurence in the Parish Church of Stirling. Stirling, 28th February, 1388-9.

ROBERTUS, Dei gratia, Rex Scottorum: Omnibus probis hominibus tocius terre sue, clericis et laicis, salutem.   Sciatis quod ratificauimus, approbauimus et confirmauimus illas donacionem et concessionem, bone memorie, quas dominus Rex Dauid, avunculus et prediecssor noster, pro salute anime sue, predicessorum et successorum suorum, Regum Scotie, fecit et concessit in honorem indiuidue Trinitatis, Beate Marie et omnium sanctorum, altari Sancti Laurencij in ecclesia parochiali de Striuelyne, et vni capellano ibidem diuina celebranti, de passagio batcllo aeque de Forth iuxta Striuelyne, vna cum crofta eiusdem passagii; cum omnibus annuis redditibus per Johaunem de Burgo, militem bachelarium nostrum, eidem altari collatis, videlicet, de vndecim solidis sterlingorum percipiendis annuatim de tertij [tribus] particatis terre iacentibus in burgo de Striuelyne in barenia senescalli Scocie, inter terram Johannis Michael ex parte occidentali ex parte vna et terram Johannis Gourlay ex parte orientali ex parte altera, et de octo solidis sterlingorum percipiendis annuatim de quatuor particatis terre illius tenementi quondam ipsius Johannis

ROBERT, by the grace of God, King of Scots: To all good men of his whole land, clerics and laics, greeting.   Know ye that we have ratified, approved and confirmed the donation and grant which the lord King David, of good memory, our uncle and predecessor, for the weal of his soul, the souls of his predecessors and successors, Kings of Scotland, made and granted in honour of the undivided Trinity, of Saint Mary, and all saints, to the altar of Saint Laurence, in the parish church of Strivelyn, and to one chaplain celebrating divine service there, of the ferry of the water of Forth near Strivelyn, together with the ferry croft thereof; with all annualrents bestowed by John of Burgh, our knight bachelor, on the said altar, to wit eleven shillings sterling, to be uplifted yearly from three particates of land lying in the burgh of Strivelyne, in the barony of the steward of Scotland, between the land of John Michael on the west side on the one part, and the land of John Gourlay on the east side on the other part, and of eight shillings sterling to be uplifted yearly from four particates of land of that tenement of the said deceased

de Burgo predicti in quo inhabitat Matheus Ferrour, in vico australi burgi predicti, et de sex solidis et octo denariis percipiendis annuatim de duabus particatis terre iacentibus in eodem vico australi burgi predicti inter terram Johannis Scot, sutoris, ex parte occidentali ex parte vna et terram Willelmi Dauid ex parte orientali ex parte altera. Nosque ex vberiori gracia, diuinum seruicium ampliare volentes, dedimus et concessimus, ad instanciam domini Thome de Erskyne et parentum et amicorum dicti quondam Johannis de Burgo, Deo et Beate Marie, semper virgini, et Beato Laurencio, et vni capellano celebranti ad altare predictum, omnes redditus ipsius passagii et ipsi passagio pertinentes seu pertinere valentes in futurum, vna cum crofta eiusdem passagii, per ipsos capellanos nostros seu per ipsorum procuratores leuandos, sine intromissione alicuius ministrorum nostrorum infra burgum vel extra ; ita quod ipse capellanus noster qui pro tempore fuerit de batella ministris batelle ciusdem et aliis prefato passagio necessariis sufficienter faciat deseruiri. Tenendas et habendas cisdem capellanis nostris qui pro tempore fuerint, cum omnibus et singulis commoditatibus, aysiamentis, rectis, consuetudinibus hucusque consuetis et iustis pertinenciis, libere et quiete, plenarie, integre, bene et in pace imperpetuum. Faciendo inde, dicti capellani nostri qui pro

John of Burgh in which Matthew Ferrour dwells, in the Southgait of the foresaid burgh, and of six shillings and eight pennies to be uplifted yearly from two particates of land lying in the said Southgait of the foresaid burgh between the land of John Scot, shoemaker, on the west side on the one part and the land of William David on the cast side on the other part. And we of ampler grace, willing to increase divine service, have given and granted, at the instance of Sir Thomas of Erskyn and of the parents and friends of the said deceased John of Burgh, to God and Saint Mary, ever virgin, and Saint Laurence, and one chaplain saying mass at the foresaid altar, all the rents of the said ferry, and pertaining or that may pertain to the said ferry in time coming, together with the ferry croft thereof, to be uplifted by our said chaplains, or by their procurators, without interference of any of our officers within or without the burgh; provided that our said chaplain for the time being may cause the foresaid ferry to be sufficiently served with a boat, attendants of the said boat, and other necessaries for the foresaid ferry. To hold and to have to our said chaplains for the time being, with all and sundry commodities, easements, rights, customs hitherto in use and just pertinents, freely

tempore fuerint, seruicium missarum cotidianum cum dispositi fuerint
ibidem pro salubri statu nostro liberorumque nostrorum, nec non pro anima
quondam carissime consortis nostre Eufamie Regine Scocie, pro qua
volumus quod specialis memoria cotidiana in missis et aliis obsequiis diuinis
ad altare predictum celebrandis dicatur, ac pro animabus omnium predicessorum et successorum nostrorum, regum Scotie, dictique quondam Johannis
de Burgo predicti, et animabus omnium fidelium defunctorum. Cuius capellanie collationem ad nos et heredes nostros volumus imperpetuum pertinere,
et eandem collationem ad nos et heredes nostros imperpetuum specialiter
reseruamus. In cuius rei testimonium presenti carte nostre nostrum precepimus apponi sigillum. Testibus: Venerabilibus in Christo patribus, Waltero
Sanctiandree et Johanne Duukelder.sis, cancellario nostro, ecclesiarum episcopis;
carissimo primogenito nostro, Johanne comite de Carric, senescallo Scocie;
Roberto comite de Fyff et Meneteth, dilecto filio nostro; Archebaldo de
Douglas domino Galwidie et Thoma de Erskyne, militibus, consanguineis
nostris dilectis. Apud Striuelyne, vicesimo octauo die Februarii anno regni
nostri decimo nono.

and quietly, fully, wholly, well, and in peace for ever. Performing therefor, our said
chaplains who shall be for the time, a daily service of masses there, when they shall
be disposed, for the prosperous estate of us and our children, and for the soul of
our late beloved consort Eufamia Queen of Scotland, for whom we will that a special
daily remembrance be said in the masses and other divine services to be celebrated at the foresaid altar, and for the souls of all our predecessors and successors,
kings of Scotland, and of the said deceased John of Burgh aforesaid, and for the souls
of all the faithful dead. Of which chaplainry we will that the collation shall belong
to us and our heirs for ever, and the said collation we specially reserve to us and
our heirs for ever. In witness whereof we have commanded our seal to be appended
to our present charter. Witnesses: Venerable fathers in Christ, Walter bishop
of the church of St. Andrews, and John bishop of the church of Dunkeld, our
chancellor; our dearest first-born son, John earl of Carrick, steward of Scotland;
Robert, earl of Fyff and Menetet'h, our well beloved son; Archibald of Douglas,
lord of Galloway and Thomas of Erskyne, knights, our well beloved cousins. At
Strivelyn, on the twenty-eight day of February in the nineteenth year of our
reign.

XVIII.

PRECEPT by King Robert the Third directing Sasine to be given to the Canons of Cambuskenneth of the Hospital of St. James at the Bridge-end of Stirling. Rothesay Castle, 10th March, 1402-3.

ROBERTUS, Dei gracia, Rex Scottorum: Vicecomiti et balliuis suis de Striueling, salutem. Quia concessimus per cartam Deo et beate Marie Virgini, ac canonicis in monasterio de Cambuskynneth ibidem Deo seruientibus et imperpetuum seruituris, hospitale beati Jacobi ad finem platee pontis de Striueling infra balliam vestram, cum omnibus et singulis terris ac possessionibus suis, tam sub terra quam supra terram, mandamus vobis et precipimus quatenus eisdem canonicis vel eorum certo attornato, latori presencium, sasinam dicti hospitalis cum pertinenciis iuste liberari faciatis, et sine dilatione, secundum tenorem dicte carte nostre quam inde habent; saluo Johanni Palmer, qui dictam plateam a longo tempore sustinuit, vsufructu terrarum dicti hospitalis, in recompensationem expensarum suarum, pro toto tempore vite sue, et hoc nullo modo omittatis. Teste, meipso. Apud castrum nostrum de Rothesay, decimo die mensis Marcii anno regni nostri tercio decimo.

ROBERT, by the grace of God, King of Scots: To the sheriff and his bailies of Striveling, greeting. Whereas we have by a charter granted to God and the blessed Virgin Mary, and to the canons in the monastery of Cambuskynneth serving God there and to serve for ever, the hospital of St. James at the end of the roadway of the bridge of Striveling within your bailliary, with all and sundry its lands and possessions, as well under the ground as above the ground, we charge and command you that ye cause sasine to be justly delivered to the said canons or their certain attorney, bearer of these presents, of the said hospital with the pertinents, and without delay, according to the tenor of our said charter which they have thereupon; saving to John Palmer, who has upheld the said roadway for a long time, the usufruct for the whole of his lifetime of the lands of the said hospital, in recompense of his expenses, and this in no way ye omit. Witness, myself. At our castle of Rothesay, on the tenth day of the month of March in the thirteenth year of our reign.

XIX.

CHARTER by Robert, Duke of Albany, Governor of the Kingdom of Scotland, to the chaplain of St. Michael's Chapel within the Castle of Stirling,
of an annual rent of ten merks furth of the lands of Cragortht. Perth,
26th June, 1407.

ROBERTUS, Dux Albanie, Comes de Fyfe et de Menteth ac Gubernator regni
Scocie: Omnibus probis hominibus tocius regni predicti, clericis et laicis,
salutem. Sciatis nos dedisse, concessisse, et hac presenti carta nostra confirmasse, pro salute animarum excellentissimorum principum, bone memorie,
Roberti et Dauid de Bruys, Roberti Senescalli, progenitoris nostri, et Roberti
Senescalli, fratris nostri, quondam regum Scocie, ac eciam pro salute anime
nostre et animarum Margarete et Murielle, vxorum nostrarum, et prolum
nostrarum ac antecessorum et successorum nostrorum ac omnium fidelium
defunctorum, Deo et beate Marie Virgini et beato Michaeli, archangelo, ac vni
capellano diuina celebranti et imperpetuum celebraturo in capella Beati
Michaelis, archangeli, infra castrum de Strinelyne situata, decem marcas annualis
redditus annuatim leuandas et recipiendas de annuo redditu viginti marcarum
exeunte de terris de Cragortht cum pertinenciis, iacentibus infra vicecomitatum

ROBERT, Duke of Albany, Earl of Fyfe and of Menteth, and Governor of the kingdom
of Scotland: To all good men of his whole foresaid kingdom, clerics and laics,
greeting. Know ye that we have given, granted, and by this our present charter
have confirmed, for the salvation of the souls of the most excellent princes, of good
memory, Robert and David of Bruys, Robert Steward, our father, and Robert
Steward, our brother, sometime kings of Scotland, and also for the salvation of our
soul and of the souls of Margaret and Muriel, our wives, and of our children and
of our predecessors and successors and of all the faithful dead, to God and the
blessed Virgin Mary and Saint Michael, the archangel, and to a chaplain celebrating
and for ever to celebrate divine service in the chapel of Saint Michael, the archangel,
situated within the castle of Strivelyne, ten merks of annual rent to be yearly
uplifted and received of an annual rent of twenty merks furth of the lands of
Cragortht with the pertinents, lying within the sheriffdom of Strivelyne, by the

de Striuelyne, per manus tenencium et inhabitancium earundem. Tenendas et habendas ae percipiendas dictas decem marcas annuatim ad duos anni terminos Penthecostes, videlicet, et Sancti Martini in ycme per porciones equales, predicto capellano et successoribus suis qui pro tempore fuerint, in liberam, puram et perpetuam elemosinam, ad manum mortuam imperpetuum, cum omnibus libertatibus, commoditatibus et aysiamentis, ac justis pertinenciis quibuscunque ad dictum annuum redditum spectantibus seu iuste spectare valentibus in futurum, adeo libere et quiete, plenarie, integre, honorifice, bene et in pace, in omnibus et per omnia, sicut aliqua elemosina infra regnum Scocie per aliquem conceditur siue datur. Volumus, eciam, et concedimus quod quandocunque et quocienscunque dictum capellanum qui pro tempore fuerit decedere contigerit seu ex aliqua causa rationabili a dicta capellania ammoueri, extunc nos uel heredes nostri qui pro tempore fuerint infra mensem a tempore vacacionis huiusmodi alium capellanum ydoneum domino episcopo Sanctiandree uel eius vicario generali, sede vacante, debite presentent admittendum, pro salute omnium animarum predictarum in capella Beati Michaelis, supradicta pro perpetuo celebraturum. Et quandocunque dictum capellanum qui pro tempore fuerit ad aliquod aliud beneficium ecclesiasticum contigerit pro-

hands of the tenants and inhabitants of the same. To hold and have and uplift the said ten merks, yearly, at two terms in the year, that is to say Whitsunday and Martinmas in winter by equal portions, to the foresaid chaplain and his successors who shall be for the time, in free, pure and perpetual alms, in mortmain for ever, with all liberties, commodities and easements, and just pertinents whatsoever belonging or which may in future justly belong to the said annual rent, as freely and quietly, fully, wholly, honourably, well and in peace, in all and by all, as any alms within the kingdom of Scotland is by any one granted or given. We will, also, and grant that whensoever and as often as the said chaplain who shall be for the time shall happen to decease or from any reasonable cause remove from the said chaplainry, then we or our heirs who shall be for the time shall within a month from the time of such vacancy duly present to the lord bishop of Saint Andrews, or to his vicar general, the see being vacant, another fit chaplain to be admitted to celebrate for ever in the foresaid chapel of St. Michael for the salvation of all the foresaid souls. And whenever the said chaplain who shall be for the time shall happen to be promoted to any other ecclesiastical benefice the said chaplainry shall immediately after he shall

moueri statim postquam illud perceperit seu obtinuerit dicta capellania vacabit.
Insuper, volumus et per presentes ordinamus quod si dictus annuus redditus
decem marcarum dicto capellano qui pro tempore fuerit ad dictos terminos
bene et prompte annuatim non soluant, licet extunc eidem capellano, sine
licencia alicuius ministri, predictas terras de Craggrotht distringere et namare,
quousque de dicto annuo redditu plenarie fuerit satisfactum. Nichil inde
faciendo, dictus capellanus et successores sui, nobis et heredibus nostris qui
pro tempore fuerint, nisi missam cotidie cum dispositi fuerint in capella
supradicta et oracionum suffragia deuotarum, pro omni alio seruicio seculari,
exaccione seu demanda, que de dicto annuo redditu decem marcarum aliqualiter
exigi poterunt uel requiri. In cuius rei testimonium presenti carte nostre
sigillum officii nostri apponi fecimus. Testibus: Reuerendo in Christo patre
Gilberto episcopo Abirdonensi, cancellario Scocie; Roberto Senescalli, primogenito carissimi filii nostri et heredis, Murdaci Senescalli, militis; Johanne
Senescalli, filio nostro, domino Buchanie; Alexandro Senescalli comite de
Marr et de Garvyach, nepote nostro; Johanne Senescalli domino de Lorne;
Willelmo de Ertht, militibus: domino Donaldo de Bute, decano Dunblanensis;
et Andrea de Hawyk, secretario nostro. Apud Perth, vicesimo sexto die

have received or obtained the same become vacant. Moreover, we will and by these
presents ordain that if the said annual rent of ten merks be not well and promptly
paid yearly at the said terms to the said chaplain who shall be for the time, then it
shall be lawful to the said chaplain, without the permission of any officer, to distrain and poind the foresaid lands of Craggrotht till he shall be fully paid of the said
annual rent. Making therefor, the said chaplain and his successors, to us and our
successors who shall be for the time, nothing except a daily mass in the said chapel
when they shall be disposed and an offering of devout prayers, for all other secular
service, exaction or demand, which can in any way be asked or required of the said
annual rent of ten merks. In witness whereof we have caused the seal of our office
to be appended to our present charter. Witnesses: The reverend father in Christ
Gilbert bishop of Aberdeen, chancellor of Scotland; Robert Steward eldest son of
our dearest son and heir, Murdoch Steward, knight; John Steward our son, lord
of Buchan; Alexander Steward earl of Marr and of Garvyach, our nephew; John
Steward lord of Lorne; William of Ertht, knights; Sir Donald of Bute, dean of
Dunblane; and Andrew of Hawyk, our secretary. At Perth on the twenty-sixth

mensis Junij anno Domini millesimo cccc^{mo} septimo et gubernacionis nostre anno secundo.

day of the month of June the year of our Lord one thousand four hundred and seven and of our government the second year.

XX.

CHARTER by King James the Second granting to the Provost, Bailies, Councillors, and Community of the Burgh of Stirling a New Fair to be held in the Burgh yearly at the Feast of the Ascension. Stirling, 25th October, 1447.

JACOBUS, Dei gratia, Rex Scotorum: Omnibus probis hominibus suis ad quos presentes litere peruenerint, clericis et laicis, salutem. Sciatis nos, ob fauorem dilectorum nostrorum prepositi, balliuorum, consulum et communitatis burgi nostri de Streuelyn, infeodasse, insigniuisse et dotasse, presentiumque per tenorem infeodare, insignire et dotare dictum burgum nostrum de Streuelyn, prepositumque, balliuos, consules et communitatem antedictos, Novis Nundinis temporibus perpetuis pro futuris in dicto nostro burgo et einsdem territorio annuatim in festo solempnitatis Asscencionis Domini tenendis, a. meridie, videlicet, vigilie dicti festi inchoandis et deinde per octo dies

JAMES, by the grace of God, King of Scots: To all his good men, clerics and laics, to whom the present letters shall come, greeting. Know ye that we, for the favour we bear to our lovites the provost, bailies, councillors, and community of our burgh of Strevelyn, have infeft, honoured, and endowed, and by the tenor of these presents infeft, honour, and endow our said burgh of Strevelyn, and the provost, bailies, councillors, and community foresaid, with a New Fair to be held yearly in all time coming in our said burgh and territory of the same at the feast of the solemnity of the Ascension of our Lord, that is to say beginning at noon of the vigil of the said

immediate sequentes inclusiue continuandis; cum cisdem priuilegiis, prerogativis, libertatibus et consuetudinibus, sicut dicta communitas et ipsum
burgum nostrum nundinas suas in festo nativitatis beate Virginis Marie et
per octavas ciusdem optinent et possident de presenti seu antiquitus optinere
et possidere consueuerunt, adeo libere et quiete, plenarie, integre, honorifice,
bene et in pace, in omnibus et per omnia, cum omni suo jure, proprietate et
possessione, sicut burgi cuicunque infra regnum nostrum seu cius communitas nundinis nouis gaudent aut antiquis; ipsis tamen nundinis suis
prehabitis eisdem vt hactenus gaudere soliti sunt semper saluis.   Reddendo
inde nobis et successoribus nostris jura de nundinis dicti burgi antiquitus
debita et consueta.   Quare, vniuersis et singulis legiis et subditis nostris et
aliis quibuscunque, firmiter precipimus et mandamus ne quis dictas nundinas
burgi nostri predicti, nouas aut antiquas, seu homines quoscunque aut
mercatores, in personis, bonis, mercandiis, catallis, equis aut rebus suis aliis
quibuscunque, ad ipsas nundinas progredientes, ibidem morantes aut inde
regredientes, perturbare, molestare seu quoquomodo inquietare presumat
iniuste, sub omni pena quam erga regiam majestatem amittere poterit in hac
parte.   In cuius rei testimonium hiis nostris presentibus literis magnum

feast and to be continued thence for eight days immediately following inclusive ; with
the same privileges, prerogatives, liberties, and customs wherewith the said community
and our said burgh at present hold and possess, or of old were in use to hold and possess
their fair at the feast of the nativity of the blessed Virgin Mary and during the octaves
of the same, as freely and quietly, fully, wholly, honorably, well, and in peace, in all
and by all things, with all their right property, and possession as any burghs within
our kingdom or community thereof enjoy their new or ancient fairs; but saving
always to them their fairs holden before as they have been wont to enjoy the same.
Rendering therefor to us and our successors the rights anciently due and wont from
the fair of the said burgh.   Wherefore, we strictly command and charge all and
sundry our lieges and subjects, and others whomsoever, that no one unjustly presume
to disturb, molest, or in any manner of way trouble the said fairs of our foresaid
burgh, new or old, or whatsoever men or merchants, in their persons, goods, merchandice, cattle, horses, or other things whatsoever, going to the said fair, remaining there
or returning thence, under all penalty which can be incurred towards our royal
majesty thereanent.   In witness whereof we have commanded our great seal to be

sigillum nostrum apponi precepimus. Apud castrum nostrum de Streuelyn, vicesimo quinto die mensis Octobris anno Domini millesimo quadringentesimo quadragesimo septimo et regni nostri vndecimo.

appended to these our present letters. At our castle of Strevelyn, on the twenty-fifth day of the month of October in the year of our Lord one thousand four hundred and forty-seven and of our reign the eleventh.

XXI.

CHARTER by King James the Second to the Burgesses and Community of the Burgh of Stirling, of freedom from the payment of Custom on Salt and Skins. Edinburgh, 12th January, 1451-2.

JACOBUS, Dei gracia, Rex Scotorum: Omnibus probis hominibus tocius terre sue, clericis et laicis, salutem. Sciatis nos, pro singulari fauore quem gerimus erga dilectos mercatores nostros, burgenses et communitatem burgi nostri de Striueline, pro suis gratuitis seruiciis nobis hactenus multipliciter impensis, dedisse, concessisse, et hac presenti carta nostra confirmasse, pro nobis nostrisque heredibus et successoribus, pro perpetuo, prefatis burgensibus et communitati burgi nostri de Striueline eorumque heredibus et successoribus, burgensibus eiusdem burgi, vt ipsi perpetuis futuris temporibus liberi, absoluti et quitti, sint ab omni solutione custume salis et pellium subscriptarum wlgariter dictarum skorlingis, skaldingis, futefellis, lentyrne ware, lambskynnis, todskynnis, calfskynnis, cunyngskynnis, ottirskynnis, et foumart-

JAMES, by the grace of God, King of Scots: To all good men of his whole land, clerics and laics, greeting. Know ye that, for the singular favor which we bear to our lovites, the merchants, burgesses, and community of our burgh of Striveline, for their manifold gratuitous services done to us heretofore, we have given, granted, and by this our present charter confirmed for us and our heirs and successors for ever to the foresaid burgesses and community of our burgh of Striveline and their heirs and successors, burgesses of the same burgh, that they be in all time coming free, released, and discharged from all payment of custom of salt and of the skins underwritten, commonly called skorlingis, skaldingis, futefellis, lentyrne ware, lambskynnis, todskynnis, calfskynnis, cunyngskinnis, otterskynnis, and foumartskynnis. And we release,

skynnis.   Et mercatores ac burgenses de Striuelyne eorumque heredes et
successores, dicti burgi burgenses, de solutione dicte custume salis et pellium
predictarum absoluimus et exoneramus et quittos clamamus, pro nobis et
nostris successoribus, pro perpetuo.   Preterea, volumus ac pro nobis et nostris
successoribus concedimus dictis burgensibus et communitati de Striueline
liberam potestatem atque facultatem vendendi, mercandizandi, vel in excambium aut alias permutandi, tam extraneis personis et non liberis quam
quibuscunque aliis personis, et tam infra regnum nostrum quam extra, mercimonia predicta salis et pellium absque quacunque custuma per ipsos extraneos
aut alios quoscunque quibuscunque futuris temporibus persoluenda; ita quod
de dictis sale et pellibus per ipsos extraneos a nostris burgensibus supradictis
emptis seu acquisitis custuma nullatenus persoluetur, nisi tantum parua custuma per extraneos et non liberos dictis burgensibus et communitati de dictis
sale et pellibus retroactis temporibus hactenus debita et persolui consueta.
Quare, vniuersis et singulis quorum interest vel interesse poterit, stricte precipiendo mandamus quatenus in contrarium dicte nostre concessionis, dona-
tionis, exoneracionis et quitticlamacionis, nullatenus deuenire presumant seu
eorum aliquis deuenire presumat, sub omni pena quam erga nostram regiam
incurrere poterint maiestatem.   In cuius rei testimonium presentibus nostris

exoner, and quitclaim, for us and our successors for ever, the merchants and
burgesses of Strivelyne and their heirs and successors, burgesses of the said burgh, from
the payment of the said custom on salt and the foresaid skins. Moreover, we will and
for us and our successors grant to the said burgesses and community of Striveline free
power and privilege of selling, buying, or exchanging in barter or otherwise, as well with
strangers and unfreemen as other persons whomsoever, and as well within our kingdom as without, the foresaid merchandise of salt and skins without the payment of
any custom by the said strangers or others whomsoever in all time coming; so
that no custom shall be paid in respect of the said salt and skins bought or acquired
by the said strangers from our foresaid burgesses, except only the petty custom of
the said salt and skins used and wont in time past to be paid by strangers and
unfreemen to the said burgesses and community.   Wherefore, we strictly charge
and command all and sundry whom it does or may concern that neither they nor any
of them in any degree presume to contravene our said grant, gift, acquittance, and
discharge, under all penalty which they can incur to our royal majesty.   In witness

E

literis pro perpetuo duraturis nostrum magnum sigillum apponi precepimus.
Testibus: Reuerendis in Christo patribus, Willelmo, Johanne et Thoma,
Glasguensis, Morauiensis et Caudidecase, ecclesiarum episcopis; carissimo
consanguineo nostro Willelmo comite de Douglas et de Auandale, domino
Galwidie; Willelmo domino Creichtoune, nostro cancellario et consanguineo
predilecto; dilectis consanguiucis nostris, Willelmo domino Somervile, Audrea
domino le Gray; magistris Johanne Arous, archidiacono Glasguensi, et
Georgeo de Schoriswode rectore de Cultir, clerico nostro. Apud Edinburgh,
duodecimo die mensis Januarii anno Domini millesimo quadringentesimo
quinquagesimo primo et regni nostri decimo quinto.

whereof we have commanded our great seal to be appended to these our present
letters to endure for ever.   Witnesses: The reverend fathers in Christ, William,
John, and Thomas, bishops of the churches of Glasgow, Moray, and Galloway; our
dearest cousin William earl of Douglas and of Avandale, lord of Galloway; William
lord Creichtoune, our chancellor and beloved cousin; our beloved cousins, William
lord Somervile, Andrew lord le Gray; Masters John Arous, archdeacon of Glasgow,
and George of Schoriswode, rector of Cultir, our clerk.   At Edinburgh, on the
twelfth day of the month of January in the year of our Lord one thousand four
hundred and fifty-one and of our reign the fifteenth.

XXII.

LETTERS PATENT by King James the Second, under his Great Seal,
appointing the Parliament of the Four Burghs, of which Stirling was one,
to be held at Edinburgh yearly.   Edinburgh, 5th November, 1454.

JACOBUS, Dei gracia, Rex Scotorum: Vniuersis et singulis ligiis et subditis
nostris ad quorum noticias presentes litere peruenerint, salutem.   Quia
serenissimus princeps Jacobus Rex Scotorum, progenitor noster, cuius anime
propicietur Deus, de auisamento et deliberacione trium regni sui statuum,

JAMES, by the grace of God, King of Scots: To all and sundry our lieges and
subjects to whose knowledge the present letters shall come, greeting.   Whereas the
most serene prince James King of Scots, our father, on whose soul may God have
mercy, with the advice and consent of the three estates of his kingdom, at Perth,

apud Perth, concessit et ordinauit parliamentum Quatuor Burgorum apud
burgum nostrum de Edinburgh annuatim teneri sicut a temporibus retroactis
tenebatur. Volumus et concessimus, ac presencium tenore concedimus, pro
nobis et successoribus nostris imperpetuum, burgensibus nostris burgi nostri
de Edinburgh et eorum successoribus, vt dictum parliamentum Quatuor Burgorum in dicto burgo nostro de Edinburghe annuatim pro perpetuo teneatur,
et die statuto post festum Beati Michaelis archangeli, cum continuacione
dierum, omnino inchoetur et obseruetur. Quare magno camerario nostro et
suis deputatis qui pro tempore fuerint stricte precipiendo mandamus
quatenus curiam parliamenti Quatuor Burgorum haberi et teneri more solito
faciatis in burgo nostro antedicte, conuocatis et summonitis annuatim ad hoc
comparituris commissariis Quatuor Burgorum principalium, videlicet, Edinburgh, Striuelyn, Lithqw et Lanark, dicte curie sectatoribus siue accessoribus,
ad subeundum, ordinandum, et finaliter determinandum, de et super judiciis
burgorum vniuersalium regni nostri curiis datis siue contradictis; ac eciam
mensuram vlne, ferlote siue bolle, lagine et petre, more solito, ligiis et communibus nostris, dandum, liberandum et recipiendum ; necnon omnia alia et

granted and ordained that the parliament of the Four Burghs should be held yearly
in our burgh of Edinburgh as it was held in times past. We will and have granted,
and by the tenor hereof grant, for us and our successors for ever, to our burgesses of
our burgh of Edinburgh and their successors, that the said parliament of the Four
Burghs be held yearly in our said burgh of Edinburgh for ever, and be constantly
begun and kept on the appointed day after the feast of St. Michael the archangel,
with continuation of days. Wherefore we strictly charge and command our great
chamberlain and his deputies who shall be for the time that they cause the court of the
parliament of the Four Burghs to be had and held in the accustomed manner within
our foresaid burgh, there being called and summoned yearly to appear thereat the commissioners of the four principal burghs, that is to say, Edinburgh, Strivelyn, Lithqw, and
Lanark, with the suitors or assessors of the said court, to consider, ordain, and finally
determine, of and upon the judgments given or gainsaid in the courts of the whole
burghs of our kingdom ; and also to give, deliver, and receive the measure of the ell,
firlot or boll, stoup and stone, in the accustomed manner, to our lieges and
commons ; also to do and exercise all and sundry which in such a court of
parliament, according to the laws, statutes, and customs of burghs, are treated upon,

singula facienda et excercenda que in huiusmodi curia parliamenti, secundum leges, statuta et burgorum consuetudines, sunt tractanda, subeunda et finaliter determinanda. In cuius rei testimonium, has literas nostras, dictis burgensibus nostris eorumque successoribus pro perpetuo duraturas, sub magno sigillo nostro, fieri fecimus patentes. Testibus: Reuerendis in Christo patribus, Jacobo consanguineo nostro carissimo; Thoma, Georgeo, et Thoma, Sanctiandree, Dunkeldensis, Brechinensis, et Candidecase, ecclesiarum episcopis; dilectis consanguineis nostris, Willelmo, comite Orchadie, domino de Sancto Claro, nostro cancellario; Georgeo comite Angusie; Thoma domino Erskyn; Willelmo domino Somervele; Willelmo domino Borthwik; Willelmo Murray de Tulibardyn; et Willelmo Bonare, nostrorum compotorum rotolutore. Apud Edinburghe, quinto die mensis Nouembris, anno Domini millesimo quadringentesimo quinquagesimo quarto et regni nostri decimo octauo.

considered and finally determined. In witness whereof, we have caused these our letters to be made patent under our great seal, to endure to our said burgesses and their successors for ever. Witnesses: the reverend fathers in Christ, James our dearest cousin; Thomas, George, and Thomas, bishops of the churches of St. Andrews, Dunkeld, Brechin, and Galloway; our beloved cousins, William, earl of Orkney, lord of Saint Clair, our chancellor; George earl of Angus; Thomas lord Erskyn; William lord Somervele; William lord Borthwik; William Murray of Tulibardyn; and William Bonare, our comptroller. At Edinburgh, the fifth day of the month of November, in the year of our Lord one thousand four hundred and fifty four and of our reign the eighteenth.

XXIII.

CHARTER by King James the Second to the Provost, Bailies, Burgesses, and Community of Stirling of the right of patronage of St. James' Hospital, with the lands and others belonging thereto. Stirling, 24th June, 1456.

JACOBUS, Dei gracia, Rex Scotorum: Omnibus probis hominibus tocius terre sue, clericis et laicis, salutem. Quia considerauimus incendia, rapinas et

JAMES, by the grace of God, King of Scots: To all good men of his whole land, clerics and laics, greeting. Whereas we have considered the fireraisings, robberies

depredaciones, per nostros rebelles et proditores, Jacobum de Douglas, militem, et complices suos, super burgo nostro de Striueling et inhabitantibus ipsum burgum alias, in nostri et coroue nostre vilepensionem et contemptum, inhumaniter et crudelissime, in dictorum burgensium et ligiorum nostrorum depauperationem, lesionem et dampnum, quam maximum et grauamen, facta et perpetrata. Nos, igitur, pietate moti, considerantes quod dicti comburgenses ob nostri causam deuastati et spoliati extiterant, et quam maxima dampna sustinuerant, dedimus et concessimus, ac presentis carte nostre tenore damus et concedimus hereditarie pro perpetuo, preposito, balliuis, burgensibus et communitati dicti burgi, et eorum successoribus, burgensibus eiusdem qui pro tempore fuerint, in laudem et honorem Dei Omnipotentis, beate Virginis Marie matris sue et beati Jacobi apostoli et omnium sanctorum, ad edificationem ecclesie parochialis dicti burgi nostri et pro supportatione et sustentatione placei uulgariter dicti *Calsay* prope pontem de Striueling, jus nostrum patronatus siue donacionem et concessionem Hospitalis Beati Jacobi prope dictum pontem de Striueling; vnacum terris, obuentionibus, oblationibus, redditibus, possessionibus et proficuis quibuscumque ad dictum hospitale spectantibus. Tenendum et habendum, dictum jus patronatus siue donationem et conces-

and depredations, barbarously and most cruelly sometime done and perpetrated by our rebels and traitors, James of Donglas, knight, and his accomplices, upon our burgh of Striveling and inhabitants of the said burgh, in despite and contempt of us and our crown, to the impoverishment, hurt and exceeding great loss and damage of our said burgesses and lieges. We, therefore, moved with piety, considering that the said co-burgesses have been wasted and despoiled for our cause, and how great losses they have sustained, have given and granted, and by the tenor of our present charter give and grant heritably for ever, to the provost, bailies, burgesses and community of the said burgh and their successors, burgesses of the same for the time being, to the praise and honour of God Almighty, the blessed Virgin Mary his mother and Saint James the apostle and of all saints, for the building of the parish church of our said burgh and for the support and maintenance of the roadway commonly called the *Calsay* near the bridge of Striveling, our right of patronage or donation and gift of the Hospital of St. James near the said bridge of Striveling; together with the lands, obventions, oblations, rents, possessions and profits whatsoever belonging to the said hospital. To hold and to have, the said right of patronage or donation

sionem dicti hospitalis, dictis preposito, balliuis, burgensibus et communitati dicti burgi nostri et eorum successoribus, burgensibus dicti burgi qui pro tempore fuerint, cum vniuersis et singulis terris, redditibus, emolumentis, proficuis et pertinenciis eiusdem, ad ipsorum liberam et plenariam ordinationem et dispositionem, in feodo et hereditate imperpetuum, sine aliquo retiuemento seu obstaculo quocunque; prefatis tamen preposito, balliuis, burgensibus et communitate dicti burgi, supportantibus et sustentantibus dictam placeam et facientibus et perimplentibus omnia alia ouera dicto hospitali incumbentia, debita et consueta, juxta primeuam et antiquam fundationem eiusdem hospitalis. In cuius rei testimonium presenti carte nostre magnum sigillum nostrum apponi precepimus. Testibus: Reuerendo in Christo patre Georgeo episcopo Brechinensi; dilectis consanguineis nostris, Thoma domino Erskin, Patricio domino Grahame, Roberto domino Boide, et Alexandro Napare, nostrorum compotorum rotulatore. Apud Striueling, vicesimo quarto die mensis Junii, anno Domini millesimo quadringentesimo quinquagesimo sexto et regni nostri vicesimo.

and gift of the said hospital, to the said provost, bailies, burgesses and community of our said burgh and their successors, burgesses of the said burgh for the time being, with all and sundry lands, rents, emoluments, profits and pertinents of the same, for their free and full ordination and disposal, in fee and heritage for ever, without any hindrance or obstacle whatever; the foresaid provost, bailies, burgesses and community of the said burgh, nevertheless supporting and maintaining the said roadway and doing and fulfilling all other burdens incumbent on the said hospital, due and wont, according to the first and ancient foundation of the said hospital. In witness whereof we have commanded our great seal to be appended to our present charter. Witnesses: The reverend father in Christ George bishop of Brechin; our well beloved cousins, Thomas lord Erskin, Patrick lord Grahame, Robert lord Boide, and Alexander Napare, our comptroller. At Striveling, on the twenty fourth day of the month of June, in the year of our Lord one thousand four hundred and fifty six and of our reign the twentieth.

XXIV.

CHARTER by Macolm Flemyng to the Provost, Bailies, Councillors, and Community of Stirling, of a tenement on the south side of the High Street forming the site of the Tolbooth. Kirkintulloch, 13th November, 1473.

OMNIBUS hanc cartam visuris vel audituris: Macolmus Flemyng, filius et heres apparens Roberti domini le Flemyng, salutem in Eo qui est omnium vera salus. Noueritis me, vtilitate atique et commodo meis vndeque preuisis et pensatis, concessisse, vendidisse ac titulo vendicionis pure et imperpetuum alienasse et hac presenti carta mea confirmasse, ac per presentes concedere, vendere, alienare et hereditarie confirmare, honorabilibus, prouidis et discretis viris, preposito, balliuis, consulibus et communitati burgi de Striueline, totum et integrum tenementum meum, cum pertinenciis, jacentem infra dictum burgum ex parte australi Vici Regii inter terram Johannis Brady ex parte orientali ab vna et communem viam regiam seu venellam ducentem ad ecclesiam parochialem dicti burgi ex parte occidentali partibus ab alia, pro quadam certa summa pecunie bone et legalis monete regni Scocie michi per prefatos propositum, balliuos, consules et communitatem dicti burgi, in mea necessitate, gratanter premaribus, in summa integra persoluta, in pecunia

To ALL who shall see or hear this charter. Macolm Flemyng, son and apparent heir of Robert lord le Flemyng, greeting in Him who is the true salvation of all. Know ye that I, my use, profit and advantage, certainly in every way foreseen and considered, have given and by title of pure sale have sold and for ever alienated and by this my present charter confirmed, and by these presents grant, sell, alienate and heritably confirm to honorable, provident and discreet men, the provost, bailies, councillors and community of the burgh of Striveline, all and whole my tenement, with the pertinents, lying within the said burgh on the south side of the High Street between the land of John Brady on the east side on the one part and the common highway or vennel leading to the parish church of the said burgh on the west side on the other part, for a certain sure sum of good and lawful money of the kingdom of Scotland thankfully paid beforehand in a whole sum to me by the foresaid provost, bailies, councillors, and community of the said burgh in my necessity, in told money, and applied to my uses in various ways; of which sum of money I hold me well content and

numerata, et in vsus meos diuersimodo conuersa ; de qua quidam summa
pecunie teneo me bene contentum et pacatum per eosdem, et ipsos ac suos
successores, prepositos, balliuos, consules et communitatem dicti burgi, pro
me et heredibus meis, quittumclamo et exonero perpetuum per presentes. Tenendum et habendum, dictum totum et integrum tenementum cum pertinenciis,
profatis preposito, balliuis, consulibus et communitati, et suis successoribus
predictis, a me et heredibus meis, de supremo domino nostro Rege regni Scocie et
suis successoribus regibus eiusdem, in feodo et hereditate imperpetuum, per omnes
rectas metas suas et diuisas, nouas et antiquas, cum vlna terre precedente in
latitudine dicte venelle a radice muri dicti tenementi, per supremum dominum
nostrum Regem michi concessa, in limitibus, bondis, fronte et cauda, longitudine
ac latitudine prout jacet, in edificiis, domibus, cameris, soliis, woltis, repera-
turis, muris, tegulis, tectis, lignis, tignis, meremiis, ferro, lapidibus, sabulo et
calce in dicto tenemento edificatis et ad iidem per me ordinatis et auisatis
edificaturis ; ac cum omnibus aliis et singulis libertatibus, commoditatibus,
asiamentis ac justis suis pertinenciis quibuscunque, tam non nominatis quam
nominatis, tam sub terra quam supra terram, prope et procul, ad dictum totum

satisfied by them, and for me and my heirs by these presents for ever exoner and
discharge them and their successors, provosts, bailies, councillors, and community of
the said burgh.   To hold and to have, all and whole the said tenement with the
pertinents, to the foresaid provost, bailies, councillors, and community and their
successors foresaid, from me and my heirs, of our sovereign lord the King of the
kingdom of Scotland and his successors kings of the same, in fee and heritage for
ever, by all their right meiths and marches, new and old, with an ell of land going
out before in the breadth of the said vennel from the foot of the wall of the said
tenement, given to me by our sovereign lord the King, in the limits, bounds, fore and
back, as it lies in length and breadth, in buildings, houses, chambers, floors, vaults,
repertories, walls, tiles, roofs, timber, wood, materials, iron, stones, gravel and lime
built in the said tenement and ordained and designed by me to be built upon the same ;
and with all and sundry other liberties, commodities, easements and their just pertinents
whatsoever, as well not named as named, as well under the ground as above the
ground, far and near, belonging to all and whole the said tenement with the pertinents
or that may justly belong in any way in time to come, freely, quietly, fully, wholly,
honorably, well and in peace, without any hindrance or revocation whatsoever. Pay-

et integrum tenementum cum pertinenciis spectantibus seu quomodolibet iuste
spectare valentibus in futurum, libere, quiete, plenarie, integre, honorifice,
bene et in pace, sine retinemento vel reuocatione aliquali. Reddendo inde,
annuatim, dicti prepositus, balliui, consules et communitas dicti burgi et sui successores predicti, supremo domino nostro Regi et suis successoribus, regibus regni
Scocie, firmam regiam, cum seruicio in burgo inde debito et consueto, ac capellano
perpetuo et altari Sancti Niniani fundato et situato in dicta ecclesia parochiali sex
solidos et octo denarios annui redditus ac alios annuos redditus inde exeuntes
et debitos[1], tantum, pro omni alio onere, exaccione, seruicio seculari, exceptione,
questione seu demanda, que de dicto toto et integro tenemento cum pertinenciis
exigi poterunt quomodolibet vel requiri. Et ego, dictus Macolmus Flemyng,
et heredes mei dictum totum et integrum tenementum cum pertinenciis prefatis preposito, balliuis, consulibus et communitati dicti burgi, et suis successoribus predictis, in omnibus et per omnia vt premissum est contra omnes
mortales, warantizabimus, acquietabimus et presentis carte tenore defendemus.
In cuius rei testimonium sigillum meum presenti carte mee est appensum.

ing therefor, yearly, the said provost, bailies, councillors, and community of the said
burgh and their successors foresaid to our sovereign lord the King and his successors,
kings of the kingdom of Scotland, the royal ferme with service in burgh therefrom
due and wont, and to the perpetual chaplain and the altar of Saint Ninian founded
and situated in the said parish church six shillings and eight pennies of annual rent
and other annual rents exigible and due therefrom[1], only, for all other burden, exaction,
secular service, exception, question or demand, which can in any way be asked or
required of all and whole the said tenement with the pertinents. And I, the said
Macolm Flemyng, and my heirs shall warrant, acquit, and by the tenor of the present
charter defend all and whole the said tenement with the pertinents to the foresaid
provost, bailies, councillors and community of the said burgh, and their successors
foresaid, in all and by all, as aforesaid, against all mortals. In witness whereof my
seal is appended to my present charter. At Kirkintulloch, on the thirteenth day

[1] The property was acquired by Malcolm
Flemyng from William Bully, chaplain of the
altar of the Holy Cross in the parish church,
conform to charter dated 27th February, 1471,
which King James III. confirmed by charter
under his great seal dated 10th November,
1472. In this confirmation there is, in addition
to the annualrent of 6s. 8d. to St. Ninian's
altar, one of 26s. 8d. payable to the altar of
St. Thomas, the Apostle, in the parish church.

Apud Kirkintulloch, decimo tercio die mensis Nouembris anno Domini
millesimo quadringentesimo septuagesimo tercio, coram hiis testibus : Roberto
Boyde, Willelmo de Lethprevir, Allano de Lethprevir, dominis Thoma Axt-
kynson, Jacobo Darow, capellanis, et Willelmo Cochran, cum diuersis aliis.

of the month of November in the year of our Lord one thousand four hundred and
seventy-three, in presence of these witnesses : Robert Boyde, William of Lethprevir,
Allan of Lethprevir, Sir Thomas Axtkynsoun, Sir James Darow, chaplains, and
William Cochran, with sundry others.

XXV.

LETTERS by the Provost, Bailies, Council, and Community of the Burgh of
Stirling, adjudging possession of a tenement in Stirling to the Altar of
the Holy Trinity in the Parish Church, in default of payment of an annual
rent. Stirling, 22nd April, 1476.

VNIUERSIS ET SINGULIS ad quorum noticias presentes litere peruenerint, prepositus, balliui, consules et communitas burgi de Striuelin, salutem in Eo
qui est omni vera salus.   Cum pietatis et meriti sit opus, et nostro congruit
officio, vnicuique secundum rei geste veritatem, presertim coram nobis pro-
batam et compertam, testimonium veridicum prohibere, in casu quo per maxime
quo aguite veritatis occultatio, preiudicium, grauamen aut dispendium, generare
poterit innocenti.   Proinde est quod presentium per tenorem attestamur et fidele
prohibemus testimonium quod alias in quatuor nostris curiis et nostri burgi
predicti curiis capitalibus discretus vir, dominus Robertus Simsoun, capellanus
perpetuus altaris Sancte Trinitatis fundati in ecclesia parochiali de Striuelin,

To ALL AND SUNDRY to whose knowledge the present letters shall come, the provost,
bailies, councillors, and community of the burgh of Strivelin, greeting in Him
who is the true salvation of all.   Whereas it is a work of godliness and merit, and
becomes our office, to bear soothfast testimony to everyone according to the truth of
the fact, especially when it is proved and found before us, in a case wherein exceed-
ingly the concealment of known truth may generate damage, injury, or expense to
the innocent.   Therefore it is that by the tenor of these presents we attest and bear
faithful testimony that certain times in our four courts and in the head courts of

coram nobis in nostro pretorio consedentibus processit et processus fecit,
videlicit, in curia capitali post festum Pasche mensis Aprilis die tertio anno
Domini millesimo cccc° lxxv°, in curia capitali post festum Sancti Michaelis
archangeli, mensis, videlicet, Octobris die secundo, in curia capitali post festum
Natiuitatis Domini die decimo quinto mensis Januarij et in curia capitali post
festum Pasche die vicesimo secundo mensis Aprilis anno Domini millesimo
cccc° lxxvj° hoc, proximis successiue et immediate alternatim sequentibus, super
vno tenemento terre jacente in burgo nostro de Striuelin antedicto quod fuit
quondam Johannis Worthy, jacente infra dictum burgum in Venella Castri ex
parte occidentali Vici Regij inter terram Roberti Joffray ex parte australi ab
vna et terram Johannis Patonsonn ex parte boreali partibus ab alia, ob
defectum solutionis vnius annui redditus decem et quinque solidorum annuatim de prefato toto et integro tenemento; de quo annuo redditu nichil per
certos annos et terminos recepit aut leuauit dictus dominus Robertus Simsonn
seu recipere aut leuare potuit. Vnde prefatus dominus Robertus, Johanne Crage,
Thoma Smytht et Johanne Rodye, sergeandj, et diuersis testibus, burgi nostri
predicti burgensibus, videlicet, Michaele Patonsonn, Johanne Patonsonn, Alex-

our foresaid burgh a discreet man, Sir Robert Simsoun, perpetual chaplain of the
altar of the Holy Trinity founded in the parish church of Strivelin proceeded, and led
a process before us sitting openly in our tolbooth, namely, in the head court after
the feast of Pasch on the third day of the month of April the year of our Lord one
thousand four hundred and seventy-five, in the head court after the feast of St.
Michael the archangel, namely, on the second day of the month of October, in the
head court after the feast of the Nativity of our Lord on the fifteenth day of the
month of January, and in the head court after the feast of Pasch on this twenty-
second day of the month of April in the year of our Lord one thousand four hundred
and seventy-six, next successively and immediately following each other, concerning
a tenement of land lying in our foresaid burgh of Strivelin which belonged to the
deceased John Worthy, lying within the said burgh in the Castle Vennel on the
west side of the High Street between the land of Robert Joffray on the south side
on the one part and the land of John Patonsoun on the north side on the other part,
on account of the non-payment of an annual rent of fifteen shillings yearly from all
and whole the foresaid tenement; of which annual rent the said Sir Robert Symsoun
has received or uplifted or been able to receive or uplift nothing for certain years and

andró Cristall, Thoma Crage, Johanne Freman, Dauido Weilfeid, Georgeo Lyntoun et Alexandro Brouster, nostris auctoritate et mandato, ad predictum teuementum accesserunt vicissim, in qualibet ipsarum nostrarum curiarum, et nichil inibi preter terram et lapides vnde dictum tenementum astringi pro dicto annuo redditu aliqualiter possit iuuenerunt; qui nobis in singulis curiis nostris presentauit. Et in vltima dicta predictarum curiarum comparuit idem dominus Robertus et peciit judicium quod possessio illius tenementi cum pertineuciis sibi tanquam domino capitali et fundi eiusdem, sub Rege, in defectu dicti annui redditus non soluti, redundari et reuerti debeat; et super hoc plegium obtinuit et inuenuit, quo plegio recepto et non contradicto, parte prosequente tunc de curia exeunte, et parte aduersa et defendenti sepe vocata ad comparendum defendendumque et resistendum parti prosequenti vel ad satisfaciendum dicto domino Roberto Simsoun, capellano, de annuis redditibus ex annis et terminis preteritis non solutis, vnacum dampnis et expensis super processu antedicto factis et faciendis; qua parte aduersa non comparente, curia consulta, et parte prosequente introducta, possessio illius tenementi cum per-

terms. Whereupon the foresaid Sir Robert, John Crage, Thomas Smytht and John Rodye, sergeants, and sundry witnesses, burgesses of our foresaid burgh, namely, Michael Patonsoun, John Patonsoun, Alexander Cristall, Thomas Crage, John Freman, David Weilfeid, George Lyntoun, and Alexander Brouster, by our authority and mandate, passed one after another to the foresaid tenement, at every one of our said courts, and found nothing there except earth and stones from which the said tenement could in any way be distrained for the said annual rent; which was represented to us in our several courts. And in the last diet of our foresaid courts compeared the said Sir Robert and asked judgment that possession of the said tenement with the pertinents ought to return and revert to him as the lord in chief and of the ground of the same, under the King, in default of the said annual rent not being paid : and upon this he obtained and found a pledge, which pledge being received and not gainsaid, the party prosecuting then leaving the court, and the opposite and defending party being ofttimes called to compear and defend and oppose the party prosecuting or to satisfy the said Sir Robert Simsoun, chaplain, of the annual rents for the by past years and terms unpaid, together with the damages and expenses caused and to be caused in regard to the foresaid process ; which opposite party not compearing, the court having consulted, and the prosecuting party

tinenciis adiudicata fuit dicto domino Roberto Simsoun, capellano, et suis
successoribus perpetuis dicti altaris, imperpetuum hereditarie, per os Thome
Steynesoun, tunc dempstarij siue judiciarij dicte curie; quo adiudicato Dauid
Murray, tunc temporis vnius balliuorum burgi prefati, statum, saisinam, et
possessionem realem, actualem et corporalem, illius tenementi cum pertinenciis,
saluo jure cuiuslibet, per terre et lapidis tradicionem, vt moris est burgorum,
prefato domino Roberto Symsoun, capellano, tradidit vt congruit atque
donauit; publiceque proclamare fecit quod si quis uel qua jus uel interesse
ad predictum tenementum cum pertinenciis vindicare aut reclamare
voluerit aut reclamauerit habere, infra tempus legittimum et jure statutum
et indultum veniret et de annuis redditibus preteritis, expensis et aliis, refun-
dendis satisfaceret, et quod dictum tenementum cum pertinenciis haberet
solutum et quietum et possiderit pro perpetuo, prout expostulat et requirit juris
ordo. Et hoc omnibus quorum interest uel interesse poterit notificamus per
presentes. In cuius rei testimonium sigillum nostrum commune dicti burgi
nostri, vnacum sigillo dicti Dauid Murray, balliui nostri, qui dictam, nostris ex
mandato et precepto, contulit possessionem et saisinam prefati tenementi cum

being brought in, by the mouth of Thomas Steynesoun, then dempster or judiciar
of the said court, possession of the said tenement with the pertinents was adjudged
to the said Sir Robert Simsoun, chaplain, and his perpetual successors at the said
altar, heritably for ever; on which adjudication David Murray, then one of the
bailies of the foresaid burgh, delivered and gave as became, to the foresaid Sir Robert
Symsoun, chaplain, state, sasine, and real, actual and corporal possession of the said
tenement with the pertinents, saving the right of every one, by delivery of earth and
stone as the manner of burghs is; and caused it to be publicly proclaimed that if any
one, man or woman, shall wish to challenge or claim, or shall claim to have right or
interest in the foresaid tenement with the pertinents, he or she shall come within the
lawful time appointed and allowed by law and make payment of the bypast annual
rents, expenses and others, to be refunded, and that he shall have and possess the
said tenement with the pertinents free and quit for ever, as the order of law demands
and requires. And this to all who have or may have interest we notify by these
presents. In witness whereof to these presents we have caused to be appended our
common seal of our said burgh, together with the seal of the said David Murray,
our bailie, who at our command and precept gave possession and sasine of the fore-

pertinenciis, presentibus apponi fecimus.   Apud dictum burgum nostrum
vicessimo secundo die mensis Aprilis anno Domini millesimo cccc° lxxvj°.

said tenement with the pertinents.   At our said burgh on the twenty second day
of the month of April in the year of our Lord one thousand four hundred and
seventy-six.

XXVI.

INSTRUMENT setting forth the Union of the Altars of the Holy Trinity
and of St. Thomas in the Parish Church of Stirling and the Institution
of a Chaplain thereto.   Stirling, 6th November, 1490.

IN DEI NOMINE, amen.   Per hoc presens publicum instrumentum cunctis
pateat euidenter quod anno incarnacionis Dominice millesimo quadringentesimo monogesimo, die vero mensis Nouembris sexto, indictione octaua,
pontificatus sanctissimi in Christo patris ac domini domini Innocencii, diuina
prouidencia, Pape, octaui, anno septimo, ac regni excellentissimi principis
supremique domini nostri regis Jacobi quarti Scotorum regis illustrissimi anno
tercio : In mei, notarii publici, et testium subscriptorum, presencia personaliter
constitutus venerabilis vir, magister Duncanus Bully, archidiaconus Dunblanensis, accedens ad insulam Sancte Trinitatis situatam et fundatam in ecclesia
parochiali de Striueling, et ibidem cum consensu et assensu preposti et

IN THE NAME OF GOD, amen.   By this present public instrument be it manifestly
known to all that on the sixth day of November in the year of the incarnation
of our Lord one thousand four hundred and ninety, in the eighth indiction, the
seventh year of the pontificate of the most holy father in Christ and lord, lord Innocent
the eighth, by divine providence, Pope, and in the third year of the reign of the
most excellent prince and our sovereign lord King James the Fourth, most illustrious
King of Scots : In presence of me, notary public, and witnesses underwritten, personally compeared a venerable man master Duncan Bully, archdeacon of Dunblane,
passing to the aisle of the Holy Trinity situated and founded in the parish church of

ballivorum necnon et consilio burgi antedicti de Striueling, vt ipse asseruit se
esse patronum altarium Sancte Trinitatis et Sancti Thome, apostoli, et ibidem
vniuit et coniuxit altare Sancti Thome, apostoli, ad altare Sancte Trinitatis,
quia annui redditus eorundem fuerunt districte per combustionem ville quod
non potuerunt sustinere duos capellanos, sed minime vnum. Et immediate
dictus magister Duncanus Bully, cum consensu et assensu propositi et ballu-
orum necnon et consilio burgi antedicti de Striueling contulit et dedit
institucionem discreto viro, domino Roberto Symsoun, capellano de dictis
altaribus, per tradicionem cornu altaris, semper et quousque dictus magister
Duncanis potuit optinere certos annuos redditus de bonis suis sibi a Deo
collatis, ad sustencionem duorum capellanorum.   De et super quibus, omnibus
et singulis, dictus dominus Robertus Simsoun a me notario publico subscripto
sibi fieri peciit vnum aut plura publicum seu publica instrumentum aut
instrumenta. Acta fuerunt hec apud insulam antedictam in ecclesia parochiali antedicta de Striueling hora quasi decima ante merediem vel circirca,
sub anno, die, mense, indictione et pontificatu quibus supra. Presentibus :
Duncano Forester de Torwode, Johanne Stewart de Jhonnestoun, Waltero

Striueling and there with consent and assent of the provost and bailies and also with
the council of the foresaid burgh of Striueling, as he asserted himself to be patron of
the altars of the Holy Trinity and St. Thomas, the apostle, and there united and
conjoined the altar of St. Thomas, the apostle, to the altar of the Holy Trinity, because
the annual rents of the same were destroyed by the burning of the town so that they
were unable to sustain two chaplains, but one only. And immediately the said
master Duncan Bully, with consent and assent of the provost and bailies and also with
the council of the foresaid burgh of Striueling bestowed and gave institution to a
discreet man, Sir Robert Symsoun, chaplain of the said altars, by delivering the
horn of the altar, always and vntil the said master Duncan could obtain certain
annual rents of his goods bestowed on him by God, for the support of two chaplains.
Whereupon, all and sundry, the said Robert Simsoun asked from me notary public
subscribing to make to him one or more public instrument or instruments. These
things were done at the foresaid aisle in the foresaid parish church of Striueling the
tenth hour before noon or thereabout, in the year, day, month, indiction and
pontificate aforesaid. Present : Duncan Forester of Torwode, John Stewart of
Jhonnestoun, Walter Forester, Thomas Forester, Adam Bully, Alexander Nortoun,

Forester, Thoma Forester, Adam Bully, Alexandro Nortoun, Jacobo Dausoun, Roberto Simsoun, Thoma Cragyngelt de eodem, Johanne Crag, domino Dauid Robertsoun, vicario de Kirkintulloch, domino Roberto Mure, rectore de Glendovane et Willelmo Speyr, cum diuersis aliis vocatis, rogatis et requisitis in fidem et testimonium omnium et singulorum premissorum.

Et ego, Alexander Fresser, presbyter, Sanctiandree diocesis, publicus auctoritatibus imperiali ac regali notarius, quia prefatis omnibus et singulis dum sic ut premittitur nec non et vnioni eorundem altarumi presens personaliter fui ; eaque omnia et singula sic fieri, vidi, sciui, et audiui, ac in notam recepi, indeque presens publicum instrumentum, alterius manu me aliis prepedito peragendis fideliter scriptum confeci, et hic me manu mea propria subscribendo in hanc publicam formam redegi, signoque ac nomine meis solitis et consuetis signaui, rogatus et requisitus, in fidem et testimonium omnium et singulorum premissorum.

ALEXR. FRESSER.

James Dausoun, Robert Simsoun, Thomas Cragyngelt of that ilk, John Crag, Sir David Robertsoun, vicar of Kirkintulloch, Sir Robert Mure, rector of Glendovane, and William Speyr, with sundry others, called, asked and required, in faith and testimony of all and sundry the premises.

And I, Alexander Fresser, priest, of the diocese of St. Andrews, notary public by imperial and royal authority, because I was personally present at all and sundry the foresaid things while done as aforesaid and also at the union of the said altars; and I saw, knew and heard the same, all and sundry, so done, and took a note thereupon ; and therefrom have made this present public instrument, faithfully written by the hand of another, I being occupied in doing of other things, and hereon subscribing my proper hand have reduced into this public form, and signed with my sign and name used and wont, being asked and required in faith and testimony of all and sundry the premises.

ALEXR. FRESSER.

XXVII.

CHARTER by Richard Crystysone, Canon of the Collegiate Church of Abernethy, giving and confirming certain annual rents to the Altar of St. James
in the Parish Church of Stirling and appointing the Community of
Stirling patrons of the Altar. Stirling, 2nd April, 1492.

OMNIBUS hanc cartam visuris vel audituris. Ricardus Crystysone, canonicus
ecclesie collegiate de Abernethy, salutem et mutuam in Domino caritatem.
Nouerit vniuersitas vestra me, zelo et instinctu deuocionis et compunctionis
motum, in potestate legali existentem, pro salubri statu et regimine supremi
domini nostri domini Jacobi quarti Scotorum Regis illustrissimi meorumque
consanguineorum et successorum, saluteque animarum ipsius Regis nostri
parentumque amicorum, predicessorum et successorum, ac omnium fidelium
defunctorum, in laudem, gloriam et honorem Dei Omnipotentis, beate Virginis
Marie matris sue gloriose, Sancti Jacobi apostoli et omnium sanctorum, dedisse,
concessisse, assignasse, et hoc presenti scripto meo confirmasse Deo et beato
Jacobo apostolo et ipsius beati Jacobi altari situato et locato infra nauem
ecclesie parochialis de Strineling, et vni capellano inibi in diuinis perpetuo
celebraturo, annuos redditus subscriptos:—In primis, vnum annuum redditum

To ALL who shall see or hear this charter. Richard Crystysone, canon of the collegiate
church of Abernethy, greeting and mutual love in the Lord. Be it known to you
all that I, moved with zeal and prompting of devotion and compunction, being in
legal power, for the salutary state and government of our sovereign lord, lord James
the fourth, most illustrious king of Scots, and of my kinsmen and successors, and for
the salvation of the souls of our said King and of my parents, friends, predecessors and
successors, and of all the faithful dead, to the praise, glory and honour of God Almighty,
of the blessed Virgin Mary, his glorious mother, of St. James the apostle and of all
saints, have given, granted, assigned, and by this my present writing have confirmed
to God and Saint James the apostle and to the altar of the said Saint James situated
and placed within the nave of the parish church of Striveling, and to one chaplain
perpetually to celebrate divine service therein, the annualrents underwritten :—
In the first, an annualrent of thirty shillings from the Hospital of St. James ; also an

G

de hospitali Sancti Jacobi, triginta solidorum ; item, vnum annuum redditum
quinque solidorum de terris jacentibus ex parte boriali pontis de Strineling ;
item, de vno orto pertinente Sancto Jacobo jacente ex parte australi pontis
de Striueling, vnum annuum redditum triginta solidorum ; item, vnum annuum
redditum decem et octo denariorum de vna crofta jacente prope *le Borowmyll*
ex parte australi eiusdem ; item, vnum annuum redditum duorum solidorum
de terra pertinente Roberto Greg jacente in Alto Vico ex parte boriali inter
terram quondam Willelmi Benneis ex parte occidentali et terram Willelmi Luter
ex parte orientali ; item, vnum annuum redditum decem et trium solidorum
ac quatuor denariorum de terra Thome Crag jacente in Alto Vico ex parte
boriali eiusdem ; item, vnum annuum redditum de terra Walteri George sex
solidorum et octo denariorum jacente in Alto Vico ex parte boriali eiusdem ;
item, vnum annuum redditum quinque solidorum et sex denariorum de terra
Mathei Forestare jacente in *le Mary Wynde;* item, vnum annuum redditum
sex solidorum et octo denariorum de terra Johannis Adamsone in *le Castell
Wynde*; item, vnum annuum redditum viginti solidorum et octo denariorum
de terra Johannis Crag jacente in Alto Vico ex parte boriali eiusdem inter
terram quondam Ricardi Mure ex parte orientali et terram Johannis Forestare

annualrent of five shillings from lands lying on the north side of the bridge of
Striveling : also from a garden belonging to Saint James lying on the south side of
the bridge of Striveling an annualrent of thirty shillings ; also, an annualrent of
eighteen pennies from a croft lying near the Borowmyll on the south side of the same ;
also, an annualrent of two shillings from a land belonging to Robert Greg lying in
the High Street on the north side between the land of the deceased William Benneis
on the west side and the land of William Luter on the east side ; also, an annualrent
of thirteen shillings and four pennies from the land of Thomas Crag lying in the High
Street on the north side of the same ; also, an annualrent of six shillings and eight
pennies from the land of Walter George lying in the High Street on the north side
of the same; also, an annualrent of five shillings and six pennies from the land of
Mathew Forestare lying in the Mary Wynde ; also, an annualrent of six shillings
and eight pennies from the land of John Adamsone in the Castell Wynde ; also, an
annualrent of twenty shillings and eight pennies from the land of John Crag lying
in the High Street on the north side of the same between the land of the deceased
Richard Mure on the east side and the land of John Forestare on the west side ; also

ex parte occidentali; item, vnum annuum redditum decem solidorum de terra
Johannis Crag jacente in *le Mary Wynde;* item, vnum annuum redditum
viginti solidorum de vna terra jacente in *le Bakraw* inter terram quondam
Magistri Roberti Forestare ex parte occidentali et terram quondam Johannis
Robisone ex parte orientali; item, vnum annuum redditum decem et sex solidorum de terra Johannis Robysone jacente super *le Bakraw* jacente inter
terram Ricardi Crystysone ex parte occidentali et terram Ricardi Curry ex
parte orientali; item, vnum annuum redditum decem et sex solidorum de
terris Roberti Lawsone jacentibus in *le Myddylraw* inter terram Alexandri
Cossoure ex parte occidentali et terram Johannis Modane ex parte orientali;
item, de terra Johannis Crag in Alto Vico ex parte boriali jacente infra terram
quondam Ricardi Mure ex parte orientali et terram Johannis Forestare ex
parte occidentali vnum annuum redditum decem et trium solidorum ac quatuor
denariorum, pro obitu meo. Tenendos et habendos omnes et singulos predictos annuos redditus beato Jacobo apostolo altarique suo prefato, et vni
capellano inibi in diuinis perpetue celibraturo, et successoribus suis qui pro
tempore fuerint, de Deo et beato Jacobo, in puram, piam et perpetuam
elimosinam, in feodo et hereditate imperpetuum, per omnes rectas metas suas

an annualrent of ten shillings from the land of John Crag lying in Mary Wynde;
also, an annualrent of twenty shillings from a land lying in the Bakraw between the
land of the deceased Mr. Robert Forestare on the west part and the land of the
deceased John Robisone on the east part; also, an annualrent of sixteen shillings from
the land of John Robysone lying upon the Bakraw lying between the land of Richard
Crystysone on the west part and the land of Richard Curry on the east part; also
an annualrent of sixteen shillings from the land of Robert Lawsone, lying in the
Myddylraw between the land of Alexander Cossoure on the west side and the land
of John Modane on the east side; also, from the land of John Crag in the High
Street on the north side lying within the land of the deceased Richard Mure on the
east part and the land of John Forestare on the west part an annualrent of thirteen
shillings and four pennies, for my obit. To hold and to have all and sundry the
foresaid annualrents to St. James the apostle and his altar foresaid, and to a chaplain
for ever to celebrate divine service there, and to his successors who shall be for the
time, of God and St. James, in pure, pious and perpetual alms, in fee and heritage
for ever, by all their right meiths and marches, with all and sundry liberties, com-

et diuisas, cum omnibus et singulis libertatibus, commoditatibus, aysiamentis,
ac iustis pertinentiis suis quibuscunque, adeo libere, quiete, plenarie, integre,
honorifice, bene et in pace, sicut aliqui annui redditus cum pertinentiis per
quemcunque cuicunque capellanie seu altari aut aliis quibusuis piis vsubus
infra hoc regnum Scotie conceduntur, assignantur, dantur et confirmantur.
Faciendo inde, annuatim et indies, capellanus dicte capellanie qui pro tempore
fuerit, apud dictum altare missarum priuatarum et aliarum precinm et
oracionum suffragia deuotarum; nec non supportando et celebrari faciendo
annuatim idem capellanus, per capellanos celebrantes in choro ecclesie parochialis
de Striueling, in die obitus mei, exequias cum nouem lectionibus missisque
priuatis; et vna missa de requie cum nota in crastina, vt moris est, cereis
accensis et campanis solemniter pulsatis, tantum, pro omni alio ouere,
exaccione, questione, seruicio seculari seu demanda, que de dictis annuis
redditibus exigi poterunt quomodolibet vel requiri. Quos quidem annuos
redditus predictos cum pertinentiis, ego Ricardus Crystesone antedictus, suc-
cessoresque mei, et communitas dicti burgi de Striueling qui pro tempore
fuerint, dicto beato Jacobo altarique suo predicto et capellano eiusdem qui
pro tempore fuerit, in omnibus et per omnia vt premissum est, contra omnes
mortales warrantizabimus, acquietabimus et imperpetuum defendemus et

modities, easements and their just pertinents whatsoever, as freely, quietly, fully,
wholly, honourably, well and in peace, as any annualrents with the pertinents are
granted, assigned, given and confirmed by any one to any chaplainry or altar or to
any other pious uses whatever within this kingdom of Scotland. Giving therefor,
the chaplain of the said chaplainry who shall be for the time, yearly and daily at
the said altar, suffrages of private masses and other prayers and devout supplications;
the said chaplain also supporting and causing to be celebrated yearly by the chaplains celebrating in the choir of the parish church of Striveling, on the day of my
obit, exequies with nine lessons and private masses; and with one mass of requiem,
with note, on the morrow, as the manner is, with wax candles kindled and bells
solemnly rung, only, for all other burden, exaction, question, secular service or demand,
which can be any way asked or required of the said annualrents. Which foresaid
annualrents with the pertinents, I, Richard Crystesone foresaid and my successors
and the community of the said burgh of Striveling who shall be for the time, shall
warrant, acquit, and for ever defend to the said St. James and his foresaid altar and

defendent. Donationem vero dicte capellanie, dum eam tociens quociens quouismodo de iure et de facto vacare contigerit, communitas dicti burgi et successores sui ipsam dent et conferant capellano ydoneo examinato et sufficienti saltem in litteratura ad diuina inibi ministranda reperto, quos patronos, protectores et defensores eiusdem facio, deputo, specialiter et ordino. In cuius rei testimonium sigillum meum et sigillum commune dicti burgi de Striueling presenti carte mee sunt appensa, apud pretorium eiusdem secundo die mensis Aprilis anno Domini millesimo quadringentesimo nonogesimo secundo. Presentibus: Honorabilibus et prouidis viris, Duncano Forestare de Torwode, Johanne Stewart de Johonstoune, Patricio Redhucht, Johanne Patonsone, Johanne Aysone, Alexandro Nortoune, Johanne Crag, et Thoma Narne, burgensibus dicti burgi, cum diuersis aliis.

the chaplain of the same who shall be for the time, in all and by all as aforesaid, against all mortals. But the donation of the said chaplainry, while and so often as it shall happen in any way by right and by fact to fall vacant, the community of the said burgh and their successors, whom I make, depute and specially ordain, to be patrons, protectors and defenders thereof, shall give and confer the same on a fit chaplain examined and found sufficient at least in literature to minister divine service thereat. In witness whereof my seal and the common seal of the said burgh of Striveling are appended to my present charter, at the tolbooth of the same on the second day of April the year of our Lord one thousand four hundred and ninety-two. Present : Honourable and provident men, Duncan Forestare of Torwode, John Stewart of Johnstoune, Patrick Redhucht, John Patonsone, John Aysone, Alexander Nortoune, John Crag and Thomas Narne, burgesses of the said burgh, with divers others.

XXVIII.

DECREE of the Lords Auditors of Causes and Complaints, ordaining certain persons to desist from occupying the fishings of the Water of Forth belonging to the burgh of Stirling. Edinburgh, 12th December, 1494.

THE lordis auditouris decrettis and deliueris that William Michelson, Johnne Bennate, Adam Wise, Johnne Cowy, Johnne Higgin, William Wilson, William Yong, Robert Dauidsoun, Johnne Wilsoun, Hew Adamsoun, Alexander Mortoun, William Stevin, Johnne Rannaldsone, James Brechin, Thomas Michelson, Johnne Wilson, Johnne Tynklare, and ane callit Primros, sall decest and ces fra the occupatioun and intromctting with the fischings of the watter of Forth pertening to the toun and burgh of Striucling, to be broikit and joisit be the prouest, bailyeis, and communite of the said burgh of Strineling, efter the forme and tenour of the charter and infeftment maid to thaim thairupon of auld be our Soucrane Lordis predecessour, vnder his grcte sele, schewin and producit before the lordis; and als decrettis and deliueris that the saidis personis sall content and pay to the said prouest, bailyeis, and communite of Striueling the fische and profitis of the said fisching insafer as thai may sufficiently pref that the saidis personis hes takin up and intromettit with of the ix yeris clamit on thaim in the summondis; to the productioun of the quhilk preif the lordis assignis to the said prouest bailyeis and communite the ix day of Marche nixt tocum, with continuatioun of daiis; and ordinis thaim to haf lettres to summond thair witnes and to warne the partij to here thaim sworn.

XXIX.

DECREE by the Lords of the King's Council ordaining that the Provost, Bailies, and Community of Stirling cease to occupy certain fishings which are to be enjoyed by the Abbot and Convent of Cambuskenneth. Edinburgh, 19th February, 1495-6.

AT Edinburgh, the nyntene day of Februar the yeir of God ane thousand foure hundreth fourscore and fyftene yeris, the lordis of the counsale vnderwrittin, that is to say, nobill and mighty lordis Archibald erle of Angus, &c., chancellare of Scotland, Archibald erle of Argile, &c., maister of houshald to oure Soucrane Lord, Patrik erle of Bothuile, lord Halis, &c., ane venerabill fader in God, Johne prior of Sanctandros, William lord Borthuik, John lord Drummond, Laurence lord Oliphant, William lord Sanct Johnns, Johnne Ogilby of Fingase, maister Richard Lausone, and maister James Henrison, decretis and deliueris that for ocht that thai haue yit sene, the provest, baillies and communite of Striueling sall desist and cess fra the occupatioun of the fischeing of the watter of Forth betuix the abbay of Cambuskynneth and Polmais, and of

the fischeing of the watter of Kersy and Tulibody, to be broukit and joisit
be ane venerabill fader in God, Henry abbot of Cambuskynneth, and the
convent of the samyn, eftir the forme of the charteris and eiudentis maid to
thame tharupone, schewin and producit before the lordis; and als decretis and
deliueris that the said provost, baillies and communite sall content and pay to
the saidis abbot and conuent the proffittis of the saidis fischeings in sa far as
thai may sufficientlie preif the saidis prouest, baillies and communite, hes taken
vp and intromettit with the samyn of the twenty-five yeris contenit in the
summondis; to the production of tae quhilk preif the lordis assignis to the
saidis abbot and conuent the xxi day of Maii nixt to cum, with continuatioun
of days; and ordanis thame to haue lettres to summond thare witnes and the
party to heir thaim sworne.

XXX.

INSTRUMENT setting forth the Institution by the Provost, Bailies, and
    Community of Stirling of a Chaplain to St. James' Altar in the Parish
    Church.   Stirling, 19th April, 1496.

IN DEI NOMINE, amen.   Per hoc presens publicum instrumentum cunctis
pateat eiudenter quod anno incarnationis Dominice millesimo quadringintesimo
nonagesimo sexto, mensis vero Aprilis decimo nono die, indictione decima
quarta, pontificatus sanctissimi in Christo patris et domini nostri domini
Alexandri, diuina prouidencia Pape, sexti, anno tercio: In mei notarii publici
et testium subscriptorum presentia personalter constitutus nobilis et honorabilis

IN THE NAME OF GOD, amen.   By this present public instrument be it manifestly
known to all men that in the year of the incarnation of our Lord one thousand four
hundred and ninety-six, on the nineteenth day of the month of April, in the fourteenth indiction, in the third year of the pontificate of the most holy father in Christ
and our lord, lord Alexander the sixth, by divine providence Pope : In presence of
me notary public and of the witnesses underwritten, personally compeared a noble

vir Jacobus Mentetht, vnus balliuorum burgi de Strincling, accedens ad altare Sancti Jacobi, apostoli, situatum et fundatum in ecclesia Sancti Crucis dicti burgi, ex speciali mandato preposti, ballini [et] communitatis dicti burgi, instituit [et] induxit in realem, actualem et corporalem possessionem, discretum virum, dominum Jacobum Crage, in dicto altari, per traditionem calicis, libri, et cetera ornamenta altaris, vnacum cornua eiusdem. Super quibus, omnibus et singulis, prefatus dominus Jacobus Crage, a me, notario publico subscripto, sibi fieri peciit, vnum aut plura publicum seu publica instrumentum aut instrumenta, cum appensione sigilli dicti Jacobi Mentetht, balliui, communienda. Acta fuerunt hec in dicta ecclesia, hora decima ante merediem vel cacirea, sub anno, die, mense, indictione et pontificatu, quibus supra. Presentibus : Honorabilibus et prouidis viris, Duncano Forstar de Skipincht, milite, Waltero Forstar, Thoma Forstar, Johanne Lokart, Jacobo Spitale, Roberto Simsoue ; dominis Jacobo Franche, Thoma Joffrasoue, Johanne Aisoue et domino Alexandro Fresale, capellanis ; cum diuersis aliis, testibus ad premissa vocatis specialiter atque rogatis.

Et ego, Thomas Kircaldy, presbiter, Sanctiandree diocesis [etc.]

and honourable man James Mentetht, one of the bailies of the burgh of Striveling, passing to the altar of Saint James, the apostle, situated and founded in the church of the Holy Cross of the said burgh, by special command of the provost, bailies and community of the said burgh, instituted and inducted a discreet man, Sir James Crage, in the real, actual and corporal possession in the said altar by delivery of the chalice, book, and other ornaments of the altar, together with the horns of the same. Whereupon, all and sundry, the foresaid Sir James Crage asked from me, notary public subscribing, to make to him one or more public instrument or instruments, to be confirmed with appending of the seal of the said James Mentetht, bailie. These things were done in the said church, the tenth hour before noon, or thereabout, the year, day, month, indiction and pontificate, as above. Present: honourable and prudent men, Duncan Forstar of Skipincht, knight, Walter Forstar, Thomas Forstar, John Lokart, James Spitale, Robert Simsoue ; Sirs James Franche, Thomas Joffrasone, John Aisoue and Sir Alexander Fresale, chaplains; with sundry others, witnesses to the promises specially called and asked.

And I Thomas Kircaldy, priest, of the diocese of St. Andrews [etc., being usual docquet.]

XXXI.

SUBMISSION and Compromise between the Abbot and Convent of Cambuskenneth and the Community of the Burgh of Stirling as to Fishings
in the Water of Forth. Edinburgh, 31st March, 1501.

AT EDINBURGH, the last day of Marche the yere of God jm vc and ane yere, ane
venerabill fader in God, Henry abbot of Cambuskynneth, for him self and as
lauchfull procuratour for the convent of the samyn on the taparte, and richt
honorabill men, Sir Duncan Forester of Skippinche, knycht, James of Mentetʒ,
provest of Strinelling, and George of Crechtoun of Brethirtoun, for thaim self and
in the name and behalue as lauchfull procuratouris for the haile communite
of the burgh of Strinelling on the tother parte, ar fully compromittit till abide
and vnderly the' counsale, decrete, ordinance and finall deliuerance of thir
persouns vnderwrittin, that is to say, ane reuerend fader in God, William
bischope of Abirdene, richt venerabill men Sir Robert Wallis, archedene of
Sanctandros, maister Richard Murcheid, dene of Glasgow and secretar till our
Soucrane Lord, maister Walter Drummond, dene of Dunblane and clerk of the
register, and Maister Gawane of Dunbar, dene of Murray, as jugis arbitrato ris
and amicabill componitouris evinly and indeferentlie chosin be the partijs
forsaidis to knaw and decide apoun the retreting of ane act gevin be the
lordis of our Soucrane Lordis counsale for the saide venerabill fader and convent
of Cambuskynneth anent the fisching of ane parte of the wattir of Forth
clamit to pertene to thame ; and in likewis to knaw and decide apoun all
and sundry the poyntis and artielis contenit in our Soucrane Lordis letteris
of summondis for the retreting of the saide act, raisit be the saide prevest,
bailyeis, counsale and communite of the said burgh of Strinelling, and in all
vther poyntis that they haue to say or allege aganis the saide act for the
retreting of the samyn ; and als to knaw and decide apoun the principale
ground richt of the saide fisching of the saide parte of wattir of Forth clamit
be athir of the saidis partijs te pertene to thame ; and quhat the saidis jugis
chosin decretis and delineris in the premissis baith the saidis partijs ar laundin,
oblist and sworne, lelelie and treulie, be the faithis and trouthis in thar bodeis,
the haly ewangellis tuichit, finalie and perpetually to obserue, kepe and fulfill,

II

for thame and thare successouris, but apellatioun or reuocatioun in tyme tocum.
The quhilkis jugis arbitratouris and amicabill componitouris sall convene and
forgaddir in Edinburgh the tend day of Maij nixt to cum and sall tak the saide
mater debatabill in and apoun thame, and salbe sworne in clikewis lelelic and
treulie be thare conscience and knaulege to counsale, decrete and diliuer
thairintill, and sall geif furth thare decrete and finale deliuerance in the saide
mater within the space of xx dais nixt eftir following the saide tend day of Maij,
but ony langar delay. And gif it happinis any of the saidis jugis arbitratouris
to be absent the saidis partijs sall cheis ane vther siclike juge in his stede quhilk
salbe suorne in clikewis, but preiudice of partij. And in the meynetyme it is
finalie appoyntit and concordit betuix the saidis partijs that the proffite of the
fisching of the saide parte of wattir sall stand and remain as it now dois, but
ony nouatioun, ay and quhill the saide mater debatabill be decidit be the
saidis jugis and to the saide day of the saide decisioun.   In witnes of the
quhilk thing baith the saidis partijs has subscriuit this compromiss with thare
handis, yere, day and place foresaidis, befor thir witnes: maister Henry Quhite,
persoun of Rothes, Johanne Leslie of Wardross, Johnne Month, maister
Alexander Leslie, Robert Hammiltoun, Richard Mekle and William Clerk,
publict notaris, with vtheris diuers. (Signed) H. abbas de Cambuskynneth ;
Duncan Forester of Garden.

XXXII.

DECREET pronounced by the Bishop of Aberdeen and others in Submission
between the Community of the Burgh of Stirling and the Abbot and
Convent of Cambuskenneth as to Fishings in the Forth. Edinburgh,
20th July, 1501.

In the name of God, amen. We, William bischop of Abirdene, James abbot
of Skone, Recharde Murchede dene of Glasgw, Gawane of Dunbar dene of
Murraye, Walter Drummond dene of Dunblane, Rechard Lausoun and James
Henrisoun, jugis arbitratouris and amycable compositouris, evinly chosin betuix
ane venerable fadir in God, Henry abbot of Cambuskenneth, for himself and
his convent of the samyn, haffand sufficient power tharto, on the tane parte,

and James of Menteth, provest of Striueling, Sir Duncan Forestare of Skip
Incb, knycht, Alexander Levingstoun of Donypace, Edwerde Spittaile and
Patrick Redehuch, as procuratouris and commissionaris for the burgh and
communite of Striueling, hauand sufficient commissioun, autorite and power,
for the tothir parte, becam faithfullie compromittit, bundin and oblist, for
thame, thar successouris and eftircummaris, to abide, vndrelie and fulfill oure
decrete, deliuerance and counsale; and we, takand in and apone us to decerne,
deliuer and counsale betuix the saidis partijs in ane actioun and caus mevit
betuix thame anent the fisching of the watter of Forth, etc.—The forsaidis
partiis thar allegeance, richtis and euidentis, herde, sene and vnderstand, and
thaireftir examinand and diligentlie assayand concord betuix the saidis partiis
in the name of God incallit, procedand to our deliuerance be consent and
commonyng of the saidis partiis, decernis, deliueris and counsalis that the
saidis abbot, convent, and thar successouris, sall hafe perpetualie the fisching
of five cobillis vp and doun at the plesour of thame in the said watter of Forth,
in the quhilkis five cobillis ar includit and contenit the twa cobillis that the said
place had of befor, to be brukit and joisit perpetualy, with all fredomes and
commodites, be the saidis abbot and convent and thar successouris; and als the
said communite and rovne of Striueling sall pay to the said Henry, abbot of
Cambuskenneth, the sovme of twenty pundis at his will, for the quhilkis the
said communite and toun of Striueling sall peciable bruke and jois in tyme
cummyn the remanent of the saidis fischingis and cobillis of the said watter
of Forth, with sic like fredomes and priueleges as thai brukit of befor, but
impediment, vexaticun or tribull to be done or maid be the saidis abbot and
convent or thar successouris or ony vtheris in thair behalf. And als the said
venerable fader be this decrete and counsale tendis nocht to gif our the effect
of the decrete of parliament gottin in the tyme of King Dauid anens his
cruffis vnder the said abbaye, bot reseruis the samyn efter the forme of the
commoun law. And als the said venerable has nocht compromittit him nor
his convent in ony maner of waye tueching his tende salmond of the said
watter. And als the said venerable fader for him self and his convent sall
renunce and gif our the tenor of the decrete gevin at Edinburgh the xix day
of Februar the yer of God j^m iiij^c nynte and fife yeris, except the said five cobillis
and the will of the said xx li. and the articulis aboue expremit; and dischargis

the said toun and commonite of all sovincs and proffetis that he or his convent
may requir in ony tymes bipast. And elikewis the saidis communite and
toun dischargis and quitclames the said venerable fader and convent of all
soviñes, clames and questiones of the saidis fischingis abone expremit, or ony
clame that thai may ask at thame in ony tyme bipast, but fraude or gile.
In witnes of the quhilk thing, to the parte of this deliuerance and decrete
remanand with the said tovne and commonite of Striueling the said venerable
fadir has appendit and tohung the common sele of thar said place and abbay
with the subscriptioun of our handis; and elikewis to the tothir parte of this
deliuerance and decrete remanand with the saidis venerable fader and convent
the said commonite of the tovne of Striueling has appendit and tohung the
commoun sele of the said tovne with our saidis subscriptiouns. At Edinburgh
the tuenty day of Julij the yere of God j^m v^c and ane yere. (Signed) Will^s
Aberdonensis; Jacobus abbas de Scona; Ricardus Muirheid, decanus
Glasgensis; Gavauus Dunbar, decanus Morauensis; Walterus Drummonde,
Dunblanensis decanus; R. Lausoun.

XXXIII.

CHARTER by King James the Fourth to the Provost, Bailies, Councillors,
and Community of the Burgh of Stirling, of the office of Sheriff within
the burgh and territory and liberty of the same. Stirling, 12th October,
1501.

JACOBUS, Dei gracia, Rex Scotorum : Omnibus probis hominibus tocius terre
sue, clericis et laicis, salutem. Sciatis quod pro singulari fauore quem gerimus
erga burgum nostrum de Striueling, et pro communi commodo et vtilitate
ciusdem, necnon pro fideli et gratuito seruicio nobis per dilectos nostros prepositum, ballinos, consules et communitatem dicti nostri burgi, impenso, dedimus,

JAMES, by the grace of God, King of Scots: To all good men of his whole land,
clerics and laics, greeting. Know ye that for the singular favor which we bear
towards our burgh of Striveling, and for the common weal and advantage of the
same, and for the faithful and gratuitous service done to us by our lovites the

concessimus et commisimus, et hac presenti carta nostra damus, concedimus et committimus, dictis preposito, balliuis, consulibus et communitati, officium vice-comitatus de Strineling infra burgum nostrum de Strineling, territorium et libertatem eiusdem, cum omnibus et singulis libertatibus, priuelegijs, pro-ficuis et denorijs dicti officij. Quod quidem officium fuit Alexandri Cunyng-hame de Polmays, militis, vicecomitis nostri de Strineling et sibi pertinebat per donationem eiusdem ei et vni heredi sibi proxime et immediate successuro desuper confectam; et quod officium idem Alexander, non vi aut metu ductus nec errore lapsus, sed sua mera et spontanea voluntate, in manus nostras apud Strineling, per fustem et baculum, et suos procuratores ad hoc legittime con-stitutos, sursum reddidit pureque simpliciter resignauit, et totum jus et clameum quod in eodem habuit seu habere potuit pro se et heredibus suis omnino quittumclamauit imperpetuum.[1] Et nos igitur fecimus, constituimus et ordin-auimus, et hac presenti carta nostra facimus, constituimus et ordinamus, pre-positum et balliuos dicti nostri burgi de Strineling, nunc presentes, et

provost, bailies, councillors and community of our said burgh, we have given, granted and committed, and by this our present charter give, grant and commit to the said provost, bailies, councillors and community, the office of sheriff of Striveling within our burgh of Striveling, territory and liberty of the same, with all and sundry liberties, privileges, profits and dues of the said office. Which office belonged to Alexander Cunynghame of Polmays, knight, our sheriff of Striveling, and pertained to him by gift of the same made to him thereupon and one heir next and immediately to succeed to him ; and which office the said Alexander, not led by force or fear nor fallen in error, but of his mere and spontaneous will, by staff and baton, and by his procurators to that effect lawfully constituted, gave up and purely and simply resigned in our hands at Striveling, and for him and his heirs he wholly quit-claimed for ever all right and claim which he had or could have had in the same.[1] And we therefore have made, constituted and ordained, and by this our present charter make, constitute and ordain, the provost and bailies of our said burgh of

[1] In a "Note of the Burgh of Sterling their Securities," 17th century handwriting, the following occurs:—"Item, ane Resignatione by Sir Alexander Cuninghame of Polmais Cuning-hame, Sheriff of Sterlingshire, of the Sheriff-ship within the toun of Sterling, in the hands of King James the Fourt, upon which the King's Gift of Sherifship is granted to the toun, dated 11th October, 1501." The document itself seems to be amissing.

successores suos, prepositum et ballinos eiusdem qui pro tempore fuerint, vicecomites nostros de Striueling infra dictum nostrum burgum, territorium et libertatem eiusdem, imperpetuum. Tenendum et habendum dictum officium vicecomitatus nostri de Striueling infra burgum nostrum de Striueling, terri- torium et libertatem eiusdem, dictis preposito, balliuis, consulibus et com- munitati prefati nostri burgi, nunc presentibus, et successoribus suis, preposito, balliuis, consulibus et communitati eiusdem qui pro tempore fuerint, de nobis et successoribus nostris, in feodo et hereditate imperpetuum, cum consimilibus et eisdem priuelegijs, libertatibus, potestate, proficuis et deuorijs, sicut prepositus, ballini, consules et communitas burgi nostri de Edinburgh, seu alicuius burgi infra regnum nostrum, habent, gaudent et possedent, ex officio vicecomitatus infra burgum, et adeo libere sicut aliquis burgorum predictorum inde liberius infeodatur. Cum plenaria potestate et mandato speciali dictis preposito et balliuis burgi nostri de Striueling, nunc presentibus, et successoribus suis qui pro tempore fuerint, ad exercendi dictum officium vicecomitatus infra burgum debiteque in eodem ministrandi, curias vicecomitatus de Striueling infra dictum nostrum burgum territorium et libertatem eiusdem ordinandi, inchoandi, affirmandi, tenendi, et tociens quociens opus fuerit continuandi;

Striveling, now present, and their successors, the provost and bailies of the same for the time, our Sheriffs of Striveling within our said burgh, territory and liberty of the same, for ever. To hold and to have the said office of our sheriff of Striveling within our burgh of Striveling, territory and liberty of the same, to the said provost, bailies, councillors and community of our foresaid burgh, now present, and their successors, the provost, bailies, councillors and community of the same who shall be for the time, of us and our successors, in fee and heritage for ever, with the like and the same privileges, liberties, power, profits and dues, as the provost, bailies, coun- cillors and community of our burgh of Edinburgh, or any burgh within our kingdom, have, enjoy and possess from the office of sheriff within burgh, and as freely as any one of the foresaid burghs is therein most freely infeft. With full power and special command to the said provost and bailies of our burgh of Striveling, now present, and their successors who shall be for the time, for exercising the said office of sheriffship within burgh and duly ministering in the same, to ordain, begin, affirm, hold, and as often as need shall be to continue sheriff courts of Striveling within our said burgh, territory and liberty of the same; suits cause to be called,

sectas vocari faciendi, absentes amerciandi, transgressores et delinquentes pro
quantitate delicti secundum juris exigenciam puniendi vel justificandi, plegios
recipiendi et vocari faciendi; amerciamenta, eschaetas et exitus curiarum predictarum leuandi et recipiendi et pro eisdem si opus fuerit distringendi;
eademque amerciamenta, eschaetas et exitus curiarum, ad vtilitatem dicti
nostri burgi de Striueling policiam et opera publica eiusdem applicandi;
breuia capelle nostre regia eis directa et presentata recipiendi, aperiendi,
proclamandi et debite deseruiri faciendi; lites et questiones in dictis curijs
motas seu mouendas, ad officium vicecomitatus infra burgum spectantes,
audiendi, decidendi et fine debito terminandi; seriandos et alios officiarios
pro exercitacione dicti officij necessarios faciendi, constituendi et ordinandi; et
generaliter, omnia alia et singula faciendi, gerendi, excercendi, perimplendi et
exequendi, que ad officium vicecomitatus infra burgum de jure seu consuetudine dinoscuntur pertinere. Ratum, gratum, firmum et stabile habentes et
habituros totum et quicquid dicti prepositi et balliui et successores sui, vicecomites nostri antedicti, eorumque seriandi et officiarij, conjunctim vel diuisim,
in dicto officio vicecomitatus infra burgum rite duxerint faciendi, sine aliquo
impedimento, renouatione, aut contradictione quacunque. In cuius rei testi-

absentees to amerciate, transgressors and delinquents according to the nature of the
fault to punish or justify as the law requires, pledges to receive and cause be called;
fines, escheats and issues of the foresaid courts to levy and receive and if need shall
be to distrain for the same; and to apply the said fines, escheats and issues of courts,
to the use of our said burgh of Striueling, policy and public works of the same; to
receive, open, proclaim and cause to be duly served royal brieves of our chapel
directed and presented to them; to hear, decide and with due end terminate pleas
and questions belonging to the office of sheriffship within burgh moved or to be
moved in the said courts; to make, constitute and ordain serjeants and other officers
necessary for the exercise of the said office; and generally to make, do, exercise,
perform and execute all other and sundry things that to the office of sheriff within
burgh is of right or custom known to belong. Ratified, thankful, firm, and stable,
holding and for to hold all and whatsoever the said provosts and bailies and their
successors, our sheriffs foresaid and their serjeants and officers, conjunctly or severally,
in the said office of sheriffship within burgh shall rightly lead to be done, without
any impediment, revocation, or contradiction whatsoever. In testimony whereof we

monium presenti carte nostre magnum sigillum nostrum apponi precepimus.
Testibus: Reuerendissimo in Christo patre nostroque carissimo fratre,
Jacobo Sanctiandree archiepiscopo; reuerendo in Christo patre Willelmo
episcopo Aberdonensi, nostri secreti sigilli custode; dilectis consanguineis
nostris Archibaldo comite de Ergile domino Campbell et Lorn, magistro hospicij
nostri; Alexandro domino Hume, magno camerario nostro; Andrea domino
Gray, justiciario nostro; venerabilibus in Christo patribus, Georgeo abbate
Sancte Crucis, Jacobo abbate de Scona, et dilecto clerico nostro, magistro
Ricardo Murehede, decano Glasguensi, secretario nostro. Apud Strineling,
duodecimo die mensis Octobris anno domino millesimo quingentesimo primo
et regni nostri decimo quarto.

have commanded our great seal to be affixed to our present charter. Witnesses:
the most reverend father in Christ and our dearest brother, James archbishop of St.
Andrews; the reverend father in Christ, William bishop of Aberdeen, keeper of
our privy seal; our beloved cousins, Archibald earl of Ergile lord Campbell and
Lorn, master of our houshold; Alexander lord Hume, our great chamberlain;
Andrew lord Gray, our justiciar; the venerable fathers in Christ, George abbot of
Holy Rood, James abbot of Scone, and our beloved clerk, master Richard Murehede,
dean of Glasgow, our secretary. At Striveling, on the twelfth day of the month
of October in the year of our Lord one thousand five hundred and one and in the
fourteenth of our reign.

XXXIV.

CHARTER by King James the Fourth to the Provost, Bailies, Councillors,
and Community of Stirling of the Right of Patronage of the Altar
of St. Laurence in the Parish Church. Stirling, 7th March, 1501-2.

JACOBUS, Dei gracia, Rex Scotorum: Omnibus probis hominibus tocius terre
sue, clericis et laicis, salutem. Sciatis nos, pro speciali fauore quem gerimus
erga dilectos nostros, prepositum, ballinos, consules et communitatem burgi

JAMES, by the grace of God, King of Scots: To all good men of his whole land,
clerics and laics, greeting. Know ye that, for the special favor which we bear
towards our lovites, the provost, bailies, councillors, and community of our burgh of

nostri de Striueling, et pro ipsorum bono et gratuito seruicio nobis impenso,
dedisse, concessisse, et hac presenti carta nostra confirmasse eis et ipsorum
successoribus, dicti burgi nostri, prepositis, balliuis, consulibus et communitati,
nostrum jus patronatus, aduocationem et donationem, capellanie · altaris
Sancti Lawrencij, martiris, infra ecclesiam parochialem de Strineling
fundati. Tenendum et habendum jus patronatus, advocationem [et donacionem,] dicte capellauie altaris Sancti Lawrencij dictis preposito, balliuis,
consulibus et communitati prefati burgi nostri de Strineling, et successoribus suis, de nobis et successoribus nostris, in feodo et hereditate
imperpetuum. Cum potestate dictam capellaniam, toticns quotiens ipsam
vacare contigerit, capel ano ydonea ad dictum altare et in choro dicte ecclesie
diuina pro nobis celebraturo et dictas nostris successoribus conferre et disponere,
libere, quiete, bene et in pace, sine aliqua reuocatione, impedimento seu contradictione, nostri aut successorum nostrorum, quouismodo inde faciendi in
futurum, et adeo libere in omnibus et per omnia sicut jus patronatus alicuius
capellanie infra dictam ecclesiam liberius possedent aut tenent. In cuius rei
testimonium presenti carte nostre magnum sigillum nostrum apponi precepimus. Testibus: Reucrendissimo in Christo patre nostroque carissimo fratre,

Striveling, and for thei= good and gratuitous service rendered to us, we have given,
granted, and by this our present charter confirmed to them and their successors,
provosts, bailies, councillors, and community of our said burgh, our right of patronage, advocation, and donation of tue chaplainry of the altar of St. Lawrence, the
martyr, founded withi a the parish church of Striveling.   To have and to hold the
right of patronage, advocation, and donation of the said chaplainry of the altar of
St. Lawrence to the said provost, bailies, councillors, and community of our foresaid
burgh of Striveling, a id their successors, of us and our successors, in fee and heritage
for ever. With power, as often as it shall happen to become vacant, to bestow and dispone the said chaplainry to a preperly qualified chaplain to celebrate divine service
at the said altar and in the choir of the said church, for us and our said successors,
freely, quietly, well, and in peace, without any revocation, impediment, or gainsaying
of us or our successors, to be made thereanent in any manner of way in time to
come, and as freely in all and by all as they most freely possess or hold the right of
patronage of any chaplainry within the said church.   In witness whereof we have
commanded our great seal to be appended to our present charter. Witnesses: the most

Jacobo Sanctiandree archiepiscopo, cancellario nostro; reuerendo in Christo patre Willelmo episcopo Aberdonensi, nostri secreti sigilli custode; dilectis consanguineis nostris Archibaldo comite de Ergile domino Campbele et Lorn, magistro hospicij nostri; Patricio comite de Boithuile domino Halis, etc.; Alexandro domino Hume, magno camerario nostro; Andrea domino Gray, justiciario nostro; et dilectis clericis nostris magistris Ricardo Murehed, decano Glasguensi, secretario nostro, et Gawino Dunbar, decano Morauiensis nostrorum rotulorum et registri ac consilij clerico. Apud Striueling, septimo die mensis Martij anno Domini millesimo quingentesimo primo et regni nostri decimo quarto.

reverend father in Christ and our dearest brother, James archbishop of St. Andrews, our chancellor; the reverend father in Christ William bishop of Aberdeen, keeper of our privy seal; our beloved cousins Archibald earl of Ergile lord Campbele and Lorn, master of our household; Patrick earl of Bothuile lord Hales, etc.; Alexander lord Hume, our great chamberlain; Andrew lord Gray, our justiciar; and our beloved clerks, masters Richard Murehed, dean of Glasgow, our secretary, and Gavin Dunbar, dean of Moray, clerk of our rolls and register and council. At Striueling, on the seventh day of the month of March in the year of our Lord one thousand five hundred and one and in the fourteenth of our reign.

XXXV.

COMMISSION by the Provost, Bailies, Council, and Community of the Burgh of Stirling, empowering certain persons in their name to pursue the Abbot and Convent of Cambuskenneth before the Lords of Council as to Fishings in the Forth. Edinburgh, 4th June, 1504.

BE IT KENND till all men be thir present lettres, ws the prouest, ballies, counsale, and communite of the burgh of Striueling, ilkane with ane consent and assent, to haue maide, constitut and ordanit, and be thir oure present

lettres makis, constitutis and ordanis, richt honorable men and traiste nychtbouris and comburgessis, Sir Duncane Forestare of Garden, knicht, James
of Menteth, Robert the Bruis, George of Crechtoun and Edwarde Spetale,
coniunctlie and seueralie, oure verray lauchfull and vndoutit commissioneris
and procuratouris, actouris, factouris speciale messingeris and craud beraris,
gevand, grantand and committand, to the saidis our commissioneris and
procuratouris and til ilkane of thain , coniunctlie and seueralie, oure full fre
place, irreuocable power, speciale mandment, expres bidding and charge, to
compere for ws in our name and apone our behalue befor oure souerane lord
the King and his lordis of counsale at Edinburgh, or quhare it sall happin
thame to be for the tyme, the vj day of Junij nixt tocum, with continuatioun
of dais, and thare in oure name and apone oure behalue to persew and follow
ane venerable fadir in God, Dauid abbot of the abbay of Cambuskenneth, and
the convent of the samyn, for the wraugws postponying and deferring to
append the common sele of thair said abbaye to the parte of the sentence and
decrete arbitrale to remane to ws and oure said burgh, gevin at Edinburgh
the xx day of Julij the yere of God j^m v^e and ane yeris be ane reuerend fader
and venerable faderis in God and discrete and honorable clerkis, that is to say,
William bishop of Abbirdene, James abbot of Skone, vmquhile maister
Richerd Murcheid, dene of Glasgow secretare to our Souerane Lord, maister
Gawane of Dunbar, dene of Murray, maister Walter Drummond, dene of
Dublane, maister Rechard Lausen and maister James Heurison, jugis
arbitratouris and amycable compositouris evinly chosen betuix vmquhile
ane venerable fader in God, Henry abbot of Cambuskenneth forsaid for the
tyme, for himself and his convent of the samyn, havand sufficient [authoritie]
and power tharto, on the ta parte, and James of Menteth, prouest of the said
burgh, Sir Duncan Forster of Garden, knicht, Alexander Levingston of
Donypace, Edward Spittale and Patrick Redehuch, as procuratouris for ws
and our said burgh, havand sufficient commissioun and power tharto, on the
tother parte, in the action and caus movit betuix the said venerable fader
and convent and ws anent the fise ing of the watter of Forth ; and for the
wrangws deferring to obserue and fulfill the tenour and effect of the saidis
sentence and decrete arbitrale gevin be the saidis jugis and subscriut with
thair handis.   And als to persew and follow the saidis venerable fader and

convent for the wrangws intromettin, vptakin and withaldin fra ws of the fisch
and proffctis of the fischingis of ellevin cobillis and half ane coble apone the
said watter of Forth pertenyng to ws and the fredom of our said burgh, in
contrar the tenour of the said sentence and decret, and attour the fife cobillis
fisching apon the said watter decernit to the saidis venerable fadir and convent
be the said sentence, be the space of ane yere last bipast, extendin the profet
of ilk cobillis fisching to the sovme of xx s.; and als to persew and follow the
said venerable fadir and convent apone all poyntis and articulis contenit in
the saidis summondis and efter the forme and tenour of the samyn; and als
to answer to the said venerable fadir and convent to all vther summondis
quhatsumcuir raisit or to be raisit quhatsumcuir day or place befor quhatsumcuir juge or jugis in the premissis; our absence to excuis, litiscontestations
to mak, the aith of faithfulnes in our saulis to suore, oure partijs aduersar to
here be suorne, our resonis and rychtis to schaw, oure pruffiis, witnes, writtis,
documentis and munimentis to produce and lede, and aganes thame producit
and led be my partj aduersar till obiect, except and aganesay, to repley,
dupley, tripley, and quadrupley, protestacions to mak, actis, instrumentis and
decretis to ask, list, rais and here be gevin; with power to wyn and tyne and
to trete, compone, compromit, continow, conclude, concord and finally to end;
and generaly al vther and sindry thingis to do, haut, exers and vse, that to
the office of lauchfull commissioneris and procuratouris of law or consuetud
in sic thingis is knawin to pertene or yit that we ourself mycht do and we war
present in proper persoun; ferm and stable haldand and for to hald al and
quhatsumcuir thingis the saidis our commissioneris and procuratouris coniunctly and seueraly in the premissis in our name ledis to be done, vnder
oblising of al our gudis present and tocum. In witnes hereof we haue appensit
our common sele of our said burgh, at the tolbuth of the sammyn, the ferd day
of Junij the yere of God j^m v^c and four yeris.

XXXVI.

CHARTER by King James the Fourth to the Burgesses and Community of Stirling of the Lands called the Ald Park and the Patronage of the Altar of St. Michael in the Parish Church. Edinburgh, 28th January, 1505-6.

JACOBUS, Dei gracia, Rex Scotorum: Omnibus probis hominibus totius terre sue, clericis et laicis, salutem. Quia pro singulari favore quem gerimus erga dilectos nostros burgenses et communitatem burgi nostri de Striveling, et in recompensacionem pro terris suis communibus de Gallowhillis dicti nostri burgi, per ipsos nobis concessis, et nunc vallo per nos castro et parche nostris de Striveling inclusis, dedimus et concessimus, hereditarie, dictis burgensibus et communitati totas et integras acras nostras ter-rarum que olim fuerunt de le Ald Park prope Striveling, jacentes inter murum lapidium nove parche nostre antedicte ex parte occidentali et terras nuncupatas Benneis Croft ac Croftam Leprosorum ex parte australi et terras nuncupatas le Rude Croft ex parte boreali; unacum jure patronatus et donacione capellanie altaris Sancti Michaelis per quondam magistrum Thomam Carmichell, vicarium de Striveling, infra ecclesiam parochialem euisdem fundate, ad nostram disposicionem et donacionem

JAMES, by the grace of God, King of Scots: To all good men of his whole land, clerics and laics, greeting. Wherers for the singular favor which we bear towards our lovites the burgesses and community of our burgh of Striveling, and in recom-pense for their common lands of the Gallowhillis of our said burgh granted by them to us, and now inclosed by us in a wall to our castle and park of Striveling, we have given and granted, heritably, to the said burgesses and community all and whole our acres of land which were formerly of the Ald Park near Striveling, lying between the stone wall of our New Park aforesaid on the west side and the lands called Benneis Croft and the Lepers Croft on the south side and the lands called the Rude Croft on the north side; together with the right of patronage and donation of the chaplainry of the altar of St. Michael founded by the deceased master Thomas Carmichell, vicar of Striveling, within the parish church of the same, now belonging to our disposition and donation as often as it shall fall vacant. To

quociens vacaverit nunc spectantis.   Tenendas et habendas, totas et
integras predictas acras terrarum cum pertinenciis, necnon jus patronatus et donacionem dicti altaris capellanie, prefatis burgensibus et communitati burgi nostri de Striveling et eorum successoribus, prefatas
acras in libero burgagio et hereditate imperpetuum per omnes rectas
metas suas antiquas et divisas, prout jacent in longitudine; cum omnibus et
singulis libertatibus, commoditatibus, asiamentis ac justis suis pertinenciis
quibuscumque, tam non nominatis quam nominatis, tam subtus terra quam
supra terram, procul et prope, ad predictas acras cum pertinenciis spectantibus
seu juste spectare valentibus quomodolibet in futurum, adeo libere, quiete,
plenarie, integre, honorifice, bene et in pace, sicut burgenses et communitas
prefati nostri burgi per progenitores nostros de aliquibus aliis terris in burgagio liberius infeodavit.   Faciendo inde annuatim, dicti burgenses et communitas nunc existentes et eorum successores, nobis et successoribus nostris,
tale servicium temporibus affuturis sicut pro dictis terris de Gallowhillis temporibus elapsis prestiterunt, tantum.   Et cum potestate eisdem capellaniam
dicti altaris, quociens vacare contigerit, capellano idoneo disponendi, infra
dictam ecclesiam pro nobis et successoribus nostris aliisque ipsius altaris

hold and to have, all and whole the foresaid acres of land with the pertinents, and also
the right of patronage and donation of the said altar of the chaplainry, to the foresaid
burgesses and community of our burgh of Striveling and their successors, the foresaid
acres in free burgage and heritage for ever by all their right meiths old and divided,
as they lie in length; with all and sundry liberties, commodities, easements and their
right pertinents whatsoever, as well not named as named, as well under the ground
as above the ground, far and near, belonging or that may justly belong in any
manner of way in time to come to the foresaid acres with the pertinents, as freely,
quietly, fully, wholly, honorably, well and in peace, as the burgesses and community
of our foresaid burgh were most freely infeft by our progenitors in any other
lands in burgage.   Doing therefor yearly, the said burgesses and community now
being and their successors, to us and our successors, such service in times coming as
they performed for the said lands of Gallowhillis in times by past, only.   And with
power to them to dispone the chaplainry of the said altar, as often as it shall happen
to fall vacant, to a fit chaplain, to celebrate divine service within the said church for
us and our successors and other founders of the said altar, according to the tenor of

fundatoribus, secundum tenorem ciusdem fundacionis, divina celebraturo, adeo libere et quiete in omnibus et per omnia sicut jus patronatus cuiuscunque alterius capellanie infra dictam ecclesiam liberius possedunt.   In cuius rei testimonium presenti carte nostre magnum sigillum nostrum apponi precepimus.   Testibus : Reuerendo in Christo patre, Willelmo episcopo Aberdonensi, nostri secreti sigilli custodie; dilectis consanguineis, Archibaldo comite de Ergile domino Campbele et Lorne magistro hospicii nostri; Patricio comite de Boithuile domino Halys, etc.; Matheo comite [de Levenex domino Dernlie; Alexandro domino Hume,] camerario nostro; Andrea domino Gray, justiciario nostro; venerabili in Christo patre Jacobo abbate [de Dunfermline, thesaurario nostro]; Magistro Gavino Dunbar archidiacono Sanctiandriee, nostrorum rotulorum [clerico].   Apud Edinburgh, vicesimo octavo die mensis Januarii anno Domini millesimo quingentesimo quinto et regni nostri decimo octavo.

the foundation thereof, as freely and quietly in all and by all as they most freely possess the right of patronage of any other chaplainry within the said church.   In witness whereof we have commanded our great seal to be affixed to our present charter.   Witnesses: the reverend father in Christ, William bishop of Aberdeen, keeper of our great seal; our beloved cousins Archibald earl of Ergile lord Campbele and Lorne, master of our household; Patrick earl of Borthuile lord Halys, etc.; Matthew earl of Lennox lord Dernlie; Alexander lord Hume, our chamberlain; Andrew lord Gray, our justiciar; the venerable father in Christ, James abbot of Dunfermline, our treasurer; master Gavin Dunbar, archdeacon of St. Andrews, clerk of our rolls.   At Edinburgh, the twenty-eighth day of the month of January the year of our Lord one thousand five hundred and five, and of our reign the eighteenth.

XXXVII.

INDENTURES between the Abbot and Convent of the Abbey of Dunfermline and the Provost, Bailies, Council and Community of the Burgh of Stirling, as to building a Choir in the Parish Kirk of Stirling. Dunfermline, 3rd May, 1507.

THIR INDENTURIS, maid at Dunfermlyne the thrid day of the moneth of Maij the yeir of God ane thousand fyve hundreth and sevin yeris, proportis, contenis and beris witnes that it is appointit and finalie concordit betuix ane honorable

fadir in God, James abbot of Dunfermlyne, thesaurar to our souerane lord the
the King, etc., and the convent of the said abbay on the ta part, [and] the provest,
ballies, counsale and communite of the burght of Striueling on the tothir
part, in maner and forme eftir following, that is to say that the saidis provest,
ballies, counsale and communite of the said burgh, has takin apon hand to big
and compleitlie edifye and end ane gud and sufficient queyr conformand to
the body of the peroch kirk of the said burgh or bettir, and sall deliuer to the
saidis abbot and convent the said body of thair peroch kirk of Striueling frely
to remane with thame as ane queir ay and quhill the said queyr now to be
biggit be fullely completit and endit ; for the quhilk bigging of the said queyr
to be biggit and completlie endit be the saidis provest, balyeis, counsale and
communite of the said burgh of Striueling in maner foirsaid, the saidis abbot
[and] convent of the said abbay of Dunfermlyne or thair successouris sall thank-
fullie content and pay to the saidis provest, ballies, counsale and communite
of the said burgh of Striueling, quhilk for the tyme sall be, the soume of twa
hundreth pundis gud and vsuale money of Scotland at thir termes vndir-
writtin, that is to say, at the feist of Witsonday nixt to cum eftir the dait of
thir present indenturis tuenty pundis, and at the feist of Sanct Martyne in
winter nixt thareftir followand twenty pundis, and swa furth termlie ilk
terme of Witsonday and ilk terme of Martynmes twenty pundis ay and quhil
the foirsaid hail soume of twa hundreth pundis be fullely assith, content and
pait ; and that the saidis abbot and convent sall deliuer and geif to the saidis
provest, ballies, counsale and communite of the said burgh of Striueling, for
the reparatioun of the said queir and hie altare of the samyn, all ornamentis
necessar baith for haly dais and wark dais that thai aucht to haue as efferis,
togiddir with ane infeftment yerlie of fourty schillingis vsuale money foirsaid
to the vphalding of the said queir and anourmentis of the said altare; and
frathineefurth the saidis provest, ballies, counsale and communite of the said
burgh of Striueling, sall vphald the said queir perpetualy in all thingis and als the
anormentis belanging the samin, swa that the hie altare thairof sall be honestly
and honorablie vphalding in the saidis anourmentis as thai resaue the samyn
thairte fra the saidis abbot and convent; and dischargis thame and thair
successouris perpetualy of all vphalding of the said queyr or the hie altare
thairof in ony maner of ornamentis in tyme tocum or ony vther thingis except

the payment of the said twa hundreth pundis and the iufeftment of the said
fourty schilliugis be yeir to be maid with the saidis oruamentis anis to be gevin
to the said altar as said is. And that all thir coudicionis and appointmentis
aboue writtin sall lelely and treulie be obscruit, kepit and fulfillit, in forme
and effect foirsaid, athir party ar burdin, oblist and sworne, ilk ane to vtheris
be the faithis and treuthis in thair bodeis in the sikkerrest forme and stile of
obligacioun that can be maid or diuisit, but canillacioun, fraud or gile. In witnes
of the quhilk thiug, to the part of thir indenturis remainand with the saidis
abbot and convent of the said abbay of Dunfermlyne, the saidis provest,
ballies, counsale and communite of the said burgh of Striueling has to hnnging
thair commoun sele of the said burgh; and to the part hereof remainand with
the saidis provest, ballies, counsale and communite foirsaid, the saidis abbot
and convent has to hunging the commoun sele of the cheptour of thair said
abbay, cheptourlie gaderit, day, yeir, and place foirsaid.

XXXVIII.

COMMISSION by the Provost, Brilies, Council, and Community of Stirling,
empowering certain persons in their name to pursue Alexander Elphin-
stone and to answer before the Lords of Council as to Fishings in the
Forth. Edinburgh, 15th March, 1508-9.

BE IT KEND to all men be thir present letteres, ws, prouest, ballies, counsale
and communite of the burgh of Striueling, to haue maid, constitut and ordauit,
and be thir oure present letteres makis, constitutis and ordanis, richt honorable
men and oure traist nychtbouris and comburgessis, Sir Duncane Forestare of
Garden, Sir Walter Forestare, his sone and apperand aire, knichtis, James of
Menteth, prouest of the said burgh, Robert the Brus, George Creehtoun,
Edwerd Spetale, maister Walter Layng and Androu Nortoune, coniunctlie
and scueralie, oure werray lauchfull and vndoutit irreuocable commissaris and
procuratouris, actouris, factouris, speciale messingeris and erand beraris;
gevand, grantand and committand to the saidis oure procuratouris and commissaris, or to ony ane of thaim, coniunctlie and scueralie, oure full, fre, plane
power, speciale and generale mandment and expres bidding, to compere befor
oure souerane lord the King and his counsaile at Edinburgh the xvij day of

K

March nixt tocum, with continuacioun of dais, and thare for ws and apone oure behalfis to follow and persew Alexander Elphinstoun, sone and apperand air to Sir Johne Elphinstoun of that ilk, knycht, for the wrangwis and maister-full biggin and recentlie insetting of certane cruflis in and throw the watter of Forth within the boundis of the samyn thareof pertenying to ws be auld infeftment of vmquhile oure souerane lordis noble progenitouris of gud memor, quham God assolye, and for the wrangwis makin of innouatioun tharein be his awne auctorite, spulyeing and putting of ws fra our auld peciable possessioun of our saidis fischingis insafer as in him is, without ony cognitioun of the caus; and forthir eftir the tenor of oure souerane lordis summondis in all poyntis raisit be ws tharupon. And als to compere befor our said souerane lord and his counsale at Edinburgh the xxᵗⁱ day of the moneth of Aprile nixt tocum, etc., with continuation of dais, to ansuer at the instance of his hienes, that is to say to se and here as his grace allegis all and hale our saidis fischingis of the watter of Forth, begynnand at Polmais Vndre and ascendand vnto the Red Croft, and abon the Red Croft passand to the hede of the samyn watter, like as at mare lynth contenit in our said souerane lordis summondis raisit apon ws thareupon ; oure absence to excuse, our resonis, rychtis, writtis, euidentis, documentis and munimentis to schaw and produce, witnes previs in maner of prefe to produce and lede, and be our partj aduersar producit or led to except and impunge, to repley, duply, triply and gif mister be quadruply, letteres, actis, instruments and decretis to ask and rais, protestations and allegations to mak, with litiscontestacion, the aith of faithfulnes in our saulis to suere, and with power to trete, concorde, com-pone, compromit, conclud and finaly to end; and with power to wyn and tyne, and generaly al vther and sindry thingis to do, haut and vse, that to the office of lauchful commissaris and procuratouris of law and consuetud ar knawin to pertene, and it to do in the said office as we war present in propir person; ferme and stable haldand and for to hald al and quhatsumeuir thingis the saidis our commissaris and procuratouris coniunctly and seueraly in oure name lodis to be done; and we sall relefe our saidis commissioneris that thai or ony ane of thame are adiugit in til vndre oblising of al oure gudis present and tocum. In witnes of the quhilk, to thir oure present letteres we haue appen-sit and to hungin oure common sele. At our tolbuth of the samyn, the xv day of Merch the yere of God jᵐ vᶜ and acht yeris.

XXXIX.

ACT of the Lords of Council as to Summons at the instance of the Abbot and Convent of Cambuskenneth, and the Tenants of their Fishings on the Forth, against the Bailies of Stirling and others, for despoiling the tenants of their cobles and nets.   Edinburgh, 27th February, 1531-2.

At Edinburgh, the twenty-sevint day of Februar, the yeir of God ane thousand fyve hundreth and thretty ane yeris, anent the summondis rasit at the instance of ane venerabill fader in God, Alexander abbot of Cambus-kynneth, and convent thairof, and of Andro Cowy, Huchcoun Mathow, Johnne Ewin, and Robert Ewin, his sone, pure tenentis and fischearis to the said venerabill fader and convent of thare fischeing on the watter of Forth, aganis Johnne Forestar, Walter Grahame, baillies of Strineling, James Dreg-horne, Thomas Paterson, James Drew, Duncan, Drew, James Suerd, Johnne Pennck, Alexander Bauerage, William Watson, Walter Ewison, Duncane Ewison, his bruthir, James Lamb, John M'Ky and Thomas Duncaneson, for the wrangus, violent and maisterfull spoliatioun, be thameselff, thare seruandis and complicis being with thame in company, in thare names, of thare causing, command, assistance and ratihabitioun, away taking and withalding fra the saidis pure tenentis recently vpon the xxvi day of Julii last bipast, vnder silence of the nicht, out of the said venerabill fader and convent landis callit Abbotishude, liand within the schirefdome of Clakmannane, of cobillis and nettis, as at mair lenth is contenit in the summondis thairvpoun, the said venerabill fader comperand for himself and his convent, and the pure tenentis comperand be maister Henry Lauder, and the saidis John Forestar, Walter Grahame and thare collegis comperand be maister Henry Spittall, thare pro-curatour, quhilk referrit the saidis personis anent the said summondis to the said venerabill faderis conscience and will; tharefore the said venerabill fader assignis to the saidis personis the xxvi day of Marche nixt tocum, with con-tinuatioun of dayis, to compere in Strineling, and to heir and se him declare his will anent the said summondis, and lettres to be directit heirupoun, gif neid beis, in forme as effeiris.

XL.

INSTRUMENT narrating Grant by the Provost, Bailies, Councillors, and
Community of Stirling to the Altar of St. Katherine in the Parish
Church of a Piece of Waste Land lying near the Church. Stirling,
28th February, 1536-7.

In Dei nomine, amen.   Per hoc presens publicum instrumentum cunctis
pateat euidenter quod anno incarnacionis Dominice millesimo quingentesimo
trigesimo sexto, mensis vero Februarii die vltimo, indictione decima, pontificatus
sanctissimi in Cristo patris et domini nostri domini Pauli, diuina prouidencia
Pape, tertii, anno tertio: In mei notarii publici et testium infrascriptorum,
presentia personaliter constituti honorabiles viri, prepositus, balliui, consules
et communitas burgi de Striuelyng, judicialiter in eorum pretorio burgi
eiusdem repetitis vicibus ad hoc bene congregati, attendentes· et pio corde
gestantes modicum illud patrimonium et annuum commodum altaris diue
Katherine, martiris, infra suam perrochialem ecclesiam Sancte Crucis, bone
memorie, antiquitus fundati, apud idem quotidianum laudabile seruicium
in choro et extra absque supplemento minime supportare poterit, vtilitate
que huiusmodi premisa, matura deliberatione longo desuper prehabito tractatu,
ad plenum ut asseruerunt auisiati et in hac parte consulti, vnauimi consensu

In the name of God, amen.   By this present public instrument be it evidently known
to all that on the last day of the month of ·February, in the year of the incarnation
of our Lord one thousand five hundred and thirty six, the tenth indiction, the third
year of the pontificate of the most holy father in Christ and our lord, Paul the
Third, by divine providence Pope: In presence of me notary public and witnesses
underwritten, personally compeared honorable men, the provost, bailies, councillors,
and community of the burgh of Striveling, properly assembled judicially in their
tolbooth of the said burgh sundry times for the purpose, regarding and with pious
heart considering that the little patrimony and annual profit of the altar of Saint
Katherine the martyr, of good memory, anciently founded within their parish church
of the Holy Cross, was not able to support the laudable daily service at the same in
the choir and outwith without supplement, and the utility thereof foreseen, mature
deliberation and long dealing had thereupon, being fully advised and consulted in that

et assensu, nullo reclamante, concesserunt, dotarunt et donarunt, et per presentes concedunt, dotant, et pro se et successoribus suis donant predicto altari
diue Katherine, martiris, in augmentum patrimonii eiusdem, illam suam communem terram vastam, cum pertinenciis, jacentem infra dictum burgum in
capite eiusdem, apud chorum prefate sue ecclesie ex parte boreali eiusdem
chori, inter *le stile* passagii ducentis ad boreale hostium memorati chori ex
australi parte ab vna et tenementum Roberti Callendar de Maner ex dicta
boreali partibus ab altera ; annexando et incorporando huiusmodi terram
vastam cum nonnullis pedibus me isure cimiterii, perprius orti dicte vaste
terre, existentibus ex parte occidentali eiusdem, cum pertinenciis.   Tenendam
et habendam dicto altari Sancte Katherine, virginis, a se et successoribus
suis, de Deo Omnipotenti, beata que Virgine Maria, omnibus sanctis et Sancta
Katherina, virgine, in puram et perpetuam elimosinam ad manum mortuam
in augmentum predicti [patrimonii].   Eciam obligarunt se et successores suos,
et per presentes fide media obligant se strictiore forma obligacionis, predictam
huiusmodi terram vastam cum dictis pedibus mensure irreuocabiliter et inuio-
labiter prefato altari Sancte Katherine et capellano eiusdem qui pro tempore

behalf, as they asserted, with unanimous consent and assent, none gainsaying, granted,
gave and bestowed, and by these presents grant, give, and for them and their successors
bestow to the foresaid altar of Saint Katherine the martyr, in augmentation of the
patrimony of the same, their common waste land, with the pertinents, lying within
the said burgh at the head of the same, at the choir of their foresaid church on the
north side of the said choir, between the stile of the passage leading to the north
entrance of the beforementioned choir on the south side on the one part and the
tenement of Robert Callendar of Maner on the said north side on the other part;
annexing and incorporating the said waste land with some feet of measurement of
the cemetery, formerly a garden of the said waste land, lying on the west side of
the same, with the pertinents.   To hold and have to the said altar of Saint Katherine, the virgin, from them and their successors, of God Almighty, and the blessed
Virgin Mary, all saints and St. Katherine the Virgin, in pure and perpetual alms in
mortmain in augmentation of the foresaid patrimony.   They also bound them and their
successors, and by these presents on oath bind themselves in stricter form of obligation,
to keep such foresaid waste land with the said feet of measurement irrevocably and
inviolably to the foresaid altar of Saint Katherine and chaplain of the same who

fuerit, libere, annuatim et terminatim de futuro ab omni solucione, precepcione
et leuacione annuorum, reddituum tam regiorum quam aliorum quorumcunque,
per quoscunque inde exigi poterunt quomodolibet vel requiri obseruare. Premissis peractis, honorabilis vir, Robertus Arnot, tunc temporis vnus balliuorum
dicti burgi, vigore et potestate sui officii ballie et de speciali mandato dictorum
prepositi, balliuorum, consulum et maioris ac digioris partis communitatis
eiusdem inibi presentium, per terre et lapidis exhibitionem, tocius et integre
predicte terre vaste cum nonnullis pedibus mensure ex parte posteriore eiusdem,
discreto viro, domino Jacobo Nycholsone, capellano dicti altaris Sancte Katherine,
nomine et ex parte eiusdem, statum et sasinam, hereditariam pariter et
possessionem corporalem, in puram et perpetuam elimosinam et ad manuum
mortuam ac in augmentum patrimonii dicti altaris imperpetuum, contulit
et tradidit pariter et deliberauit cum effectu. Super quibus, omnibus et
singulis, dictus Jacobus, capellanus dicti altaris, a me, notario publico subscripto, sibi fieri peciit vnum seu plura publicum aut publica instrumentum
vel instrumenta, vnacum appensione sigilli communis dicti burgi in signum
donacionis dicte terre vaste prefato altari, necnon appensione sigilli dicti
Roberti, balliui, in signum donacionis sasine huiusmodi et vtrique promitten-

shall be for the time, free, yearly and termly in the future from all payment, up-
lifting and levying of annualrents, as well royal as others whatsoever, by whomsoever
they could be exacted therefrom or required in any manner of way. Which things
foresaid being done, an honorable man Robert Arnot, then one of the bailies of the
said burgh, by virtue and power of his office of bailie and by special command of
the said provost, bailies, councillors, and the greater and more worthy part of the
community of the same there present, by presenting of earth and stone, bestowed and
gave and also delivered with effect to a discreet man, Sir James Nycholsone, chaplain of the said altar of Saint Katherine, in name and on the part of the same, state
and sasine and also heritable and corporal possession of all and whole the foresaid
waste land with certain feet of measurement on the back part of the same, in pure
and perpetual alms and in mortmain and in augmentation of the patrimony of the
said altar for ever. Whereupon, all and sundry, the said Sir James, chaplain of the
said altar, asked from me, notary public subscribing, one or more public instrument
or public instruments to be made to him, together with the appending of the common seal of the said burgh in token of the bestowal of the said waste land to the

tes presenti instrumento comuniri.   Acta erant hec super solum predicte terre
vaste, hora octaua ante merediem, vel cocirca, sub auno, die, mense, indictione
et pontificatu quibus supra.   Presentibus ibidem: prouidis viris, Thoma
Michaell, Jacobo Watsoun, Malcolmo Kinros, burgensibus dicti burgi, Thoma
Bargille, lathomo, ciue ciuitatis Glasgaensis et Willelmo Aisoun, seriando prefati burgi, testibus, cum multis aliis communitatis predicti burgi ad premissa
vocatis pariter et rogatis.

> Et ego, Willelmus Litstar, presbyter, Sanctiandree diocesis, publicus,
> sacra auctoritate apostolica, notarius, quia premissis omnibus et singulis
> dum sic ut premittitur, dicerentur, agerentur et fierent, vnacum pre-
> nominatis testibus presens interfui, eaque omnia et singula sic fieri et
> dici, vidi, sciui et audiui ac in notam cepi: ideoque hoc presens publi-
> cum instrumentum, manu mea propria fideliter scriptum, exinde
> confeci, et hic me subscribendo iu hanc publicam formam redegi,
> signoque subscriptione et nomine meis, solitis et consuetis, vnacum

foresaid altar, and also with appending of the seal of the said Robert, bailie, in
token of giving of sasine and promising to confirm the present instrument.   These
things were done on the ground of the said waste land at the eighth hour before
noon or thereabout, in the year, day, month, indiction and pontificate above mentioned.   Present there: provident men, Thomas Michaell, James Watsoun, Malcolm
Kinros, burgesses of the said burgh, Thomas Bargille, mason, citizen of the city of
Glasgow, and William Aisoun, serjant of the foresaid burgh, witnesses to the premises, with many others of the community of the foresaid burgh, likewise called and
required.

> And I, William Litstar, priest, of the diocese of St. Andrews, by sacred
> apostolic authority, notary public, because I was present with the fore-
> named witnesses at all and sundry the premises while they were so said,
> done, and transacted as above written, and saw, knew, and heard the same,
> all and sundry, so done and said and took a note of them; and thereupon I
> have made this present public instrument faithfully written with my own
> hand, and by subscribing here have reduced it into this public form, and
> have signed with my sign, subscription and name, used and wont, together

appensionibus dictorum sigillorum, signaui, rogatus et requisitus in
fidem et testimonium omnium et singulorum premissorum.

WILLELMUS LITSTAR.

with the appending of the said seals, being asked and required in faith and
testimony of all and sundry the premises.

WILLIAM LITSTAR.

XLI.

CHARTER by King James the Fifth ratifying certain Acts and Statutes
as to the exercise of Trade and Merchandise, and also confirming Letters
by the Privy Council charging the Provost, Dean of Guild and Bailies of
Stirling, to enforce the laws against unfreemen.   Edinburgh, 8th July,
1540.

JACOBUS, Dei gracia, Rex Scotorum: Omnibus probis hominibus suis ad quos
presentes litere peruenerint, salutem.   Sciatis nos, post nostras legitimam et
perfectam etatem viginti quinque annorum completorum reuocationemque
generalem, quedam acta parliamenti et alia laudabilia statuta subscripta,
vnum, videlicet, parliamenti actum factum per quondam Jacobum secundum
Scotorum Regem, bone memorie, cuius anime propicietur Deus, apud Edinburgh sexto die mensis Marcii anno Domini millesimo quadringentesimo
quinquagesimo septimo, proportans in effectu quod nullus tinctor pannum per
ipsum rursus vendi emat, sub pena confiscationis eiusdem; aliud parliamenti

JAMES, by the grace of God, King of Scots: To all his good men to whom the present letters shall come, greeting.   Know ye that, after our lawful and perfect age of
twenty-five years complete and general revocation, we have clearly understood certain acts of parliament and other lauable statutes underwritten, namely, an act of
parliament made by the late James the second King of Scotland, of good memory,
on whose soul may God have mercy, at Edinburgh on the sixth day of the month of
March in the year of our Lord one thousand four hundred and fifty-seven, in effect
porporting that no dyer buy cloth to be sold again by himself under pain of escheat

actum factum per quondam Jacobum tertium Scotorum Regem, bone memorie,
cuius anime propicietur Deus, apud Edinburgh nono die mensis Octobris anno
Domini millesimo quadringentesimo sexagesimo sexto, proportans in effectu
quod nullus artifex vtatur mercanciis per seipsum, suos factores aut famulos,
nisi suam dimiserit artem et eidem renunciauerit, absque colore seu dissimulatione; aliud parliamenti actum factum per prefatum Jacobum tertium in
parliamento suo tento apud Edinburgh decimo tertio die mensis Octobris
anno Domini millesimo quadringentesimo octuagesimo septimo, proportans in
effectu quod parliamenti actum suprascriptum concernens artifices executioni
demandaretur sit, quod quisquis artifex aut desinat a mercanciis seu arti
remunciet sue, absque colore aut dissimulatione, sub pena confiscationis
mercanciarum quibus vtitur suum artificium occupando nostro vsui im-
portandarum, ac compotum de eisdem annuatim nostro in scaccario fiendum;
acetiam vnum parliamenti actum factum per quondam carissimum patrem
nostrum Jacobum quartum Scotorum Regem vltimo defunctum, cuius anime
propicietur Deus, apud Edinburgh vndecimo die mensis Martii anno Domini
millesimo quingentesimo tertio, proportans in effectu quod omnes mercatores
regni nostri habebunt et possidebunt priuilegia et libertates eiis per
nobilissimos suos progenitores concessos et quod eadem ipsis obseruabuntur

of the same; another act of parliament made by the late James the third, King of
Scots, of good memory, on whose soul may God have mercy, at Edinburgh on the
ninth day of the month of October in the year of our Lord one thousand four
hundred and sixty-six, in effect proporting that no craftsman use merchandise by himself, his factors or servants, unless he shall have left his craft and renounced the same,
without colour or dissimulation; another act of parliament made by the foresaid James
the Third in his parliament held at Edinburgh on the thirteenth day of the month of
October in the year of our Lord one thousand four hundred and eighty-seven, in effect
proporting that the act of parliament above written concerning craftsmen may be
put to execution, so that every craftsman either forbear his merchandise or renounce
his craft without colour or dissimulation, under pain of escheat of the merchandise
which he uses occupying his craft to be inbrought to our use, and an account of the
same to be made yearly in our exchequer; also an act of parliament made by our
late dearest father James the Fourth King of Scots, last deceased, on whose soul
may God have mercy, at Edinburgh on the eleventh day of the month of March in

L.

et custodientur, et quod nulle persone extra burgos moram trahentes
vtentur marcauciis, nec vinum, ceram, serica, aromata, nec stapule bona, nec in
villa de Leith nec aliis locis extra burgos, emant, pak nec pele, sub pena confiscationis prefatorum bonorum nostro vsui: De mandato nostro, visa, lecta, in-
specta, et diligenter examinata, per dilectum familiarem clericum et consiliarum
nostrum, magistrum Jacobum Foulis de Colintoun, nostrorum rotulorum,
registri et consili clericum, subscriptum, vtique intellexisse, sub hac verborum
forma:—In Parliamento excellentissimi principis, domini Jacobi secundi, Dei
gratia, Regis Scotorum, tento et inchoato apud Edinburgh sexto die mensis
Marcii anno Domini millesimo quadringentesimo quinquagesimo septimo.
Item, it is sene speidfull that lyt be eryit vp as it wes wont to be, and that
na litstare be drapar nor by claith to sell agane nor yit tholit thairto, vnder
the pane of eschete thairof. In parliamento excellentissimi principis, domini
Jacobi tertii, Dei gratia, Regis Scotorum, tento apud Edinburgh nono die
mensis Octobris anno Domini millesimo quadringentesimo sexagesimo sexto.
Item, it is statut and ordinit that na man of craft vse marchandice be himself,
his factouris or seruandis, bot gif he leif and renunce his craft, but colour or
dissimulatioun. In parliamento dicti excellentissimi principis, domini Jacobi
tertii Dei gratia, Regis Scotorum, tento apud Edinburgh decimo tertio die
mensis Octobris anno Domini millesimo quadringentesimo octuagesimo septimo.

the year of our Lord one thousand five hundred and three, in effect proporting that
all merchants of our kingdom shall have and possess the privileges and liberties
granted to them by his most noble progenitors, and that the same be observed and
kept to them, and that no persons dwelling without burghs use merchandise, nor buy,
pak or pele wine, wax, silk, spicery, or staple goods, neither in the town of Leith
nor other places without burghs, under the pain of escheat of the foresaid goods to
our use: By our command seen, read, inspected, and diligently examined by our
beloved familiar clerk and councillor, Master James Foulis of Colintoun, clerk of our
rolls, register and council, subscribing, in this form of words:—In the parliament of
the most excellent prince lord James the second, by the grace of God, King of Scots,
held and begun at Edinburgh on the sixth day of the month of March in the year
of our Lord one thousand four hundred and fifty-seven. Item, it is sene speidfull
[etc., as above]. In the parliament of the most excellent prince lord James the
third, by the grace of God, King of Scots, held at Edinburgh on the ninth day of

Item, it is statute and ordinit that the act of parliament tuiching craftismen vsand and deland with marchandice mycht be put to executioun, sa that he that is craftisman ovthir forbeir his marchandice or ellis renunce his craft, but ony dissimulatioun or colour, under the pane of eschete of the marchandice that he vsis occupiand his craft, and this eschete to be inbrocht be the saidis sercheouris to our Souerane Lordis vse, and compt thairof to be made in his chekker. In parliamento excellentissimi principis, domini Jacobi quarti, Dei gratia, Regis Scotorum, tento apud Edinburgh vndecimo die mensis Marcii anno Domini millesimo quingente-imo tertio. Item, it is statut and ordinit that all the marchandis of the realme and the burrowis brouk and haif thair auld priuilege and fredomis, grantit and gevin to thame be our Souerane Lordis progenitouris, of maist nobill mynd, be obscruit and kepit to thame, and that na personis duelland ortwith the burrowis vse ony marchandice nor yit tap nor sell wyne, walx, silkis nor spicery, wad, nor siclike stuff, nor yit stapill gudis, and that nane pak nor pele in Leith nor vthir places without the Kingis borrowis, vnder the pane of escheting of the gudis to the Kingis vse that be tappit, sald, pakkit or pelit, agane this statute. Extracta de libris actorum parliamentorum per me, magistrum Jacobum Foulis de Colintoun, clericum rolutorum, registri ac consilii supremi domini nostri Regis, de mandato dominorum consilii, vicesimo octauo Decembris anno Domini millesimo quingentesimo trigesimo nono, sub meis signo et subscriptione manualibus.

the month of October in the year cf our Lord one thousand four hundred and sixty-six. Item, it is statut and ordinit that na man of craft [etc., as above]. In the parliament of the said most excellent prince lord James the third, by the grace of God, King of Scots, held at Edinburgh on the thirteenth day of the month of October in the year of our Lord one thousand four hundred and eighty-seven. Item, it is statute and ordinit that the act of parliament tuiching craftismen [etc., as above]. In the parliament of the most excellent prince lord James the fourth, by the grace of God, King of Scots, held at Edinburgh on the eleventh day of the month of March in the year of our Lord one thousand five hundred and three. Item, it is statut and ordinit that all the marchandis etc., as above]. Extracted from the books of the acts of parliaments by me, master James Foulis of Colintoun, clerk of the rolls, register and council of our sovereign lord the King, by command of the lords of council, on the twenty-eighth of December in the year of our Lord one thousand five

Quacquidem acta et statuta, ac omnia et singula in eisdem contenta, approbamus, ratificamus, ac pro nobis et nostris successoribus pro perpetuo confirmamus.   Necnon, ratificamus nostras literas per deliberationem dominorum
consilii nostri concessas, apud Edinburgh, primo die mensis Decembris anno
Domini millesimo quingentesimo trigesimo nono, precipiendo et mandando, per
publicam proclamationem apud crucem foralem burgi nostri de Striueling et
omnia alia loca necessaria, omnibus et singulis nostris ligeis, minime liberis
tam in burgo quam extra burgum moram trahentibus, quod eorum nullus
emat, *foirstaw*, *regrait* nec *cowp*, lanam, coria, pelles, pannum, seu ullas alias
mercancias, temporibus affuturis, sub pena consfiscationis earundem et suarum
personarum secundum iura et parliamenti acta punitionis.   Necon mandando
et precipiendo preposito, decano gilde et balliuis prefati burgi nostri de Striueling, quod ipsi diligenter perquirant et scrutentur prefatos lie *regratouris*,
foirstawaris et *cowparis*, ac ipsos et eorum bona *regratit* capiant et ipsos et
eadem iusticiario nostro et suis deputatis apportent pro eorum demeritis et
delictis secundum regni nostri iura ac parliamenti acta puniendos; prout in
prefatis literis lacius continetur.   In cuius rei testimonium presentibus magnum sigillum nostrum apponi precepimus.   Apud Edinburgh, octauo die

hundred and thirty-nine, under my sign and subscription manual.—Which acts and
statutes, and all and sundry contained in the same, we approve, ratify, and for us and
our successors for ever confirm.   Also, we ratify our letters given by deliverance of
the lords of our council, at Edinburgh, on the first day of the month of December in
the year of our Lord one thousand five hundred and thirty-nine, charging and
commanding, by public proclamation at the market cross of our burgh of Striueling
and all other places necessary, all and sundry our lieges, unfreemen, as well dwelling
in the burgh as without the burgh, that none of them buy, forstall, regrait or cowp,
wool, hides, skins, cloth, or any other merchandice, in times coming, under pain of
escheat of the same and punishment of their persons according to the laws and acts
of parliament.   Also commanding and charging the provost, dean of guild and
bailies of our foresaid burgh of Striuling, that they diligently inquire and search for
the foresaid regraiters, forestallers and cowpers, and apprehend them and their
regraited goods, and bring them and the same to our justicier and his deputes to
be punished for their faults and offences according to the laws and acts of parliament
of our kingdom; as in the foresaid letters is more fully contained.   In witness whereof

mensis Julii anno Domini millesimo quingentesimo quadragesimo et regni
nostri vicesimo septimo.

we have commanded our great seal to be appended to these presents.   At Edinburgh,
on the eighth day of the month of July in the year of our Lord one thousand five
hundred and forty and in the twenty-seventh of our reign.

XLII.

LETTERS by the Provost, Bailies, Councillors, and Community of the Burgh
of Stirling granting to Sir William Robesoun the Chaplainry of the Altar
of St. Michael in the Parish Church, with the Lands and others belonging thereto.   Stirling, 17th February, 1540-1.

VNIUERSIS et singulis ad quorum noticias presentes litere peruenerint: Prepositus, balliui, consules et communitas burgi de Striueling eternam in
Domino salutem.   Noueritis nos, vnanimi consensu et assensu, contulisse,
presentiumque per tenorem conferimus discreto viro, domino Willelmo Robesoun, capellano, capellaniam altaris Sancti Michaelis infra ecclesiam parrochi-
alem nostram de Striueling fundatam, in manibus nostris de jure et de facto
vacantem per dimissionem discreti viri, domini Alexandri Forsitht, capellani
vltimique possessoris eiusdem, ad nostram donationem pleno jure spectantem;
cum omnibus fructibus, terris, tenementis, annuis redditibus, juribus, obuentionibus, ornamentis, et pertinentiis suis quibuscunque ad eandem capellaniam

To ALL and sundry to whose knowledge the present letters shall come: The provost,
bailies, councillors and community of the burgh of Striueling greeting in the Lord
everlasting.   Know ye that we, with unanimous consent and assent, have granted,
and by the tenor of these presents grant to a discreet man, Sir William Robesoun,
chaplain, the chaplainry of the altar of Saint Michael founded within our parish
church of Striueling, vacant in our hands of right and of fact by dimission of a
discreet man, Sir Alexander Forsith, chaplain and last possessor of the same, being
at our lawful disposal in full right; with all fruits, lands, tenements, annual rents,
rights, obventions, ornaments and their pertinents whatsoever, belonging or which
may justly belong to the said chaplainry in any way in time coming, and specially of

spectantibus seu iuste spectare valentibus quomodolibet in futurum; et precipue de annuis redditibus de terris et tenementis subscriptis annuatim leuandis et percipiendis jacentibus infra burgum de Striueling, videlicet, de tenemento quondam Thome Joffray, jacente in le Castellwinde, nunc Margareto Joffray, duodecim denarios; de tenemento domus elimosinarum jacente penes cimitorium in ecclesia parrochiali de Striueling, duos solidos; de tenemento quondam Nicolaij Coistesoun jacente in le Bakraw, duos solidos; de tenemento Willelmi Manis jacente in eodem le Bakraw, duos solidos; de tenemento Alexandri Robesoun, quatuor solidos; de tenemento Jacobi Ferny, quatuor solidos; de duobus tenementis Walteri Cousland, octo solidos; de duobus tenementis quondam domini Jacobi Darrocht, capellani, nunc Roberti Spittell, viginti solidos; et de tenemento dicti Roberti Spittell, sex solidos; de tenemento Jacobi Duncansoun, quatuor solidos; de tenemento Georgi Creichtoun, quatuor solidos; de tenemento Thome Lauson, quatuor solidos; de tenemento Duncani Darrocht, sex solidos; et de tenemento quondam Johannis Broun nuen diuiso inter Georgium Yester et Georgium Spens, quatuor solidos, jacente contigue in occidentali parte de le Midraw; de tenemento Johannis Alexander, decim solidos; de tenemento quondam Roberti Norvell, tres

the annual rents to be uplifted and received yearly furth of the lands and tenements underwritten lying within the burgh of Striveling, namely, of the tenement of the deceased Thomas Joffray, lying in the Castle Wynd, now of Margaret Joffray, twelve pennies; of the tenement of the almshouse lying near the burying ground in the parish church of Striveling, two shillings; of the tenement of the deceased Nicholas Coistesoun, lying in the Bakraw, two shillings; of the tenement of William Mains, lying in the said Bakraw, two shillings; of the tenement of Alexander Robesoun, four shillings; of the tenement of James Ferny, four shillings; of two tenements of Walter Cousland, eight shillings; of two tenements of the deceased Sir James Darrocht, chaplain, now of Robert Spittell, twenty shillings; and of the tenement of the said Robert Spittell, six shillings; of the tenement of James Duncanson, four shillings; of the tenement of George Creichtoun, four shillings; of the tenement of Thomas Lauson, four shillings; of the tenement of Duncan Darrocht, six shillings; and of the tenement of the deceased John Brown, now divided between George Yester and George Spens, four shillings, lying contiguous on the west side of the Midraw; of the tenement of John Alexander, ten shillings; of the tenement of the deceased

solidos; et de tenemento Thome Smytht, tres solidos, jacente etiam in dicto
le Midraw; de tenemento Thome Smytht jacente apud Portem Orientalem
dicti burgi, octo decim denarios; de horreo quondam Alexandri Crag, duos solidos
et sex denarios; de horreo quondam Willelmi Cossur, duos solidos sex denarios;
de horreo Alexandri Forestar, duos solidos sex denarios; de orto quondam
Willelmi Provand, duos solidos; de cnabus particatis terre jacente ex parte
boreali horrei dicti Alexandri Forester et quondam Dauid Crag, tres solidos,
jacente etiam apud finem orientalem dicti burgi; de terra vocata le Milhill
jacente apud le Burrowm ll, tres solidos; de duobus tenementis quondam
Alexandri Evingsoun, vndecim solides sex denarios; de tenemento Johannis
Aitkin jacente apud locum Fratrum Predicatorum, duodecim denarios; de
tenemento quondam Alexandri Patersoun jacente apud le Havin, nunc
Roberto Spittell pertinente, viginti denarios; de tenemento Georgii Smytht,
viginti denarios; et de horreo Johannis Cragiugelt, sex solidos, jacente apud
finem orientalem dicti burgi; de horreo Rechardi Narne jacente ex parte
boreali dicti burgi, tres solidos et quatuor denarios; de tenemento et crofta
Alexandri Schaw de Sauchy jacente apud finem borealem de le Mary Winde,

Robert Norvell, three shilliıgs; and cf the tenement of Thomas Smytht, three
shillings, lying in the said Midraw; of the tenement of Thomas Smytht, lying at the
East Port of the said burgh, eighteen pence; of the barn of the deceased Alexander
Crag, two shillings and six pennies; of the barn of the deceased William Cossur, two
shillings six pennies; of the barn of Alexander Forestar, two shillings six pennies;
of the yard of the deceased William Provand, two shillings; of two particates of land
lying on the north side of the barn of the said Alexander Forester and the deceased
David Crag, three shillings, lying also at the east end of the said burgh; of the land
called the Millhill lying at the Burrownhill, three shillings; of two tenements of the
deceased Alexander Evingsoun, eleven shillings six pennies; of the tenement of John
Aitkin lying at the place of the Friars Preachers, twelve pennies; of the tenement of
the deceased Alexander Patersoun lying at the Havin now belonging to Robert
Spittell, twenty pennies; of the tenement of George Smitht, twenty pennies; and of
the barn of John Cragingelt, six shillings, lying at the east end of the said burgh;
of the barn of Richard Name lying on the north part of the said burgh, three
shillings and four pennies; of the tenement and croft of Alexander Schaw of Sauchy
lying at the north end of the Mary Wynd, three shillings; and of the house or

tres solidos; et de domo seu tenemento altari Sancti Andree pertinente jacente in dicto le Mary Wynde, duos solidos; de terra Margarete Bell jacente etiam in dicto le Mary Wynde ¹ de tenemento jacente ex parte orientali de le Tour de Ballat in Mary Wynde, sex denarios; de tenemento Johannis Kar jacente in dicto le Mary Wynde, duodecim solidos quatuor denarios; de tenemento domini Jacobi Nicolsoun jacente ex parte, boreali ecclesie parrochialis de Striueling, nouem solidos; de tenemento anteriori Rechardi Narne, duos solidos; de tenemento Dauid Greg, septem solidos, jacente in dicto le Middillraw; de tenemento Gilberti Brady, sex solidos octo denarios; de terra quondam domine de Cummyrnald, nunc ¹ pertinentiis ¹ solidos; pro toto tempore vite antedicti domini Willelmi. Faciendo inde, annuatim, idem dominus Willelmus ad idem altare per se quotidie missam ad horam ¹ cum dispositus fuerit, et per alium idoneum capellanum onera et seruicia secundum ritum chori dicte ecclesie in ebdomadalibus, tantum. Prouidendo etiam quod dictus dominus Willelmus nobis seruiet et successoribus nostris in officio magistri fabrice dicti burgi durante tempore vite sue, diligenter et fideliter, prout coram Deo et homine

tenement belonging to the altar of Saint Andrew lying in the said Mary Wynd, two shillings; of the land of Margaret Bell lying also in the said Mary Wynd, ¹ of the tenement lying on the east side of the Tour de Ballat in Mary Wynd, six pennies; of the tenement of John Kar lying in the said Mary Wynd, twelve shillings four pennies; of the tenement of Sir James Nicolsoun lying on the north side of the parish church of Striueling, nine shillings; of the fore tenement of Richard Nairne, two shillings; of the tenement of David Greg, seven shillings, lying in the said Middleraw; of the tenement of Gilbert Brady, six shillings eight pennies; of the land of the late lady of Cummyrnald now ¹ with the pertinents ¹ shillings; for the whole lifetime of the foresaid William. Performing therefor, yearly, the said Sir William by himself a daily mass at the said altar at the hour of ¹ when he shall be disposed, and by another sufficient chaplain the burdens and services according to the custom of the choir of the said church every week, only. Providing also that the said Sir William shall serve us and our successors in the office of master of work of the said burgh during his whole lifetime, diligently and faithfully, as he

¹ Blank in original.

respondere voluerit. In cuius rei testimonium sigillum nostrum commune presentibus est appeusum. Apud dictum burgum, decimo septimo die mensis Februarii anno Domini millesimo quingentesimo quadragesimo.

shall wish to answer before God and man. In witness whereof our common seal is appended to these presents. At the said burgh, the seventeenth day of the month of February in the year of our Lord one thousand five hundred and forty.

XLIII.

GRANT by the Provost, Bailies, Council and Community of the Burgh of Stirling to John Grahame of the office of Clerk of the Burgh Court. Stirling, 9th November, 1542.

VNIUERSIS et singulis presentes litcras inspecturis: Propositus, balliui, counsall et communitas burgi de Striueling, salutem in Domino sempiternam. Noueritis nos, presentium per tenorem, dare et concedere Johanni Grahame, notario, officium clerici seu scribe curie nostre burgalis; cum quatuor libris monete Scocie et botha orientali anterioris tenementi pretorii dicti burgi, in feodo, pro toto tempore vite sue, cum ceteris emergentibus, eschætis, libertatibus, commoditatibus, preuilegiis et proficuis, dicto officio pertinentibus, vsitatis et consuetis; cum scriptione omnium cedularum conquerentium ac cum testificatione omnium sasinarum infra libertatem dicti burgi per balliuos eiusdem tradendarum. Faciendo inde, annuatim, dictus Johannes Grahame, per se vel substitutum seu substitutos, de quo et de quibus faciendis sibi ad vitam

To ALL and sundry who shall see the present letters: The provost, bailies, council, and community of the burgh of Striveling, greeting in the Lord everlasting. Know ye that we, by the tenor of these presents, give and grant to John Grahame, notary, the office of clerk or scribe of our burgh court; with four pounds Scots money and the east booth of the fore tenement of the tolbooth of the said burgh, in fee, for the whole of his lifetime, with the other issues, escheats, liberties, commodities, privileges and profits, belonging to the said office, used and wont; with the writing of all schedules of complaints and with the attesting of all sasines within the liberty of the said burgh to be given by the bailies of the same. Performing therefor, yearly, the said John Grahame, by himself or a substitute or substitutes, whom to make we

M

suam facultatem liberam impertimur, seruitia in curiis et extra infra libertatem burgi debite et consuete, tantum. In cuius rei testimonium sigillum nostrum commune presentibus est appensum. Apud dictum burgum nostrum nono die mensis Nouembris anno Domini millesimo quingentesimo quadragesimo secundo.

impart free power during his life, the services in and outwith the courts within the liberty of the burgh used and wont, only. In witness whereof our common seal is appended to these presents. At our said burgh on the ninth day of the month of November in the year of our Lord one thousand five hundred forty-two.

XLIV.

PRECEPT by King Francis and Queen Mary, commanding a Charter to be made confirming a Grant by the Friars Preachers of Stirling and Convent thereof to Alexander Erskin, of the lands and others formerly belonging to them. Edinburgh, 10th May, 1560.

FRANCISCUS ET MARIA, Dei gracia, Rex et Regina Gallie et Scocie, etc.: Nostri magni sigilli gardiano, salutem. Quia approbauimus, ratificauimus, ac pro nobis et successoribus nostris pro perpetuo confirmauimus chartam, preceptum et feudifirmam in eadem contenta, factam per nostros oratores, fratrem Andream Makneill, priorem Fratrum Predicatorum de Striuiling et eiusdem loci conuentum, dilecto nostro familiari seruitori, Alexandro Erskin de Cangnoir, fratri germano dilecti nostri consanguinei Johannis domini Erskin, et Margarete Home, ipsius coniugi, ac eorum altera diutius viuenti,

FRANCIS AND MARY, by the grace of God, King and Queen of France and Scotland, etc.: To the keeper of our great seal, greeting. Whereas we have approved, ratified, and for us and our successors for ever confirmed a charter, precept and feu-farm contained in the same, made by our orators, brother Andrew Makneill, prior of the Friars Preachers of Striveling and convent of the same place, to our beloved familiar servitor, Alexander Erskin of Cangnoir, brother german of our well beloved cousin John lord Erskine, and to Margaret Home, his spouse, and

in coniuncta infeodatione, et heredibus in dicta carta contentis, de totis et integris dictorum fratrum terris olim, pomario, molendinis, piscariis, cum pertinentiis subscriptis, videlicet, toto et integro ipsorum olim pomario, nunc vastis terris, ac totis et integris terris siue crofta nuncupata the Freris Croft dicto olim pomario adiacente, inter molendinarium aqueductum qui a molendino lie Burrow Mylne vocata defluit ex oriente, viam publicam qua a burgo de Striuiling ad Cambuskynneth itur ex occidentali et croftam Bawenis Croft vocatam ex boriali ac monasterium dictorum fratrum ex australi partibus; acetiam, de totis et integris terris de Broun Yardis, vnacum dimidietate piscarie vnius cymbe super aquam de Forth et piscaria vnius alterius cymbe super dictam aquam de Forth; et dictorum fratrum molendino the Burrow Mylne appellato, jacente prope dictum burgum de Striuiling, ac de totis et integris terris nuncupatis Sanct Michaellis Hill and Riallis Croftis dicto molendino contigue adiacentibus; necnon de alio dictorum fratrum molendino illic jacente the Brig Mylne nuncupato, infra vicecomitatum nostrum de Striuiling; et de prefatorum fratrum acris jacentibus prope villam de Dunfermling nuncupatis the Hawank, infra dominium et regalitatem eiusdem. De dictis priore et conuentu loci Fratrum Predicatorum de Striuiling et eorum successoribus in

the longer liver of them, in conjunct fee, and to the heirs mentioned in the said charter, of all and whole the lands sometime of the said friars, the orchard, mills, fishings, with the pertinents underwritten, that is to say, all and whole their late orchard, now waste lands, and all and whole the lands or croft called the Friars Croft lying near the said late orchard, between the mill lade which flows from the mill called the Burrow Mill on the east, the public road which leads from the burgh of Striveling to Cambuskynneth on the west and the croft called Bawenis Croft on the north and the monastery of the said friars on the south side; also, of all and whole the lands of Broun Yards, together with the half of the fishing of one boat upon the water of Forth and the fishing of another boat on the said water of Forth; and the mill of the said friars called the Burrow Mill lying near the said burgh of Striveling, and of all and whole the lands called Saint Michaels Hill and Rials Crofts lying next to the said mill; also of another mill of the said friars lying there called the Brig Mill, within our sheriffdom of Striveling; and of the acres of the foresaid friars lying near the town of Dunfermling called the Hawank, within the lordship and regality of the same. To be held of the said prior and convent of the

perpetua feudifirma tenendis, prout in dictis carta et precepto desuper
confectis plenius continetur. Saluis nobis et successoribus nostris, juribus,
seruiciis et deuotarum orationum suffragis de dictis terris, molendinis, pomariis,
piscariis cum suis pertinencijs, nobis a dictis priore et conventu eorumque
successoribus ante presentem nostram confirmacionem debitis et consuetis
respectiue. Vobis precipimus et mandamus quatenus cartam nostram confirmacionis in maiori forma capelle nostre debita sub prefato nostro magno
sigillo dictis personis super premissis fieri faciatis. Datum sub nostro secreto
sigillo, apud Edinburgh, decimo die mensis Maij anno Domini millesimo
quingentesimo sexagesimo et regnorum nostrorum annis, videlicet, Gallie
primo et Scocie secundo et decimo octauo.

place of the Friars Preachers of Striveling and their successors in feu farm for ever,
as in the said charter and precept made thereupon is more fully contained. Saving
to us and our successors the rights, services and offerings of devout supplication
from the said lands, mills, orchards, and fishings with their pertinents, respectively
due and accustomed to us by the said prior and convent and their successors before
our present confirmation. We charge and command you that ye cause to be made
to the said persons our charter of confirmation upon the premises in greater and due
form of our chancery under our foresaid great seal. Given under our secret seal, at
Edinburgh, on the tenth day of the month of May in the year of our Lord one
thousand five hundred and sixty and in the years of our reigns, that is to say, of
France the first and of Scotland the second and the eighteenth.

XLV.

CHARTER by Queen Mary to the Provost, Bailies, Councillors, and Community of Stirling of the Church Property and Revenues within the
Burgh, for the support of the Ministry and maintenance of Hospitals
for the poor and infirm. Edinburgh, 15th April, 1567.

MARIA, Dei gratia, Regina Scotorum: Omnibus probis hominibus totius terre
sue, clericis et laicis, salutem. Sciatis quia nos, impensius munus nostrum

MARY, by the grace of God, Queen of Scots: To all good men of her whole land,
clerics and laics, greeting. Know ye whereas we, more carefully reflecting upon our

erga diuinum seruicium pependentes, et pro ardenti zelo quem ob intertenendam policiam et equabilem ordinem inter subditos nostros, precipue vero infra burgum nostrum de Striueling, preseruandum habemus; considerantes nos, itaque, ex officio teneri munus erga Deum complecti debere, cuius prouidentia regimini huius regni preponimur, satque nobis ex officio incumbere, omni honesto modo, pro ministris verbi Dei prouidere, et quod hospitalia pauperibus, mutilatis et miseris personis, orphanis et parentibus destitutis infantibus, infra dictum nostrum burgum preseruentur, post nostram perfectam etatem, cum auisamento dominorum secreti consilii nostri, dedimus, concessimus, disposuimus, ac pro nobis et successoribus nostris pro perpetuo confirmauimus, ac tenore presentium damus, concedimus, disponimus, ac pro nobis et nostris successoribus pro perpetuo confirmamus predilectis nostris preposito, balliuis, consulibus et communitati dicti nostri burgi de Striuiling, et eorum successoribus imperpetuum, omnes et singulas terras, tenementa, domos, edificia, ecclesias, capellas, hortos, pomeria, croftas, annuos redditus, fructus, deuorias, proficua, emolimenta, firmas, elemesinas *lie dailsiluer*, obitus et anniuersaria quecunque que quouismodo pertinuerunt aut pertinere dinoscuntur ad quascunque capellanias, alteragia, prebendarias in quacunque ecclesia, capella aut

duty towards divine service, and out of the ardent zeal which we have for maintaining civil polity and preserving good order among our subjects, but especially within our burgh of Striveling; considering, therefore, that we by our office are bound and ought to be careful of our duty towards God, by whose providence we are set over the government of this kingdom, and that it is incumbent on us, in virtue of our office, by all honest means to provide for the ministers of the word of God, and that hospitals for poor, maimed and miserable persons, orphans and children deprived of their parents, may be maintained within our city, did, after our perfect age, with the advice of the lords of our privy council, give, grant, dispone and for us and our successors for ever confirm, and do by the tenor of these presents give, grant, dispone and for us and our successors for ever confirm to our well-beloved the provost, bailies, councillors and community of our said burgh of Striviling, and their successors for ever, all and sundry lands, tenements, houses, buildings, churches, chapels, yards, orchards, crofts, annual rents, fruits, duties, profits, emoluments, rents, alms, daill-silver, obits and anniversaries whatsoever, which anywise belonged to or were known to belong to any chaplainries, altarages, prebends founded by whatsoever patron

collegio, infra libertatem dicti nostri burgi de Striuiling fundata seu fundatas
per quemcunque patronum, in quarum possessione capellani et prebendarii
carundem perprius fuerant, vbicunque prefate domus, tenementa, edificia,
pomeria, horti, annui redditus, anniuersaria, fructus, prouentus et emolimenta,
jacent aut prius leuata fuerunt respectiue, cum maneriebus locis, pomeriis,
terris, annuis redditibus, emolimentis et denoriis quibuscunque que Fratribus
Dominicalibus seu Predicatoribus et Minoribus seu Franciscanis dicti nostri
burgi de Striuiling perprius pertinuerunt; vnacum omnibus et singulis terris,
domibus, tenementisque, jacentibus infra dictum nostrum burgum et libertatem
eiusdem, cum omnibus annuis redditibus de quacunque domo, terris et tenemento,
infra dictum nostrum burgum leuandis, datis, donatis et fundatis, quibuscunque
capellaniis, altaragiis, ecclesiis, mortuariis aut anniuersariis vbicunque sint infra
regnum nostrum; acetiam cum omnibus et singulis annuis redditibus et aliis
denoriis solitis aut que per quamcunque ecclesiam extra dictum nostrum
burgum a preposito et balliuis eiusdem de communi redditu eiusdem, pro suffra-
giis celebrandis, demandari poterint, cum pertouentiis. Tenendas et habendas
omnes et singulas prefatas terras, tenementa, domos, edificia, pomeria, hortos,
croftas, annuos redditus, fructus, denoria, proficua, emolimenta, firmas, elemosinas,

in any church, chapel, or college within the liberty of our said burgh of Striviling,
in possession of which the chaplains and prebendaries of the same formerly were,
wheresoever the foresaid houses, tenements, buildings, orchards, yards, annualrents, anniversaries, fruits, profits, and emoluments lie or were formerly uplifted
respectively, with manor-places, orchards, lands, annualrents, emoluments and
duties whatsoever which formerly belonged to the Dominican or Preaching
Friars and to the Minorites or Franciscans of our said burgh of Striviling;
together with all and sundry lands, houses and tenements, lying within our said
burgh and liberty of the same, with all annualrents leviable from whatsoever
house, lands and tenement, within our said burgh, given, granted and founded
to whatever chaplainries, altarages, churches, burials or anniversaries wheresoever they may be within our kingdom; and also with all and sundry annual
rents and other duties customary or that could be demanded by any church outwith
our said burgh from the provost and bailies of the same from the common good
thereof, for celebrating suffrages, with the pertinents. To hold and to have all and
sundry the foresaid lands, tenements, houses, buildings, orchards, yards, crofts,

obitus, anniuersaria, ecclesias, capellas, fratrum loca, hortos, cum pertinentiis,
prefatis preposito, balliuis, consulibus et communitati et eorum successoribus,
de nobis et successoribus nostris imperpetuum, prout eadem jacent in longitudine et latitudine, in domibus, edificiis, muris, muremis, lignis, lapide et calce,
cum libero introitu et exitu, etc.; ac cum omnibus aliis et singulis libertatibus,
commoditatibus, proficius et asiamentis, ac iustis suis pertinentiis quibuscunque,
tam non nominatis quam nominatis, tam sub terra quam supra terram, ad predictas terras, tenementa, domos, edificia, pomeria, hortos, croftas, annuos redditus,
fructus, deuorias et alia prescripta cum pertinentiis spectantibus seu iuste
spectare valentibus quomodolibet in futurum; libere, quiete, plenarie, integre,
honorifice, bene et in pace, absque reuocatione aut contradictione quacunque.
Cum potestate memoratis preposito, balliuis, consulibus et communitati, et
ipsorum successoribus, per seipsos et ipsorum collectores quos constituent,
prefatos annuos redditus, fructus, deuorias, proficua [et] emolimenta quecunque,
leuandi et recipiendi, vbicunque perprius leuata fuerant, prefatas terras et
tenementa locandi et remouendi, loca diruta extruendi et reparandi, eademque
in hospitalia aut alios similes vsus legitimos, prout ipsis cum auisamento

annual rents, fruits, duties, profits, emoluments, rents, alms, obits, anniversaries,
churches, chapels, places of friars, yards, with the pertinents, to the foresaid provost,
bailies, councillors and community and their successors, of us and our successors for
ever, as they lie in length and breadth, in houses, buildings, walls, timber, wood,
stone and lime, with free ish and entry, etc., and with all and sundry other liberties,
commodities, profits and easements and their just pertinents whatsoever, as well not
named as named as well under the ground as above the ground, belonging or which may
in time to come justly belong in any manner of way to the foresaid lands, tenements,
houses, buildings, orchards, yards, crofts, annual rents, fruits, duties and other things
foresaid with their pertinents; freely, quietly, fully, wholly, honorably, well and in
peace, without revocation or challenge whatsoever.   With power to the above
mentioned provost, bailies, councillors, and community, and their successors, by
themselves and their collectors whom they shall appoint, to uplift and receive the foresaid annual rents, fruits, duties, profits, and emoluments whatsoever wherever they
were formerly uplifted, to let and remove from the foresaid lands and tenements, to
build and repair the ruinous places, and to restore and apply the same to hospitals,
or other similar lawful uses, as to them, with the advice of the ministers and elders

ministrorum et seniorum dicti nostri burgi videbitur, reducendi et applicandi ;
adeo libere in omnibus sicuti prefati prebendarii, capellani et fratres proscripti,
eisdem perprius gaudere easdemque possidere potuissent.   Memorati, autem,
prepositus, balliui, consules et eorum successores, tenebuntur et astricti erunt,
ministros,lectores,et alia ecclesiastica onera, prefatis annuis redditibus,proficuis,
et denoriis, secundum valorem et quantitatem earundem, sustinere, locaque et
edificia reparanda in hospitalitatem et alios vsus prescriptos applicare.   Considerantes, itaque, quanta fraude ingens numerus dictorum prebendariorum,
capellaniorum et fratrum prescriptorum, qui post alterationem religionis,
terras, annuos redditus et emolimenta, ipsorum capellaniis, prebendis, et aliis
locis respectiue perprius mortificatas, disposuerunt, alienarunt, et in manibus
quorundem particularium virorum extradonarunt ; acetiam quod plerique
ligei, quarundem terrarum, tenementorum et annuorum reddituum peripsorum
predecessores mortificatarum, jus sibi acclamarunt, per breuia capelle nostre,
aut alias sasinam tanquam heredes suorum predecessorum qui easdem
ecclesie perprius dotarunt, recuperarunt ; quod euenit partim negligentia
officiariorum dicti nostri burgi et partim collusione dictorum prebendariorum
et capellanorum et fratrum prescriptorum ; quocirca, cum auisamento pre-

of our said burgh, shall seem fit ; as freely in all respects as the foresaid prebendaries,
chaplains and friars before written, might have enjoyed or possessed the same afore-
time.   Moreover, the said provost, bailies, councillors and their successors, shall be
holden and obliged to support the ministers, readers, and other ecclesiastical charges,
out of the foresaid annual rents, profits and duties, according to the value and
quantity of the same, and to apply the places and buildings to be repaired for
hospitality and other uses foresaid.   Besides, considering how dishonestly a great
number of the said prebendaries, chaplains and friars foresaid, have, since the change
of religion, disponed, alienated and given away into the hands of certain private
persons the lands, annualrents and emoluments previously mortified to their chaplainries, prebends and other places respectively; and also that very many of the
lieges have claimed for themselves, by brieves of our chancery, the right to certain
lands, tenements and annualrents mortified by their predecessors, or otherwise have
again obtained sasine as heirs of their predecessors who previously gifted the same
to the church ; which has happened partly through the negligence of the officers of
our said burgh and partly through the collusion of the said prebendaries, chaplains

scripto, omnes et singulas huiusmodi alienationes, dispositiones et sasinas, quibus primum propositum et animus fundatorum infringitur, alteratur et variatur, diducendo easdem in particulares vsus, ad effectum quod eedem in vsus suprascriptos conuerte poterunt, per presentes, rescindimus et annullamus; quamquidem hanc nostram declarationem volumus tanti esse roboris et efficacie acsi persone que easdem dispositiones obtinuerunt particulariter citate essent ipsarumque infeofamenta absque vlteriori processu rescinderentur. Acetiam, cum anisamento prescripto, vnimus et incorporamus omnes et singulas terras, tenementa, domos, edificia, ecclesias, cymiteria, capellas, pomeria, hortos, croftas, annuos redditus, fructus, deuorias, proficua, emolimenta, firmas, elemosinas, obitus auniuersaria, fratrum loca, hortos earundem, cum suis pertinentiis, in vnum corpus imposterum appellanda Fundatio nostra Ministerii et Hospitalitatis de Striueling. Volumus, etiam, quod vnica sasina per prefatos prepositum et ballinos aut eorum aliquem, dicti ministerii et hospitalitatis nomine, apud pretorium dicti nostri burgi semel accepta, tam sufficiens erit sasina perpetuo in futurum acsi eadem super particulares terras ad dictos capellanos, prebendarios et fratres, pertinentes, aut ipsis in prefatos annuos redditus, anniuersaria, firmas, proficua et deuoria prescripta debitas,

and friars foresaid; wherefore, with advice foresaid, we, by these presents, rescind and annul all and sundry such alienations, dispositions and sasines, by which the first purpose and will of the founders is infringed, altered and changed, by perverting the same to private uses, to the effect that the same may be converted to the purposes above set forth; and this our declaration we will to be as strong and effectual as if the persons who obtained the said dispositions had been particularly cited and their infeftments rescinded without further process. As also, with advice foresaid, we unite and incorporate all and sundry lands, tenements, houses, buildings, churches, churchyards, chapels, orchards, yards, crofts, annual-rents, fruits, duties, profits, emoluments, rents, alms, obits, anniversaries, friars' places, yards of the same, with their pertinents, in one body in all time coming, to be called our Foundation of the Ministry and Hospitality of Striviling. We will, also, that one sasine taken once for all at the tolbooth of our said burgh by the foresaid provost and bailies, or any of them, in name of the said ministry and hospitality, shall be as sufficient a sasine in all time coming as if the same were taken upon the particular lands belonging to the said chaplains, prebendaries and friars, or in the

N

sumeretur, non obstante locorum distantia. Preterea, per presentes nolumus capellanos, prebendarios et fratres qui ante dictam alterationem pronisi erant, per hoc presens nostrum infeofamentum, proiudicari, sed reseruamus illis vsum dictorum fructuum et deuoriarum durante eorum vita tantum. Precipiendo, itaque, nostrorum computorum rotulatoribus, presentibus et futuris, ipsorum collectoribus, factoribus et aliis quorum interest in genere necnon in specie, vt ne quis eorum recipere aut leuare presumat dictos fructus particulariter suprascriptos pro quouis tempore, preterito seu futuro, neue impediant aut impedimentum vllum faciant memoratis preposito, balliuis, consulibus, communitati, et eorum successoribus, in pacifica possessione earundem. Requirendo et ordinando etiam dominos nostre sessonis quatenus literas in omnibus quatuor formis, ad instantiam dictorum prepositi, balliuorum, consulum, communitatis, et ipsorum successorum, ad effectum suprascriptum dirigant. Necnon precipiendo quibuscunque intromissoribus cum dictis fructibus quatenus ipsis de eisdem prompte intendant, pareant et gratam solucionem faciant. In cuius rei testimonium huic presenti carte nostre magnum sigillum nostrum apponi precepimus. Testibus: Reuerendissimo in Christo patre, Johanne archiepiscopo Sanctiandree, etc.; dilectis nostris consanguineis, Georgio

foresaid annualrents, anniversaries, rents, profits and duties foresaid due to them, the distance of the places notwithstanding. Besides, by these presents we will that no prejudice be done to the chaplains, prebendaries and friars who were in possession before the said change, by this our present infeftment, but we reserve to them the use of the said fruits and duties during their lives only.   Directing, accordingly, our comptrollers, present and future, and their collectors, factors, and others whom it concerns in general as well as in special, that none of them presume to receive or to levy the said fruits particularly above described for any time whatever, past or future, or offer any obstruction or impediment to the foresaid provost, bailies, councillors, community and their successors, in the peaceable possession of the same.   Requiring and ordaining also our lords of session that they direct letters in all the four forms, at the instance of the said provost, bailies, councillors, community and their successors to the effect above written. Also commanding all intromitters with the said fruits that they give prompt attention, obey and make willing and ready payment to them of the same. In witness whereof we have commanded our great seal to be appended to this our present charter. Witnesses: The

comite de Huntlie domino Gordoun et Badyenach, cancellario nostro; Jacobo
comite de Boithuile domino Halis, Creichtoun et Liddisdale, regni nostri
magno admirallo; dilectis nostris familiaribus consiliariis, Richardo Maitland
de Lethingtoun, nostri secreti sigilli custode; Jacobo Balfoure de Pettindreich,
nostrorum rotulorum, registri et consilii clerico; et Johanne Bellenden de
Auchnoule, nostre iusticiarie cleric, equitibus auratis.   Apud Edinburgh,
decimo quinto die mensis Aprilis, anno Domini millesimo quingentesimo
sexagesimo septimo et regni nostri vicesimo quinto.

most reverend father in Christ, John archbishop of Saint Andrews, etc.; our beloved
cousins, George earl of Huntlie lord Gordoun and Badyenach, our chancellor; James
earl of Boithuile lord Halis, Creichtoun and Liddisdale, great admiral of our kingdom; our beloved familiar councillors, Richard Maitland of Lethingtoun, keeper of
our privy seal; James Balfoure of Pittendreich, clerk of our rolls, register and
council; and John Bellenden of Auchnoule, our justice clerk, knights. At Edinburgh,
the fifteenth day of the month of April, in the year of our Lord one thousand five
hundred and sixty-seven and of our reign the twenty-fifth year.

XLVI.

DECREE by the Lords Interpreters of the Law of Oblivion as to an Annual-
     rent claimed by William Galane, Master of the Grammar School and
     Chaplain of the Altar of St. Lawrence in the Parish Kirk of Stirling,
     from the tacksman of St Laurance's Croft.   Stirling, 30th August,
     1569.

AT STRIUELING, the penult day of August the yeir of God j^m v^c lxix yeiris.
The lordis interpretouris of the law of obliuioun vnderwrittin, thai ar to say the
nobill and michtie lord, James erle of Murray lord Abirnethy, etc., Regent to
oure Soueraue Lord his realme and ligies; James erle of Mortoun lord Da.keith,
chancellar of this realme; Alexander erle of Glencarne lord Kilmawris; Johne
erle of Mar lord Erskin; maister Robert Rechartsoun, commendatar of Sanct

Marie Ilo, thesaurar to oure said Soueraue Lord; and Sir Johnne Ballenden
of Auchnowll, knycht, justice clerk: Anent the supplicatioun maid be maister
Williame Gulane, maister of the Grammer Scole of Striueling, makand mentioun
that he is lauchfillie prouidit of auld to the chaiplaurie of Sanct Laurence
foundit within the paroche kirk of Striueling and hes bene in peccabill possessioun of vptaking of the males, annuellis, fruittis and rentis pertening thairto
thir nyntene yeiris bigane, lyke as he is presentlie, except that Dauid Ker,
burges of Striueling, occupear and takkisman of ane croft callit Sanct Laurence
Croft, perteniug to the said chapellanrie, for the quhilk he is obleist in his
assedatioun to pay yeirlie four pundis vsuale money of this realme, haldis fra
the said maister Williame nyntene pundis money for termes bigane at this last
Witsonday; and quhen he did call and persew the said Dauid for payment
contenit in the assedatioun of the said croft befoir the provost and baillies of
the burgh of Striueling he wranguslie refuisit to do the samin be proponing
of the act and law of obliuioun, quharthrow the saidis provost and baillies
wald nocht proceid to the geving of thair interloquutour in the said actioun
quhill the samin be interpretit be the lordis interpretatouris quhether the
samin suld be comprehendit vnder the said law or nocht; and anent the
chairge gevin to the said Dauid to compeir before the saidis lordis interpretatouris this day to heir and se the actione abonementionat ressonit and thair
declaratioun gevin quhether gif the samin aucht or suld becum vnder the said
law or nocht, with certificatioun and he compeirit nocht the saidis lordis wald
proceid as accordis; as at mair lenth is contenit in the said supplicatioun and
indorsatioun thairof; baith the parteis comperand personalie the lordis interpretatouris of the law of obliuioun findis that the males and dewitie of the said
croft extending to four pundis of the [crope and] yeir of God j^m v^c lix yeiris
aucht and suld be comprehendit vnder the said law of obliuioun, and that all
vtheris males and dewiteis of all vtheris yeiris and termes contenit in the said
maister Williames libell aucht nocht to bruik nor jois the priuilege thairof;
bot the saidis lordis hes remittit and remittis the samin to the saidis provest
and baillies to be decydit be thame as accordis of the law nochtwithstanding
the said allegeance.   Extractum de libro actorum per me, Alexandrum Hay,
deputatem in hac parte honorabilis viri, magistri Jacobi Makgill de Rankelour
Nether, clericum rotulorum, registri ac consilii, S.D.N. Regis, sub meis signo

et subscriptione manualibus.   [Extracted from the book of acts by me, Alexander Hay, depute of an honourable man, James Makgill of Rankelour Nether, clerk of the rolls, register and council, of our sovereign lord the King, under my sign and subscription manual.]

ALEXANDER HAY.

XLVII.

INSTRUMENT embodying Protest as to Warrandice given by the Provost, Bailies, and Town of Stirling, to Mongo Grahame, of the Friars Lands and the meadow lying contiguous thereto.   Stirling, 8th March, 1576-7.

In Dei nomine, amen.   Per hoc presens publicum instrumentum cunctis pateat cuidenter et sit notum quod anno incarnationis Dominice j^m v^c septuagesimo sexto, mensis vero Martii die octauo, et regni supremi domini nostri regis Jacobi, Dei gratia Scotorum Regis, sexti, anno eius decimo: In mei, notarii publici, et testium subscriptorum, presentia personaliter constitutus, Alexander Wysser, vnus balliuorum burgi de Striuiling, protestatus est solemniter vt sequitur in vulgari:—Forsamekill as this sasing that I instantle giff to Mongo Graheme of the landis callit the Frers landis, with the medow lyand contigue thairto, lyand within the terretorie of the bruch of Striuiling, sall hawe na maner of effect nor warrandice of the provost, baillies and toune off Striuiling, nor thair successouris, nor the gift gewin to ws be the Quenis grace our sowerane for the tyme may bei: and sustene; and the said Mongo anserit aganc: I am content thairoff and will seik na forder: Super quibis, premissis omnibus et singulis, dictus Alexander Wsser, ballinus, a me notario publico sub-

In the name of God, amen. By this present public instrument be it manifest and known to all that on the eighth day of the month of March in the year of the incarnation of our Lord one thousand five hundred seventy-six, and in the tenth year of the reign of our sovereign lord the king, James the Sixth, by the grace of God, King of Scots: In presence of me, notary public, and of the witnesses underwritten, personally appeared Alexander Wsser, one of the bailies of the burgh of Striveling, has solemnly protested as follows in the common language:—Forsamekill [etc., as above.] Whereupon, all and sundry the premises, the said Alexander Wsser, bailie, asked scripto sibi fieri petiit publicum seu publica instrumentum vel instrumenta vnum seu plura. Acta erant hec super fundo dictarum terrarum hora tertia post meridiem vel cocirca. Presentibus ibidem: Waltero Forester de Buquhan, preposito burgi de Striuiling; Waltero Aissone, balliuo eiusdem; Willelmo Norwell, Jacobo Edmonsone, Joanne John, Joanne Hog, Willelmo Graheme et Dauide Murray, seriando, cum diuersis aliis testibus ad premissa vocatis pariter et requisitis.

Et ego, vero, Johannes Graheme, Dunblauensis diocesis, publicus sacra apostolica auctoritate notarius, quia, premissis omnibus et singulis, dum sic ut premittitur agerentur, dicerentur et fierent, vnacum prenominatis testibus personaliter interfui, eaque omnia et singula sic fieri et dici, vidi, sciui et audiui, ac in notam cepi, ideoque hoc presens publicum instrumentum, manu alterius fideliter scriptum, exinde confeci, et in hanc publicam instrumenti formam redegi, signoque nomine, cognomine et subscriptione meis solitis ac consuetis signaui, in omnium et singulorum premissorum fidem rogatis et requisitus.

JOHANNES GRAHEME.

from me notary public subscribing one or more public instrument or public instruments to be made to him. These things were done upon the ground of the said lands at the third hour afternoon or thereabout. Present there: Walter Forester of Buquhan, provost of the burgh of Striuiling; Walter Aissone, bailie of the same; William Norwell, James Edmonsone, John John, John Hog, William Graheme, and David Murray, serjeand; with sundry other witnesses to the premises likewise called and required.

And I, John Grahame, of the diocese of Dunblane, by sacred apostolic authority, notary public, because I was present with the forenamed witnesses at all and sundry the premises while they were so transacted, said and done as above written, and saw, knew and heard the same, all and sundry, so done and said and took a note of them, and thereupon I have made the present public instrument, faithfully written by the hand of another, and have reduced it into this public form of instrument, and have signed with my sign, name, surname and subscription, used and wont, being asked and required in faith of all and sundry the premises.

JOHN GRAHEME.

XLVIII.

ACT of Parliament ordaining the Commissioners of Burghs to settle the debate between the Burghs of Perth, Dundee and Stirling, as to their respective antiquity and priority. Edinburgh, 11th November, 1579.

THE Kingis Maiestie and his thrie estaitis in this present parliament, vndir-standing the debait betwix the burrowis of Perth, Dundee and Striueling, anent the ordering of thame in thair awin places according to the auncietie of the saidis burrowis, and that thair is ane conventioun of the burrowis to to be in Glasgw the xxiiii day of Februar nixtcoum, at the quhilk tyme ordanis all the foirsaidis thrie burrowis to send commissioneris fullely instructit for thame and euerie ane of thame with the richtis and priuileges quhairby euerie ane of thame clames thair p aces in parliament; at the quhilk tyme ordanis the saidis commissioneris of burrowis to tak ordour with thame thair-anent for placeing of euery ane of thame in their awin places, and siclike the rest of the burrowis, swa that perpetuall ordour may be establishit amangis the saidis haill burrowis in tyme cuming. And his Maiestie, with anise of his saidis thrie estaitis, for performing of the premissis hes geuin full pouer and commissioun to the saidis burrowis and commissioneris thairof to tak ordour heirament as is abone writtin. And as the saidis commissioneris declaris and decernis ordanis the same to haue full effect, and they to abyd thairat in tyme cuming, with certification to thame and they failyie the remanent burrowis gevand furth thair decreit vpoun their placeing in manner foirsaid thair said decreit sall stand and haue effect in all tyme cuming.

XLIX.

ACT of Parliament whereby, *inter alia*, the Sheriff and the Provost and Bailies of Stirling were appointed the King's Justices of the Waters of the Teith, Forth, &c., for execution of certain fishery laws. Edinburgh, 29th November, 1581.

OUR Souerane Lord and thre estatis of this present parliament ratefeis and apprevis all actis maid be his Hines and his maist noble progenitouris anent

the distruction of cruuis and yaris, slauchter of reid fische, smoltis, and the fry of
all fisches, and ordanis the samyn to haue effect and executioun in tyme cuming.
And becaus it is vnderstand to his Hines and his saidis thre estatis that,
albeit panes and trauellis wes tane to cast done and distroy the saids cruuis
and yaris, yet in default of the exccusioun of the panis contenit in the saidis
actis vpoun the contraueuaries thairof, the saids cruuis and yaris ar not haldin
doun nor ouie vthir thing in effect (appointit to be done in the saidis actis)
put in executioun throw the default and negligence of the ordinar officiaris to
quhome the executioun thairof wes committit; thairfoir oure Soucrane Lord,
with aduise of his saidis thre estatis, hes maid, constitute and ordanit, and be
the tenoure of this present act, makis, constitutis and ordanis, the personis efter
specifeit, within the boundis particularlie follovand his Hines justices in that
pairt to the effect vnderwrittin:—   . . .   The stewart of Menteith and his
deputis for the heiddis of the wattir of Teith and Forth; the schiref of
Striuiling and his deputis, and provest and bailleis of Striuiling, for the
remanent of the watteris of Forth, Teith, Gudie, Carroun, Alloun, and Dovane,
and thair granis; the schiref of Linlithgow and his deputis, and the provest
and bailleis of Linlithgow, for the Watter of Avane and southsyde of Forth
within the boundis of that schireffdome. . . Gevand, grantand and committand to the saidis justices in that pairt, coniunclie and scueralie, within the
boundis particularlie aboue writtin, full power, speciall command, expres
bidding and charge, to inquire and tak vp dittay of all personis contraven-
eris of the saidis actis of parliament within the boundis particularie aboue
writtin, alsweill the principall offendaris as thair maisteris, landislordis and re-
settaris, to call thame to vnderly the law thairfoir in the tolbuyth of the heid
burgh of euerie schire or vthir place convenient at the discretioun of the
saidis justices, and put thame to the knawlege of ane assyse, as they be fundin
culpabill or innocent to minister iustice vpoun thame conform to the lawes of
this realme, the panes contenit in the saidis actis to rais and uplift and of
the samyn to mak compt, reknyng and payment, to oure Soucrane Lord and
his Hienes thesaurair in his chekker. And to the effect that the exceutioun
of the saidis actis sall not be neglectit as in tymes bypast ordanis twa ordiner
iustice courtis to be haldin yeirlie, the ane the first day of Februar and the
vthir at the first day of [August] or the nixt lawfull dayis thairefter following,

besyde vther cowrtis to be haldin át vthir dayis quhen occasioun seruis at the
discretioun of the saidis justices. . . . Be it alwayis vnderstand that this
present act nor nathing thairin contenit salbe prejudiciall to his Hines sub-
iectis being dewlie infeft and in possessioun of halding of cruuis, lynis or
loupis within fresche watteris, but that they may vse, jois, bruik and occupy
the same in tyme cuming according to thair richtis, kepand the Setterdayis
slop and sic distance betuix euerie hek as the actis of parliament appoyntis;
and in case they failye thairin to be accusabill and suffer punischment as the
remanent transgressouris of the said s acts.

L.

ACT of Parliament whereby the Fair formerly held at Stirling on 14th September was appointed to be held in future on 22nd October yearly.
Edinburgh, 29th November, 1581.

OUR Souerane Lord and thrie esta.tis of this present parliament, vnderstand-
ing the complaint gevin in be the provest, bailleis, counsell and communitie of
the burgh of Striueling, that thair hes bene twa dayis grantit to thame for
haldiu of fairis yeirlie this lang tyme bipast in the moneth of September,
viz., the ane being the letter Lad e day, the aucht day thairof, and the vther
the Ruid day, being the fourtene day of the samin moneth, being bayth within
sevin dayis efter vtheris, and swa being so neir togidder and in tyme of
harwest sua that the samin hes nawayis bene proffitabill to the said burgh
nor nawayis can serue to thair commoditie in tyme cuming quhan na resort of
pepill cumis thairto; thairfoir our said Souerane Lord, with auise foirsaid, hes
alterit and changit the said fair haldin of befoir yeirlie within the said burgh
and fredome thairof vpoun the said xiiij day of September to be haldin in
all tymes cuming vpoun the xxij day of October yeirlie thairefter; and the
first fair vsit of befoir vpoun the said viij day of September to stand and be
vsit in the same sort and maner as the samin wes of befoir.   And ordanis
letteres to be direct to mak publicatioun heirof in forme as effeiris at all places
neidfull.

o

LI.

REMISSION by King James the Sixth to the Bailies, Councillors, Community and Inhabitants of Stirling (with certain exceptions) for taking part with the Earl of Angus and others in their treasonable proceedings. Falkland, 26th June, 1584.

JACOBUS, Dei gratia, Rex Scotorum: Omnibus probis hominibus suis ad quos presentes litere pervenerint, salutem. Sciatis, quia ex nostris specialibus gratia et misericordia remisimus tenoreque presentium remittimus rancorem animi nostri, sectam regiam, et omnem actionem quem seu quas concepimus, habuimus, habemus seu habere vel clamare poterimus adversum ballivos, consules, communitatem et omnes inhabitatores, tam burgenses quam alios, burgi nostri de Striviling, eorumque uxores, proles, famulos et familias pro tempore (exceptis Joanne Muschet, Waltero Muresoun, Egidia Grahame relicta quondam Jacobi Archibald, Waltero Neische, Roberto Portarfeild, Willelmo Fairbairne, Christophero Lamb, Thomas Winyettis, Jacobo Richardsoun, Andrea Vtem, Joanne Watsoun, Joanne Duncanesoun, ministro, et Elizabetha Alschinder, relicta quondam Joannis Leischman eiusque servis et familia) quequidem persone nunc excepte sub hac nostra remissione non comprehendentur, pro arte et partis captione cum Archibaldo Angusie comite, Joanne comite de Mar, magistro Thoma Lyoun de Baldowkie magistro de Glammis,

JAMES, by the grace of God, King of Scots: To all his good men to whom the present letters shall come, greeting. Know ye, forasmuch as we of our special grace and mercy have remitted and by the tenor hereof remit rancour of our heart, royal suit, and all action which we have conceived, had, have, or may have or claim against the bailies, councillors, community and all indwellers, as well burgesses as others, of our burgh of Striviling, and their wives, children, servants and families for the time (excepting John Muschet, Walter Muresoun, Giles Grahame relict of the late James Archibald, Walter Neische, Robert Portarfield, William Fairbairne, Christopher Lamb, Thomas Winyettis, James Richardsoun, Andrew Vtem, John Watsoun, John Duncanesoun, minister, and Elizabeth Alschinder, relict of the late John Leischman, and his servants and family) which persons now excepted are not comprehended under this our remission, for art and part taking with Archibald earl of Angus, John Earl of Mar, master Thomas Lyoun of Baldowkie master of Glammis,

corum collegis et complicibus, in eorum proditoria interceptione et detentione
nostri castri et dicti burgi de Strivil:ng, ac pro receptione, supportatione, inter-
loquutione et defensione dictarum personarum et eorum sociorum in dicta
proditorio actu in mense Aprilis ultimo elapso commisso; necnon pro aliqua
prescientia seu premeditatione premissorum, aut in defensione et detentione
dicti castri et ville contra nos, nostram authoritatem et obedientiam, et pro
omnibus actione et crimine que inde sequi aut dictis ballivis, consulibus, communitati et inhabitatoribus eorumque uxoribus, prolibus [et] famulis (exceptis
personis superius particulariter nominatis solummodo) imputari poterint.   Et
supradictos ballivos, consules et communitatem, ac omnes inhabitatores, tam
burgenses quam alios, burgi nostri de Striviling antedicti, eorumque uxores,
proles, famulos et familias pro tempore (exceptis personis particulariter prenominatis) sub firma pace et protectione nostra juste suscipientes, firmiter
inhibemus ne quis eis aut eorum alicui, occasione predicte proditorie artis et
partis captionis, malum, molestiam, injuriam aut gravamen aliquod inferre,
presumat injuste, super nostram plenariam forisfacturam, aut mortem eis
aut eorum alicui inferat sub pena amissionis vite et membrorum.   In cuius
rei testimonium has literas nostras remissionis pro toto tempore vite prefa-

their colleagues and accomplices, in their treasonable taking and detention of our
castle and said burgh of Striviling, and for reception, support, intercommuning and
defence of the said persons and their associates in the said treasonable act committed
in the month of April last bypast; also for any foreknowledge or premeditation of the
premises, or in defence and withholding of the said castle and town against us, our
authority and obedience, and for all action and crime which may thence ensue or
be imputed to the said bailies, councillors, community and inhabitants, and their
wives, children, [and] servants (excepting only the persons particularly above named).
And justly taking the foresaid bailies, councillors, and community, and all the
inhabitants, as well burgesses as others, of our foresaid burgh of Striviling, and their
wives, children, servants and families for the time (except the persons particularly
before named) under our firm peace and protection, we strictly inhibit any one
wrongfully to take upon hand to inflict harm, molestation, wrong or any injury on
them or any of them because of the foresaid treasonable art and part taking, upon
our full forfeiture, or inflict death on them or any of them on pain of the loss of life
and members.   In witness whereof we have caused these our letters of remission to

tarum personarum (exceptis prius exceptis) duraturas sub nostro magno sigillo
eis fieri facimus patentes.   Apud Falkland, vicesimo sexto die mensis Junii
anno Domini millesimo quingentesimo octuagesimo quarto, et regni nostri
decimo septimo.

endure for the whole lifetime of the foresaid persons (except as before excepted) to
be made patent to them under our great seal.   At Falkland, the twenty-sixth day
of the month of June the year of our Lord one thousand five hundred and eighty-
four and of our reign the seventh year.

LII.

GRANT by Archibald Allan, burgess of Stirling, with consent of Sir John
Schaw of Arnecomrie, to the Provost, Bailies and Councillors of Stirling,
in name of the poor of the same, of the Almshouse or Hospital in Stirling
with the revenues within the Burgh belonging thereto.   Stirling and
London, 28th February and 1st May, 1610.

OMNIBUS hanc cartam visuris vel audituris: Archibaldus Allane, burgensis
burgi de Striuiling, capellanus seu prebendarius capellanie olim infra dictum
burgum situate, quo domus elimosinaria seu hospitale pro Christi pauperibus
et languentibus inibi, suscipiendis, hospitandis, et sustinendis, in dicto burgo,
nuncupatur, jacens in australi platea, ex parte orientali ecclesie perochialis
dicti burgi contigue cum cemiterio eiusdem ecclesie; cum expressis consensu et
assensu honorabilis viri, domini Joannis Schaw de Arnecomrie, militis, veri
et indubitati mei patroni dicte capellanie seu domus elimosinarie, pro ipsius

To ALL who shall see or hear this charter: Archibald Allane, burgess of the burgh of
Striuiling, chaplain or prebendary of the chaplainry sometime situated within the
said burgh, which is called the Almshouse or hospital for the admission, lodging,
and sustaining therein of Christ's poor and sick in the said burgh, lying in the
Southgait on the east side of the parish church of the said burgh, near to the
cemetery of the said church; with express consent and assent of an honorable man,
Sir John Schaw of Arnecomrie, knight, my true and undoubted patron of the said

interesse, eternam in Domino, salute m.   Quum, in laudem Dei et ad pios vsus, pro juuamine pauperum dicti burgi dicta capellania seu domus elimosinaria, cum omnibus annuis redditibus, emolumentis, et denoriis eidem spectantibus, primo constituta et dotata fuit, et nunc post abolitionem Romane seu papistice illius religionis, in quam successit hec vera ac clara lux Euangelij qua non tollitur, nequis capellanus dictum domum elimosinariam possideat prout institutio primo fundationis postulat; et quia strenuus et juuictus ille miles, quondam dominus Willelmus Edmound, preregimine Scotorum in partibus Flandrie colonellus, in laudem Dei pro multiplici erga se diuina preseruatione in quam plurimis suis periculis, apud se decreuit domum quandam elimosinariam seu hospitale infra dictum burgum propriis suis sumptibus erigere, vel magis antedictam domum elimosinariam nunc ruinosam et caducam reparare; et, pro sustentatione quorundam pauperum inibi suscipiendorum, annuos redditus seu elimosinas quasdam etiam ipsis dotare.   Igitur, cum expressis consensu et assensu predictis, dedisse, concessisse, et hac presenti carta mea confirmasse, proposito, baliuis et consulibus dicti burgi, nomine pauperum ciusdem, et eorum successoribus, hereditarie, totam et integram antedictam

chaplainry or almshouse, for his interest, greeting in the Lord everlasting.   Whereas the said chaplainry or almshouse with all annual rents, emoluments and duties belonging to the same, was first founded and endowed to the praise of God and for pious uses and for the assistance of the poor of the said burgh, and now after the abolition of that Rom sh or Popish religion, to which has succeeded this true and clear light of the Evangel which is not taken away, no chaplain can possess the said almshouse as the order of the first foundation requires; and whereas that valiant and invincible knight, the deceased Sir William Edmond, colonel of the regiment of Scots in the parts of Flanders, in praise of God for manifold divine preservation of himself in his very many perils, determined with himself to erect on his own proper charges a certain almshouse or hospital within the said burgh, or rather to repair the foresaid almshouse now ruinous and falling down; and, for the maintenance of certain poor to be admitted therein, also to bestow on them certain annual rents or alms.   Therefore, with express consent and assent foresaid, I have given, granted, and by this my present charter confirmed to the provost, bailies, and councillors of the said burgh, in name of the poor of the same, and of their successors, heritably all and whole the foresaid almshouse or hospital domum elimosinariam seu hospitale olim infra dictum burgum situatam jacentem in australi platea ex orientali parte dicte ecclesie perochialis eiusdem; cum omnibus annuis redditibus, emolumentis et deuoriis, infra dictum burgum solummodo eidem spectantibus seu iuste spectare valentibus. Quamquidem domum seu elimosinariam antedictam nos vnanimi consensu et assensu ad manum mortuum mortificamus et disponimus dictis preposito, baliuis et consulibus dicti burgi, nomine dictorum pauperum, imperpetuum. Tantum, inde faciendo, antedicti pauperes infra dictam domum elimosinariam hospitandi et sustinendi, pias ac puras preces pro libertate euangelij et amplificatione regni Dei, ac salute rei publice dicti burgi in futurum. Pauperes, autem, ita elegantur ex ciuitate Sterlinensi decrepiti viri qui aliquando ciues dicti burgi fuerant et vitam honestam duxerant, per prefatos prepositum, baliuos et consules dicti burgi, et corum successores, senatui ecclesiastico dicti burgi commendati, et per eundem senatum admissi. Et nos vero prefati capellanus ac patronus, antedicti heredes et successores nostri, totam et integram antedictam domum elimosinariam seu hospitale antedictum, cum omnibus annuis redditibus, emolumentis et deuoriis, infra dictum burgum solummodo, eidem spectantibus seu iuste spectare valentibus, prefatis preposito, baliuis et consuli-

sometime situated within the said burgh lying in the Southgait on the east side of the said parish church of the same; with all annual rents, emoluments, and duties within the said burgh only, belonging or that may justly belong to the same. Which house or alms foresaid we with unanimous consent and assent mortify and dispone in mortmain to the said provost, bailies, and councillors of the said burgh, in name of the said poor, for ever. Making therefor, only, the foresaid poor to be lodged and sustained within the said almshouse, pious and pure prayers for the liberty of the evangel and increase of the kingdom of God, and for the prosperity of the commonwealth of the said burgh in time coming. Moreover, the poor so elected from the city of Stirling shall be aged infirm men who sometime had been citizens of the said burgh and had led an honest life, recommended by the foresaid provost, bailies, and councillors of the said burgh, and their successors, to the kirk session of the said burgh and by the said session admitted. And farther, we the foresaid chaplain and patron, our foresaid heirs and successors, shall warrant, acquit, and for ever defend all and whole the foresaid alms house or hospital, with all the annual rents, emoluments, and duties within the said burgh only, belonging or that may

bus dicti burgi et eorum successoribus, a propriis nostris factis solummodo,
warrantizabimus, acquietabimus et imperpetuum defendemus. Insuper dilectis
nostris Christophero Alexander, mercatore, burgensi dicti burgi, . . . ac
vestrum cuilibet, coniunctum et diuisum, baliuis nostris in hac parte specialiter
constitutis, salutem : vobis precipimus et firmiter mandamus quatenus visis
presentibus, indilate, statum, sasinam hereditariam, pariter et possessionem
realem, actualem et corporalem, totius et integre antedicte domus elimosinarie
seu hospitalis vt supra iacentis, cum omnibus annuis redditibus, emolumentis
et denoriis, infra dictum burgum, eidem spectantibus seu iuste spectare valentibus, memoratis preposito, baliuis et consulibus dicti burgi, vel eorum certo
actornato, nomine dictorum pauperum eiusdem, per terre et lapidis fundi dicti
domus tradicionem et deliberacionem, vt moris est, tradatis et deliberetis seu
aliquis vestrum tradat et deliberet; et hoc nullo modo omittatis. In cuius
rei testimonium, presentibus manibus nostris subscriptis ac manu Alexandri
Barclay, notarij, scriptis, sigilla nostra propria sunt appensa. Apud Striuiling
et Londoun, vltimo et primo diebus respectiue mensibus Februarij et Maij
respectiue, anno Domini millesimo sexcentesimo decimo, coram his testibus:
Alexandro Auchmowtie seruitore Regis; Alexandro Drummound, eius seruitore;

justly belong to the same, to the foresaid provost, bailies and councillors of the said
burgh and their successors, from our own proper facts only. Moreover, to our well-
beloved Christopher Alexander, merchant, burgess of the said burgh, . . . and to
each of you, conjunctly and severally, our bailies in that part specially constituted,
greeting: we command and firmly charge you, or any of you, that these presents seen
yo immediately give and deliver state, heritable sasine, as well as real, actual and corporal possession, of all and whole the foresaid almshouse or hospital, lying as above,
with all annual rents, emoluments and duties belonging or that may rightly belong to
the same within the said burgh, to the foresaid provost, bailies, and councillors of
of the said burgh, or their certain attorney, in name of the said poor of the same, by
the giving and delivering of earth and stone of the ground of the said house as the
manner is ; and this in no way ye omit. In witness whereof to these presents, subscribed with our hands and written by the hand of Alexander Barclay, notary, our
proper seals are appended, at Striviling and Londoun, on the last and first days
respectively in the months of February and May respectively in the year of our Lord
one thousand six hundred and ten, before these witnesses, Alexander Auchmowtie,

magistro Joanne Archibald, scruitore Regis; Jacobo Archibald, cius scruitore; Duncane Patersone, Alexandro Patersone, mercatoribus, burgensibus dicti burgi; et dicto Alexandro Barclay. (Signed) Archibald Allane; Sir Jhone Schaw; Alexr. Auchtmoutie; Mr. Joⁿ Archebald, witnes; Alexr. Drummond, witnes; James Archibald, witnes; D. Patersone, witnes; to Archbald Allan subscription; Alexander Paterson, witnes to Archebald Alane; A. Barclay, witnes to the subscriptione of the said Archibald Allane.

servitor of the King; Alexander Drummound, his servitor; master John Archibald, servitor of the King; James Archibald, his servitor; Duncane Paterson, Alexander Patersone, merchants, burgesses of the said burgh, and the said Alexander Barclay. [Signed as above.]

LIII.

DECREE by the Lords of Council and Session annulling a pretended Gift to Robert Erskine, son of the earl of Mar, and finding that the only undoubted right of the office of Sheriffship within the Burgh of Stirling belongs to the Provost, Bailies, Council and Community thereof. Edinburgh, 29th March, 1633.

In the actioun and caus persewit at the instances of Thomas Bruce, provest, John Johnstoun, David Stevinsone, Johne Squyre and Williame Murcheid, baillies of the burgh of Striviling, for thame selffis and in name and behalff of the counsall and communitie thairof, haifing the gift of our soverane lord and his hienes most nobill progenitouris, of worthie memorie, to thame and thair successouris, provest, baillies, counsall and communitie of the said burgh, [of] all and haill the office of schereffschip of Striviling within the burgh thairof, territorie and libertie of the samin; with the lyk and the samyn priviledges, liberties, power, proffeittis and dewties, as the provest, baillies, counsall and communitie of the burgh of Edinburgh, or any vther burgh within this realm, hes [or] bruikis thair office of scherefschip within burgh; vpone the resignatioun of vmquhile Sir Alexander Cunynghame of Polmais, knight, than scheref of the scherefdome of Striviling, maid be him for himselff, his airis and successouris, of the samin in favouris of the saidis provest, baillies, counsall and communitie of the said burgh of Striviling, and thair successouris, as the chartour and infeftment maid, given and grantit, to thame and thair predicessouris thairvpone, be his hienes vmquhile darrest foirgrandschir King James the fourt, of happie memorie, vnder his hienes great seill, of the dait the tuelff day of October the yeir of God j^m v^c and ane yeiris, and of his hienes regnne the fourteine yeir, mair fullie contennes ; and thairby haifing guid and vndoubtit richt to the said office of scherefchip within the said burgh, territorie and libertie thairof, and to remove all impedimentis that may anywayes stop, hinder or prejudge, thame or thair successouris in the peaciabill possessioun, bruiking and joysing of the samin in tyme cuming, and sufficient entres to persew the actioun and caus of reductioun vnderwritten againes Jchn erle of Mar lord Erskine and Garioche, etc., Johne lord Erskine, his e'dest sone and appeirand air, pretendit heretabill schereffis of the scheref.Jome of Striviling, and to quhom and thair successouris the pretendit gift and infeftment of scherefschip thairof is alledgit maid, gevin and grantit in mauer vnderwritten, and all vtheris haifing or pretending to have entres in the mater eftermentionat, tuiching the exhibitioun and productioun with thame of the pretendit chartour and infeftment of the dait at Edinburgh the tuentie sext day of Februar the yeir of God j^m v^c and sex yeiris, alledgit maid and grantit be his hienes vmquhile darrest foirgrandschir King James the fourt, of happie memorie, to vmquhile Robert Erskine son to the said Johne er e of Mar, his airis maill and successouris, of all and haill the office of scherefschip of the said burgh of Striviling within the haill boundis thairof, quhilk pertenit of befoir to the said vmquhile Sir Alexander Cunynghame of Polmais, knight, and Robert Cunynghame, his sone and appeirand air, in lyfrent, and wer resignit be thame in favouris of the said vmquhile Robert Erskine and his foirsaidis; or of quhatsumever vther dait or daittis, tennour or contentis the samin be of, to haif beine seine and considderit be the saidis lordis and to haife hard and seine the samin reducit, retreittit, rescindit, cassit, annullit, decernit and declairit be decreit of the saidis lordis to haif beine fra the begining, to be now and in all tyme cuming, null and of nane availl, force, strenth nor effect, with all that hes followit or may follow thairvpon swa far as the samin concernes or may be extendit to the said office of scherefschip within the said burgh of Striviling, territorie and liberties thairof, or any part of the samin; and als to haif hard and seine

it fundin and declairit be decreit of the saidis lordis that the onlie vndoubtit
richt of the said office of the schirrefschip within the said burgh of Striviling,
haill boundis, territories and liberties of the samin, perteines and belongis to
the saidis provoist, baillies, counsall, communitie thairof, and thair successouris,
now and in all tyme cuming, conforme to the tennour of thair said chartour
and infeftmont, to be bruikit, joysit and exercit be thame, but any stop, troubill
or impediment, to be maid to thame thairintill be any persone or persones
quhatsumever; and the saidis Johne erle of Mar and Johne lord Erskene, thair
airis and successouris, to be perpetuallie secludit thairfra and fra all richt,
tytill and priviledges, liberties, power, proffeittis, and dewties of the samin
schirrefschip within the said burgh of Striviling, haill boundis, territories and
liberties thairof, in all tyme cuming, for the ressounes and caussis lybellit; as
at mair lenth is contenit in the said summondis, actis [and] lettres following
thairvpone: The saidis Thomas Bruce, Johne Johnstoun, David Stevinsone,
and remanent persewaris abonewrittin, compeirand be Adame Cunynghame,
thair procuratour, quha for instructing of their richt to the said office of
schirefschip of Striviling producit the foirsaid chartour maid and grantit to
the said toun of Striviling of the dait, tennour and contentis, respective
abonewrittin; and the saidis Johne erle of Mar, etc., and Johne lord Erskine,
defendaris, compeirand be maister David Primrois, thair procuratour; and all
vtheris haifand or pretendand to have entres in the said mater being
lauchfulie summond to this actioun, oftimes callit and not compeirand, the
foirsaidis parties compeirand as said is, richtis, ressounes, allegatiounes of the
saidis pairties compeirand as said is, togidder with the foirsaid chartour maid
and grantit in favouris of the said toun of Striviling of the dait and contentis
abonewrittin producit and repeittit for the pairtis of the saidis persewaris for
instructing of thair tytill and richt to the said office of scherefschip, hard,
seine, vnderstand, and the saidis lordis thairwith being ryplie advysit, the
lordis of counsall reduces, retreittis, rescindis, cassis, annullis, decernis
and declaires the foirsaid pretendit chartouris, infeftmentis, and vtheris writtis
and evidentis particularlie abonewritten, callit for to be producit to the effect
and in maner abonementionat, to have beine from the beginning, to be now
and in all tymecuming, null and of nane availl, force, strenth nor effect, with
all that hes followit or may follow thairvpone swa far as the samin concernes

or may be extendit to the said office of scherefschip within the said burgh of
Striviling, territorie and liberties thairof or any pairt of the samin; and als
findis and declaires that the onlie and vndoubtit richt of the said office of
scherefschip within the said burgh of Striviling, haill boundis, territories and
liberties of the samin, perteines and belongis to the saidis proveist, ballies,
counsall and communitie thairof, ard their successouris, now and in all tyme
cuming, conform to the tennour of the said chartour and infeftment, to be
bruikit, joysit and exercit be thame but ony stop, troubill or impediment, to
be maid to thame thairintill be any persone or persones quhatsumever. And
the saidis lordis secludis the saidis Johne erle of Mar and Johne lord Erskene,
his sone, thair airis and successouris, perpetuallie thairfra and all richt, tytill,
priviledge, liberties, power, proffeittis and dewties of the samin scherefschip
within the said burgh of Striviling, haill boundis, territories and liberties
thairof, in all tyme cuming; becaus the said Johne erle of Mar and Johne lord
Erskene, defenderis, and all vtheris haifand or pretendand to have entres in
the said mater wer divers tymes lauchfulie summond, and last be vertew of
our Soverane Lordis lettres proceiding vpone ane act of the saidis lordis to
have compeirit befoir thame, bringand and produceand with thame the
foresaidis pretendit chartouris, infeftmentis and vtheris writtis and evidentis
particularlie abonewritten, to have beine seine and considderit be the saidis
lordis to the effect abonementionat, with certificatioun to thame and thay
failyiet thairintill the saidis lordis wald reduce, find and declaire in maner
abonespecifeit; and the saidis Johne erle of Mar and Johne lord Erskene,
defenderis, thairefter compeirand be maister David Prymrois, thair procurator,
to quhom the saidis lordis haifing assignit divers termes of his awin consent
for produceing of the saidis pretendit chartouris and vtheris abonewrittin callit
for, with certificatioun to him and he failyiet thairintill the saidis lordis wald
reduce, find and declair in maner abonementionat; at the quhilkis termes the
said maister David Prymrois failyiet to produce the foirsaidis evidentis and
writtis or any of thame: In respect quhairof and of the productioun of the
saidis persewaris thair chartour and tytill producit in maner abonewrittin,
the saidis lordis reducit, fand and declairit in maner abonewrittin. And
ordaines lettres to be direct vpone the premissis gif neid beis in forme
as effeiris.

LIV.

EXCERPTS from Signature or Warrant for Charter of Confirmation of the Rights, Privileges, and Possessions of the Burgh of Stirling [No. LV.], 1641.

OURE SOUERANE LORD, calling to mynd that the burghe of Sterling, quhilk is ane of the [maist] ancient burghes of this his Hienes kingdome of Scotland, being erectet befoir the dayes of vmquhile King Alexander, of worthie memorie, wes doted with sindrie grite preveleges, liberteis and immunities, be his Hienes and his predicessouris, in respect of the commodious situatioun thairof, being placed and situate on the watter of Forthe, in that pairte of the said kingdome of Scotland to the quhilk the maist part of the hielandis of Menteythe and Ergyle resortes and repaires for making thair merchandice, be the quhilk repairing to the said burghe they ar and haif bene reducet to ane ciuile and politike forme of leving vnder his Maiestic and his predicessouris peace and obedience; and haifing alsua at the said pairte quhair the said burghe is situate ane brig on the said watter of Forthe quhilk is the commoun passage to the haill lieges cummand and gangand fra the northe and southe pairtes of his said Hienes realme, quhilk brig hes bene continuallie intertenyit vpoun the proper charges and expenssis of the prouest, baillies, counsell, communitie and inhabitantis of the said burghe; and his Hienes and his predicessouris hes euer had thair castell and palice of Sterling neir to the said burghe, within the quhilk nocht onlie had they thair residence for the maist pairte bot also the said castell and burghe adiacent thairto hes bene the place quhair his Maiestie and his Hienes predicessouris thair most sacred personeς hes bene educate and brocht vp, as being the maist fitt and proper place for that effect, baithe be ressoun of the naturall strenthe of the said castell and palace of Sterling, plesandness and amenitie of the feildes and healthsunnes of the air, and als in respect of the cairfulnes and faithfulnes of the burgessis and inhabitantes of the said burghe quha maist cairfullie and panefullie hes kepit thair dewtie and obedience to his Hienes and his predicessouris; lyke as, his Maiestie, considering that the said castell and palice of Sterling wes nocht onlie the place of his Hienes vmquhile derrest father, of maist happie memorie, his educatioun fra his infancie, bot

also the place of the birthe and educatioun of his vmquhile derrest brother
the Prince, of maist worthie memorie, quhair he remanit and wes educate fra
his infancie continuallie to his repairing to his Maiesteis kingdome of England; and his Hienes alsua considering the grite hurt, damnage, and skaithe
sustenit be the inhabitantes of the said burghe of Sterling be mony hairshipis,
burnyngis and vther depredationes vsit aganes thame in his Maiesteis predicessouris seruice, quhilk merites to be recompensit and rewairdit be his Hienes:
Thairfoir his Maiestie, being of mynd, gudewill, and affectioun toward the
inhabitantis of the said burghe, and nawyes willing that they be onywayes
preiugit of ony of thair formare liberties, preveleges, and immunities grantet
to thame, bot rather that the same be augmentit and they mentenit in thair
saidis richtis, preveleges, liberteis and immuniteis, gevin and grantet of ald
and ancient tyme to the said burghe of Sterling, burgessis and inhabitantis
thairof, his Hienes, of certane knawlege and proper motive, withe auyse and
consent of (*blank*), ordines ane charter of confirmatioun to be maid vnder his
Maiesteis grite scale in the mair forme, ratifeand, approvand, and for his Hienes
and his successouris perpetuallie confirmand the particulare infeftmentis,
charteris, preceptis, instrumentis of sesing, confirmationes, giftis, donationes,
liberteis, preveleges and immuniteis contenit thairin, maid, gevin, grantet or
confirmit be his Maiesteis maist noble progenitouris to the said burghe of
Sterling, burgessis and inhabitantis thairof, particularlie efterspecifeit, viz.,
the charter and gift maid, gevin and grantet be vmquhile Allexander King of
Scottis for the tyme, of worthie memorie, of the dait at Kincairdine the auchtene day of August and of his regnne the tuelf yeir, quhairby the said King
Allexander gave to the said burghe of Sterling and to the burgessis of the
same ane mercat day in the said burghe, to wit, Setterday oulklie, and thairwithe gave to thame his sure peace for all thame that cumes to the said
mercate, prohibiting straitlie that none commit onye wrang, truble or iniurie,
to ony that cumes to the said mercate ather in thair cuming or ganging,
vnder the pane of forfalture; and alsua straitlie prohibiting that na extraneare
merchand within the sherefdome of Sterling by or sell ony thing outwith the
said burghe vnder his defence, bot that the extraneare merchandis bring thair
merchandice to the said burghe of Sterling and thair sell the same, and gif
onye extraneare merchand be fund bying or selling onye thing within the said

sherefdome of Sterling vpoun the defence foirsaid, that the samyn be takin
and detenit quhill the Kingis will be declairit; prohibiting lykewyes that na
extraneare merchand cut his claythe to be sauld in the said burghe of Sterling
bot fra the day of the ascensioun of our Lord vnto the feist of Lambes, within
the quhilkis termes they sall cut thair claithe to be sald in the said mercat of
the burghe of Sterling, and that [thai] thair sall sell and by claithe and vther
merchandice commounlie with the burgesses; commanding also that all quha
abydes in the said burghe of Sterling and quha will communicate with the
burgessis thairof at the mercate that they communicate with thame to the
Kingis aid and help quhaes men socuer they be; gevand also to the saidis
burgessis of the burghe of Sterling libertie to haif ane merchand gildrie, except to the walkeris and wobsteris; and prohibiting that na taverne be had
in ony toun within the said sherefdome of Sterling bot quhair the lord or
maister of the toun is ane knycht and remanes thairintill, and that ane onlie
taverne salbe had thair; prohibiting alsua that nane remanyng outwithe the
said burghe of Sterling in the said sherefdome of Sterling mak or caus be
maid ony claithe cuttit or shorne within the said sherefdome of Sterling bot
onlie the burgessis of the said burghe of Sterling quha ar of the merchand
gildrie thairof and payes to the King ayde and supplie with the burgessis of
the said burghe; and sielike prohibiting straitlie that nane within the said
sherefdome of Sterling presume to mak claithe cuttit or shorne vnder the pane
of forfalture, and gif ony claithe cuttit or shorne be fund sua maid, commanding
the sheref of the said sherefdome incontinent to apprehend the same and do
thairwithe conforme to the consuetude of the tyme of King Dauid. Togidder
with the confirmatioun of King Dauid the Second of the foirsaid charter in his
parliament haldin at Scone the tuentie sext day of October and of his regnne
the threttie ane yeir, with all and sindrie consuetudes and liberteis abonwretin and vther immuniteis and previleges contenit in the said charter.
And sielyke, the charter grantet be the said vmquhile King Allexander, of
worthie memorie, to the saidis burgessis of the burghe of Sterling resident
within the same, proporting that they salbe quyte in all tyme cuming thairefter for euer of all toles and customes of thair gudes and cattell within all the
kingdome; prohibiting straitlie that nane presume to truble thame aganes the
said grant in exacting fra thame ony toles or customes of thair saidis gudes and

cattell within all the kingdome; prohibitiug straitlie that nane presume to truble thame aganes the said grant in exacting fra thame ony toles or customes of thair saidis gudes and cattell; as the said charter of the dait at Edinburghe the tuentie day of Julij and of his regnne the thrittene yeir beres. Togidder with the confirmatioun of the said charter grantet be the said vmquhile King Dauid, 2d. of that name, to the saidis burgessis of the burghe of Sterling and communitie thairof, vnder the said vmquhile King Dauidis grite scale, in his parliament haldin at Scone the tuentie sext[1] day of October and of his regnne the thretto ane yeir. And lykwyes the charter of fewferme grantet be vmquhile King Robert the secund to the burgessis of the said burghe of Sterling and communitie thairof and to thair successouris, vnder the said Kingis grite scale, off the foirsaid burghe of Sterling with the fischingis of the watter of Forthe pertenyng thairto; with the ferme of the said burghe, litle customes and pertinentis quhatsumeuer belangand thairto; as the samyn charter of the dait at Methven the threttene day of Julij and of his regnne the sextene yeir at mair lenthe proportes. [Here follow references to the charters by King James II., dated 25th October, 1447 (No. xx.), and 24th June, 1456 (No. xxiii.); the charters by King James IV., dated 12th October, 1501 (No. xxxiii.), and 7th March, 1501-2 (No. xxxiv.); and the charter by Queen Mary dated 15th April, 1567 (No. xlv.). The following also stood originally in the MS., but is deleted:—] "Item ane lettre of gift and presentatioun, maid, gevin and grantet, be vmquhile Sir Johnne Schaw of An ccomrye, knycht, vndoutet patrone of the chaplenrie vnderwretin, to vmquhi e Archibald Allane, younger, burges of the said burghe of Sterling, makand, constitutand, and ordinand him chaplene or prebendare of that chaplenrie semtyme situat within the said burghe of Sterling, quhilk being first foundin t to haif bene [ane] hospitell wes for lacke and want of mentenance thairto convertet in the ministeris manse of the said burghe, lyand on the eist pairt of the Hiegait that leadis to the kirk of the said burghe contigue to the kirk yuird thairof; quhilk lettre of gift and presentatioun is of the dait at London the first day of Januare the yeir of God j[m] vj[c] and ten yeiris; togider with the charter and fundatioun[2] maid and grantet be the said vmquhile Archibald Allane, chaplane and prebendare

foirsaid, with expres consent and assent of the said vmquhile Sir Johnne
Shaw, vndoutet patrone foirsaid of the said chaplenrie, to the saidis prouest,
baillies, and counsell of the said burghe of Sterling, and thair successouris, of
all and haill the foirsaid hospitell, now convertit for want of mentenance in
ane ministeris manse; togider with the precept of sesing contenit in the said
charter and instrument of sesing following thairvponn."] Togider with all and
quhatsumener vther charteris, infeftmentis, confirmationes, [etc., granted to
the burgh by the King's predecessors; "togidder with all mortificationes and
fundationes of hospitallis, speciallie the hospitellis callit Spittellis Hospitall
and Cowanes Hospitall, landis, tenementis, yairdis and rentis belangand
thairto."] Attoure our said Soucrane Lord, but hurt and preiudice of the foirsaidis charteris, infeftmentis, fundationes, donationes, mortificationes, giftis,
decreittis, richtis and previleges thairin contenit, and in corroboratioun of the
same, *accumulando iura iuribus*, of new, with anyse and consent foirsaid,
geves, grantis, dispones, erectis and perpetuallie confirmes to his Hienes weill-
belouit the saidis prouest, baillies, counsell, communitie and inhabitantes of
the said burghe of Sterling, present and to cum, and thair successouris, all
and haill the said Burghe of Sterling in ane frie burgh royall, with the haill
commoun faires, mercat dayes, commoun houssis, mercat places, haill territorie
of the same, landis, tenementis, aikeris, rudes, wallis, portis, calseyes, brigis,
gaittis, passages, fishingis, commoun mures, heavenes, portis, herberies, annual-
rentis, prebendareis, chaplenreis, hospitellis, patronages, and haill pertinentis
of the same; togidder with all and sindrie proffites, preveleges, toles, customes,
liberteis and immunities quhatsumener pertenyng to the said burghe and
quhairof the saidis prouest, baillies, counsell and communitie of the said burghe
and thair predicessouris hes bene in possessioun of befoir; withe speciall poware
and libertie to haif and cheis, yeirlie, prouest, baillies and counsell, for governing of the said burghe[1]; actis, statutes and ordinances to mak and caus be
published and obseruit within the said burghe, territorie and haill libertie of
the samyn, nocht repugnant alwyes to the lawes and constitutiones of this
realme; and with poware to the saidis prouest, baillies, counsell and fremen of
the said burghe, and thair successouris for euer, to haif, hant, vse and exerce,

[1] The following, originally inserted here, is tolbuithe, wallis, calseyes, and vther thair
deleted:—" and for vphald of thair kirk, brig, commoun warkis."

as they haue heirtofoir bein in vse and custome, the tred and traffik of
merchandice, blok, by, top, and sell all sorte of wares, baithe cuntrie wares
and forane wares, nocht onlie within the said burghe, territorie, and iurisdictioun thairof, bot also within all the boundis situat within the said sherefdome
of Sterling, alsueill regalitie as ryaltie, baithe breid and lenthe of the samyn
sherefdome; and with speciall prohibitioun to all persones vnfremen that nane
of thame presume or tak vpoun hand to vse and exerce the traffik of merchandice within ony pairte of the samyn sherefdome of Sterling except they
be burgessis of the said burghe of Sterling. And speciallie, but preiudice of
the generalitie foirsaid, his Maiestie with auyse and consent abonwretin, gevis,
grantis and dispones to the saidis prouest, baillies, counsell, burgessis and
communitie of the said burghe of Sterling, and thair successouris, all and
sindrie the particulare landis and vtheris aftermentionate quhilkis hes bene
bruikit and possest be thame and thair predecessouris as ane pairt of the
commoun gude [and] patrimony of the saide burghe, viz. [Here follows description of lands and possessions, and references to patronages of hospitals,
chaplainries, altars, &c., and property thereof, similar to what is contained in
Charter No. LV.][1] Attoure, his Maiestie, with auyse and consent foirsaid,
gevis, grantis and dispones to the saidis burghe of Sterling libertie to haif in
all tyme cuming ane merchand gildrie; with poware to vse and exerce all
liberteis, privileges, and immuniteis quhatsumeuer belangand to the said
merchand gildrie, sielike and in the samen maner in all respectis as they haue
heirtofoir exercit the same.[2] And sielike gevis, grantis and dispones to the

<hr>

[1] The following clause, originally inserted
here, is deleted:—" Withe poware also to the
saidis prouest, baillies and counsell of the said
burghe of Sterling and their successouris to
big and builde ather wynd or watter mylnes as
quhatsumeuer pairt or place maist commodious
within the libertie of the said burghe as they
sall think expedient."

[2] This clause originally read thus :—"Attoure
his Maiestie, with auyse and consent foirsaid,
gevis, grantis and dispones to the saidis prouest,
baillies and burgessis of the said burghe of Sterling and thair successouris libertie to haif ane
merchand gildrie, except to the wobsteris and

walkeris thairof, conforme to the charter and in
feftment abonspecifeit grantet to thame thairof
be the said vmquhile King Alexander, of worthie
memorie, and thaireftir confirmit be the said
vmquhile King Dauid in his parliament haldin
at Scone as is befoir expremit; with poware to
the saidis burgessis, except as said is, to vse
and exerce all liberteis, privileges and immuniteis quhatsumeuer, belangand to the said merchand gildrie, sielike and als frelie and amplie
in all respectis as the gildbrether of the burgh
of Edinburgh, Perthe, or ony vther burgh of this
realme, hes exercet and vsit or may exerce the
same at ony tyme bigane or to cum."

saidis prouest, baillies, counsell, communitie and burgessis of the said burghe
of Sterling and thair successouris the prevelege of tua mercat dayes oulklie
within the said burghe, the ane of thame on Wodinsday and the vther of
thame on Setterday; with foure frie faires yeirlie [each enduring for eight days.
The dates of the first two are left blank; the third, called the "Latter Ladye darn
hervist fair," to begin on 8th September; and the fourth, called the "Latter
Fair day," to begin on 22nd October.][1] With full prevelage and libertie to the
saidis prouest, baillies, counsell and communitie of the said burghe, and thair
successouris, to haif, bruke and posses, the office of shorefship within thame-
selfis in the said burgh and haill territorie thairof, for euer in all tyme
cuming. . . . And siclike his Maiestie gevis, grantis and dispones
to thame and their successouris the richt, previlage and libertie of all
[the ways and passages leading to and from the burgh; also petty
customs and dues conform to a table as in Charter No. LV.; ports,
havens and harbours, with dues thereof.][2] And siclike considering that the
brig of Sterling on the said water of Forthe and the lang calsey leading to
and fra the said brig requyres grite charges and expenssis to vphald the same,
and that the saidis prouest, baillies, counsell and communitie of the said
burghe are also burdinit with the vphald of thair walles, portes and calseyes
thairfore his Maiestie with consent foirsaid hes gevin, grantit and disponit to

the saidis prouest, baillies and counsell of the said burgh, and thair successouris, the customes of the said brig following, viz. :—[Here follows table similar to that in Charter No. LV. Also clauses of union and incorporation and holding of the burgh, lands and others, as in the charter.] Gevand thairfoir, yeirlie, the saidis prouest, baillies, counsell and commountie of the said burghe of Sterling, and their successouris, to our said Soucrane Lord and his successouris and vtheris haifand richt fra his Maiestie, as follows, viz., for the said burghe of Sterling, landis, mylnes, tenamentis, aikeris, rudes, walles, portes, herberies, lauding places, briggis, gaittis, passages, fishingis, commoun mwres, faires, oulklie mercattis and customes, proffeittis, previleges of the same and vtheris particularlie abonementiounate, the dewties and utheris contenit in the auld infeftmentis grauted to the said burgh;[1] and for the said office of sherefschip and iurisdictioun thairof abonespecifeit, dew and lauchfull administratioun of iustice in the said office and iurisdictioun; and for all and sindrie the saidis patronages, almoushoussis, hospitellis, chapleureis, kirkes, beneficcs, annuellis, and utheris abonwrittin belonging thairto, the saidis provest, baillies, counsell and communitie of the said burghe, and ministeris at the saidis kirkis and pure of the saidis hospitallis and thair successouris, makand devoite, humble and daylie prayer, to the almichtie of God for his Maiestie and his successouris, and performing all uthir dewties and burdeins if any be contenit in the auld infeftmentis thairof, alancrlie ; tegidder with service of burgh vsed and wont for all and sundrie the premissis. And that the said charter be extendit in the best forme, with extensioun of all claussis [neidfull, and] that preceptis be direct heirupounne in forme as effeires. Gevin at . . the . . day of .˙. the yeir of God j^m vj^c fourty and . yeires.

[1] The words "the dewties and wther s contenenit in the auld infeftmentis granted to the said burgh" are substituted for the following, which originally stood in the MS. :—"the soume of ten merkis money of this realme and tuentie thrie merkis to Johne erle of Mar, his aires and successouris, lordis of Cambuskeunethe, as succeeding in place of the abote and convent of Cambuskennethe to quhome the saidis tuentie thrie merkis of ald wes disponit .be his Hienes predicessouris."

LV.

CHARTER by King Charles the First, confirming previous Charters and of
new granting to the Burgh of Stirling, their several possessions, rights,
and privileges. Holyrood House, 17 November, 1641.[1]

CAROLUS, Dei gratia, Magne Britannie, Francie et Hibernie, Rex, fideique
defensor : Omnibus probis hominibus totius terre sue, clericis et laicis,
salutem. Sciatis nos, considerantes antiquum burgum nostrum de Stirling
olim erectum fuisse in liberum burgum regalem, et de tempore in tempus per
preclarissimos nostros progenitores multifariis privilegiis imbutum,[2] respectu
habito commode et opportune situationi dicti burgi et castri nostre de
Stirling eidem adjacentis, vbi multi predecessorum nostrorum nati et educati
fuerunt; necnon consideratione habita bonorum et gratuitorum servitiorum

CHARLES, by the grace of God, King of Great Britain, France, and Ireland, and
defender of the faith: To all good men of his whole land, clerics and laics, greeting.
Know ye that we, considering that our ancient Burgh of Stirling had formerly
been erected into a free Royal Burgh, and had from time to time been endowed
by our most illustrious progenitors with many various privileges, respect being
had to the commodious and accessible situation of the said burgh and of our
castle of Stirling adjacent thereto, where many of our predecessors were
born and educated ; and also consideration being had to the good and

<hr/>

[1] The original of this charter not having been
found, it has been printed from an official extract from the register of the Great Seal certified
by the late Mr. William Robertson, keeper of the
records, and the print has been collated with
the register itself.   For filling in blanks in
parts of the charter where the writing in the
register is obliterated or illegible, recourse has
been had to a precept of sasine following on
the charter, of the same date with it, and
indorsed by Lord Scotstarvet, director of
chancery, on 3rd October, 1648. The precept,
with the instrument of sasine thereon (expede
13th, and recorded in the general register of

sasines at Edinburgh 17th October, 1648), are
still preserved.
  The print has also been collated with a copy
of the charter made, in 1714, apparently from
the original. Where the variations in the
register and copy are not merely verbal, such
as the substitution of "prefatis" for "prenominatis," "vel" for "seu," "dictis" for
"predictis," &c., or arise from the transposi-
tion of words without alteration of the meaning,
the different readings are given in foot notes,
the letter "C" in these denoting "copy charter
made in 1714."

[2] "multis et variis privilegiis ornatum."—C.

nobis dictisque nostris preclarissimis progenitoribus per burgenses et incolas dicti burgi nostri assidue prestitorum et impensorum; et maxime[1] volentes affectionem nostram et gratiam dicto burgo nostro illustrare, ipsosque ad omnem debitam obedientiam et bona officia erga nos nostrosque successores imposterum animare. Idcirco nos, cum avisamento et consensu predilectorum nostrorum consanguineorum et consiliariorum Joannis comitis de Loudoun domini Terrinzeane et Mauchlin, magni nostri cancellarii huius regni nostri Scotie; Archibaldi marchionis de Ergyll comitis de Kintyre domini Campbell et Lorne; Willielmi comitis de Glencairne domini Kilmawiris; Joannis comitis de Lindsay domini Parbroith; necnen cum avisamento et consensu fidelis et predilecti nostri consiliarii, domini Jacobi Carmichaell de eodem, militis baronetti, nostri thesaurarij deputati,—nostrorum commissionariorum pro thesaurario nostro; ac etiam cum avisamento et consensu reliquorum dominorum nostri scaccarij dicti regni nostri nominatorum et appunctuatorum ad recipiendum resignationes nostro nomine et nova infeofamenta desuper concedendum, ratificasse, approbasse, et hac presenti carta nostra confirmasse, tenoreque ejusdem, ratificare, approbare, proque nobis et successoribus nostris pro

gratuitous services assiduously performed and rendered to us and our said most illustrious progenitors by the burgesses and inhabitants of our said burgh; and we specially wishing to show our affection and favour for our said burgh, and to encourage them to all due obedience and good offices towards us and our successors in time coming. Therefore we, with the advice and consent of our well-beloved cousins and counsellors, John earl of Loudoun lord Terrinyeane and Mauchlin, our great chancellor of this our kingdom of Scotland; Archibald marquis of Argyll earl of Kintyre lord Campbell and Lorne; William earl of Glencairne lord Kilmawiris; John earl of Lindsay lord Parbroith; and also with advice and consent of our trusty and well-beloved counsellor, Sir James Carmichaell of that ilk, knight baronet, our treasurer depute,—our commissioners for our treasury; and also with advice and consent of the remanent lords of our exchequer of our said kingdom named and appointed for receiving resignations in our name and for granting new infeftments thereupon, have ratified, approved, and by this our present charter confirmed, and by the tenor of the same, ratify, approve, and for us and our successors for ever confirm

---

[1] " et nos maxime "—C.

perpetuo confirmare particularia infeofamenta, cartas, precepta et instrumenta
sasinarum, confirmationes, concessiones, donationes, libertates, privilegia et
immunitates, in eisdem contentas, factas, datas et concessas seu confirmatas
per serenissimos nostros progenitores dicto burgo nostro de Stirling, burgensibus et incolis ejusdem, particulariter postea specificata, videlicet, cartam et
concessionem factam, datam et concessam, per quondam Alexandrum, Regem
Scotorum pro tempore, dignissime memorie, de data apud Kincairden
decimo octavo die mensis Augusti et anno regni sui duodecimo, virtute
cujusquidem predictus Rex Alexander dedit burgo nostro de Stirling et burgensibus ejusmodi unum foralem diem in dicto burgo, diem, scilicet, Saturni
hepdomadatim et eo cum firmam dedit suam pacem omnibus ad dictum forum
advenientibus, stricte prohibendo omnes ne injûriam, maleficium sive molestiam,
aliquam comittent quibusvis ad dictum forum advenientibus, nec in accedendo
neque in discendendo, sub pena forisfacture ; stricteque etiam prohibendo
omnes extraneos mercatores infra vicecomitatum nostrum de Stirling ne ulli
eorum vendent neque ement qnodvis extra dictum burgum sub munitione et
defensione ejusdem, sed quod dicti extranei illi mercatores mercimonia sua
adferent dicto burgo nostro de Stirling et eadem ibidem vendent; et si

the particular infeftments, charters, precepts and instruments of sasine, confirmations,
grants, gifts, liberties, privileges and immunities, contained therein, made, given, and
granted or confirmed by our most serene progenitors to our said burgh of Stirling,
the burgesses and inhabitants thereof, particularly after specified, that is to say :
a charter and gift made, given and granted, by the deceased Alexander, King of
Scots for the time, of most worthy memory, of date at Kincairden the eighteenth
day of the month of August and the twelfth year of his reign, in virtue whereof the
said King Alexander gave to our burgh of Stirling and to the burgesses of the same
a market day in the said burgh, that is to say on Saturday, weekly, and therewith
gave to them his sure peace to all coming to the said market, strictly prohibiting
all from committing any wrong, trouble or injury, to any persons coming to the said
market, either in coming thereto or going therefrom, under pain of forfeiture; also
strictly prohibiting all stranger merchants within our sheriffdom of Stirling that
none of them buy or sell anything outwith the said burgh under the protection and
defence of the same, but that the said stranger merchants shall bring their
merchandice to our said burgh of Stirling and there shall sell the same ; and if

quivis extraneus mercator vendens seu emens quidvis invenietur infra dictum
vicecomitatum nostrum de Stirling sub defensione predicta, idem apprehen-
sum et detentum erit donec regia voluntas eatenus declaretur; prohibendo
prorsus quod nulli extranei mercatores pannum suum scindent neque vendent
in dicto burgo nostro de Stirling preterquam a die ascentionis Domini nostri
usque ad festum Petri ad vincula, *lie Lambas*, inter quosquidem terminos
solummodo pannum suum vendibilem in dicto foro burgi nostri de Stirling
scindent, et ibidem pannum et alia mercimonia cum burgensibus ejusmodi
vendent et ement; mandando etiam omnibus in dicto burgo nostro de Stirling commorantibus et apud dictum forum cum burgensibus communicantibus
quod cum iis communicent ad subsidium et auxilium nostrum (qualescunque
sint); dando et concedendo etiam dictis burgensibus dicti burgi nostri
de Stirling libertatem mercatorialem gildriam, *lie merchand gildrie*, habendi
(exceptis fulonibus et textoribus); et prohibendo quod nulla taberna tenta sit
in aliqua villa infra dictum vicecomitatum nostrum de Stirling ubi dominus
et pretor dicte ville eques auratus non existit et ibidem remanet, et quod
unica solum taberna ibidem tenta sit; proviso etiam quod nulli remanentes
extra dictum burgum nostrum de Stirling infra vicecomitatum ejusdem con-

any stranger merchant shall be found buying or selling anything within our said
sheriffdom of Stirling under the defence foresaid, the same shall be seized and
detained until the royal pleasure is declared thereanent; prohibiting further that
no stranger merchants shall cut their cloth to be sold in our said burgh of Stirling
except from the day of the ascension of our Lord until the feast of Peter
ad vincula, that is of Lammas, between which terms only they shall cut their
cloth to be sold in the said market of our burgh of Stirling, and there shall buy and
sell their cloth and other merchandice with the burgesses of the same; commanding
also all abiding in our said burgh of Stirling and taking part with the burgesses at
the said market that they contribute with them towards our aid and help (whoso-
ever they may be); giving and granting also to the said burgesses of our said burgh
of Stirling the liberty of having a Merchant Guildry (excepting the walkers and
weavers): and prohibiting that no tavern be kept in any town within our said
sheriffdom of Stirling where the lord and ruler of the said town is not a knight and
remains there, and that only a single tavern be kept therein; providing also that no
persons dwelling outwith our said burgh of Stirling within the sheriffdom of the

ficient neque conficere causabunt quemvis pannum scissum et rasum, *lie cuttit et schorne*, infra dictum vicecomitatum nostrum de Stirling preter burgenses solummodo dicti burgi nostri de Stirling qui sunt ex mercatoriali gildria ejusdem et ad auxilium et subsidium nostrum cum burgensibus dicti burgi nostri solvent; stricteque similiter prohibendo quod nulli infra dictum vicecomitatum de Stirling pannum conficere audeant sive presumant scissum vel rescissum, *lie cuttit et schorne*, sub pena forisfacture; et si hujusmodi pannus scissus et rescissus ita confectus invenietur, mandando vicecomiti dicti vicecomitatus quatenus deinde eundem apprehendat et cum eo agat secundum consuetudinem tempore Regis Davidis. Vnacum confirmatione Regis Davidis ejus nominis secundi predicte carte, in parliamento suo tento apud Sconam vigesimo sexto die mensis Octobris et anno regni sui trigesimo primo; cum omnibus et singulis consuetudinibus et libertatibus suprascriptis aliisque immunitatibus et privilegiis in dicta carta contentis. Et similiter cartam concessam per dictum quondam nostrum serenissimum progenitorem Alexandrum Regem, dignissime memorie, concessam predictis burgensibus burgi nostri de Stirling ibidem residentibus, proportantem quod ipsi de omnibus tolloniis et custumis bonorum suorum et cattellorum in omnibus partibus dicti regni nostri pro perpetuo liberi et immunes

same shall make or cause to be made any cloth cut and shorn within our said sheriffdom of Stirling excepting only the burgesses of our said burgh of Stirling who are of the merchant guildry thereof and pay to our aid and supply with the burgesses of our said burgh; and likewise strictly prohibiting that no persons within the said sheriffdom of Stirling shall dare or presume to make cloth cut or shorn under the pain of forfeiture; and if cloth of this sort cut and shorn shall be found so made, commanding the sheriff of the said sheriffdom that he forthwith apprehend the same and deal therewith according to the custom in the time of King David. Together with a confirmation of King David the second of that name of the foresaid charter, in his parliament held at Scone the twenty sixth day of the month of October and in the year of his reign the thirty first; with all and sundry customs and liberties above written and other immunities and privileges contained in the said charter. And likewise a charter granted by our said late most serene progenitor King Alexander, of most worthy memory, granted to the foresaid burgesses of our burgh of Stirling residing there, proporting that they shall be free and exempt in time coming for ever of all tolls and customs of their goods and cattle within all parts of

erunt in futurum; stricte etiam prohibendo quod nulli audeant sive presumant
molestare sive inquietare eos contra dictam concessionem in exigendo ab illis
aliquas tholonias sive custumas predictorum bonorum et cattellorum; prout in
dicta carta, de data apud Edinburgum vigesimo die mensis Julij et anno regni
sui decimo tertio latius continetur. Vuacum confirmatione dicte carte concessa
per dictum quondam Davidem Regem, ejus nomine secundum, sub suo magno
sigillo, predictis burgensibus burgi nostri de Stirling et communitati ejusdem, in
parliamento suo tento apud Sconam vigesimo sexto die mensis Octobris et anno
regni ejus [trigesimo] primo. Ac etiam cartam feudifirme concessam per alium
progenitorum nostrorum, quondam Regem Robertum ejus nominis secundum,
burgensibus dicti burgi nostri de Stirling et communitati ejusdem eorumque
successoribus, sub magno suo sigillo, de predicto burgo nostro de Stirling, cum
piscationibus super aqua de Forth ad eundem pertinentibus, cum firma dicti
burgi, custumis minutis et pertinent.is quibuscunque ad eandem spectantibus;
prout eadem carta, de data apud Methven decimo tertio die mensis Julij et
anno regni sui decimo sexto, latius proportat. Item, cartam et infeofamentum
concessam per alium serenissimorum progenitorum nostrorum, Jacobum Regem

our said kingdom ; also strictly prohibiting that no persons shall dare or presume
to molest or trouble them contrary to the said grant in exacting from them any
tolls or customs of their foresaid goods and cattle ; as is more fully contained in the
said charter, of the date at Edinburgh the twentieth day of the month of July and
in the year of his reign the thirteenth. Together with a confirmation of the said
charter granted by the said deceased King David, the second of that name, under
his great seal, to the foresaid burgesses of our burgh of Stirling and to the
community of the same, in his parliament held at Scone the twenty sixth day of
the month of October and in the first year of his reign [thirty]. And also a charter
of feu-farm granted by another of our predecessors, the deceased King Robert the
second of that name, to the burgesses of our said burgh of Stirling and to the
community of the same and to their successors, under his great seal, of our foresaid
burgh of Stirling, with the fishings upon the water of Forth pertaining to the same,
with the forme of the said burgh, small customs and pertinents whatsoever belonging
thereto ; as the said charter, of the date at Methven the thirteenth day of the month
of July and of his reign the sixteenth year, more fully bears. Also, a charter
and infeftment granted by another of our most serene predecessors, King James

R

eo nomine[1] secundum, sub ejus magno sigillo, pro perpetuo, concessam in favorem prepositi, ballivorum, consulium [et] communitatis dicti burgi de Stirling, omni tempore affuturo, novarum nundinarum tenendarum in dicto burgo et territorio ejusdem annuatim ad festum ascensionis Domini nostri, videlicet, inchoandarum ad medium diem dicti festi ac deinde duraturam per spatium octo dierum immediate sequentium, inclusive; cum privilegiis, prerogativis, libertatibus et consuetudinibus, modo in dicta carta contentis, ut in eadem, sub dicto magno sigillo, de data vigesimo quinto die mensis Octobris anno Domini millesimo quadringentesimo quadragesimo septimo, latius continetur. Item, cartam per dictum Jacobum Regem[2] secundum concessam preposito, burgensibus et communitati dicti burgi nostri de Stirling, eorumque successoribus, burgensibus ejusmodi pro tempore, de jure patronatus, ordinatione et donatione, zenodochij et hospitalis Sancti Jacobi prope pontem de Stirling; unacum terris, obventionibus, redditibus, possessionibus et proficuis quibuscunque ad dictum hospitale pertinentibus; que carta est de data vigesimo quarto die mensis Junij anno Domini millesimo quadringentesimo quinquagesimo sexto. Item, cartam per alium preclarissimorum nostrorum progenitorum, Jacobum Regem the second of that name, under his great seal, in favour of the provost, bailies, councillors and community of the said burgh of Stirling, in all time coming for ever, of a new fair to be held in the said burgh and territory of the same yearly at the feast of the ascension of our Lord, that is to say, to be begun at mid day of the said feast and thereafter to continue for the period of eight days immediately following, inclusive; with the privileges, prerogatives, liberties and customs, in the manner contained in the said charter; as in the same, under the said great seal, of date the twenty-fifth day of the month of October in the year of our Lord one thousand four hundred and forty-seven, is more fully contained. Also, a charter granted by the said King James the second to the provost, burgesses and community of our said burgh of Stirling, and to their successors, burgesses of the same for the time, of the right of patronage, ordination and gift of the inn and hospital of St. James near the bridge of Stirling; together with the lands, obventions, rents, possessions and profits whatsoever pertaining to the said hospital; which charter is of date the twenty-fourth day of the month of June in the year of our Lord one thousand four hundred and fifty-six. Also, a charter granted by another of our most illustrious predecessors, King James the fourth of that name, under his

---

[1] "ejus nominis"—C.   [2] "ejus nominis"—C.

ejus nominis quartum, sub suo magno sigillo, concessam preposito, ballivis, consulibus et communitati dicti burgi nostri de Stirling, de officio vicecomitatus de Stirling infra dictum burgum et territorium ejusdem et libertatem ejusmodi; cum omnibus et singulis libertatibus, privilegiis, proficuis et divoriis dicti officij; hec vero carta est de data apud Stirling duodecimo die mensis Octobris anno Domini millesimo quingentesimo primo.   Item, aliam cartam concessam per dictum quondam Jacobum Regem ejus nominis quartum predictis preposito, ballivis, consulibus et communitati dicti burgi nostri de Stirling, corumque successoribus, sub suo magno sigillo, de patronatu, advocatione et donatione, capellanie altaris Sancti Laurentij, martyris, fundati infra ecclesiam parochialem de Stirling; quequidem carta est de data septimo die mensis Martij anno Domini millesimo quingentesimo primo.   Item, aliam cartam factam et concessam per dictum quondam Jacobum Regem quartum preposito, ballivis, consulibus et communitati dicti burgi nostri, corumque successoribus, sub magno suo sigillo, de data duodecimo die mensis Junij anno Domini millesimo quingentesimo quinquagesimo primo,[1] de tota et integra custuma salis

great seal, to the provost, bailies, councillors and community of our said burgh of Stirling of the office of sheriff of Stirling within the said burgh and territory of the same and liberty thereof; with all and sundry liberties, privileges, profits and duties of the said office; which charter is of date at Stirling the twelfth day of the month of October in the year of our Lord one thousand five hundred and one.   Also, another charter granted by the said late King James the fourth of that name, under his great seal, to the foresaid provost, bailies, councillors and community of our said burgh of Stirling, and to their successors, of the patronage, advocation and donation, of the chaplainry of the altar of St. Laurence, the martyr, founded within the parish church of Stirling; which charter is of date the seventh day of the month of March in the year of our Lord one thousand five hundred and one.   Also, another charter made and granted by the said late King James the fourth to the provost, bailies, councillors and community of our said burgh, and their successors, under his great seal, of date the twelfth day of the month of June in the year of our Lord one thousand five hundred and fifty one, of all and whole the customs of salt and

---

[1] The description of this charter is printed as in the register of the great seal and in the copy charter, but there is obviously a mistake. Probably reference was intended to be made to the charter by James II., dated 12th January, 1451-2, whereby the burgesses and community of Stirling were freed from the payment of custom on salt and skins. [Stirling Charters, No. xxi., antea, p. 32].

et corriorum infra boudas in prodicta carta mentionata et expressa. Item, aliam cartam, sub magno sigillo, de data vigesimo octavo die mensis Januarij, in favorem prodictorum burgensium et communitatis dicti burgi nostri, de totis et integris acris terrarum que olim [fuerunt de *le Ald Park* prope Striveling] jacentibus olim inter murum lapideum viridarij *lie Park de Stirling* ex occidentali, terras nuncupatas *Bennetis Croft* [ac Croftam Leprosorum ex parte australi, et] aliter boudatas modo in dicta carta specificatas; unacum jure patronatus capellanie et altaris Sancti Michaelis infra ecclesiam parochialem de Stirling per quondam magistrum Thomam Carmichaell, vicarium, fundati. Item, aliam cartam factam et concessam per charissimam nostram aviam, dignissime memorie, sub magno sigillo suc, preposito, ballivis, consulibus et communitati dicti burgi nostri de Stirling, eorumque successoribus, de omnibus et singulis terris, tenementis, domibus, edificiis, ecclesiis, capellis, hortis, pomariis, croftis, annuis redditibus, fructibus, divoriis, emolumentis, feudifirmis, elimosinis et monetis nuncupatis *lie daill silver et obite silver*, et aliis quibuscunque que ad quascunque capellanias, altaragia, prebendarios, seu ad quamcunque ecclesiam, capellam, sive collegium, pertinuerunt aut pertinere dignoscuntur, fundatas per quoscunque patronos infra libertatem dicti burgi

hides within the boundaries mentioned and expressed in the foresaid charter. Also, another charter, under the great seal, of date the twenty-eighth day of the month of January, in favor of the foresaid burgesses and community of our said burgh, of all and whole the acres of land which formerly belonged to the Ald Park near Stirling, lying between the stone wall of the Park of Stirling on the west, the lands called Bennet's Croft and the Lepers' Croft on the north, and otherwise bounded in the manner described in said charter; together with the right of patronage of the chaplainry and altar of St. Michael within the parish church of Stirling founded by the late Mr. Thomas Carmichael, vicar. Also, another charter made and granted by our dearest grandmother, of most worthy memory, under her great seal, to the provost, bailies, councillors and community of our said burgh of Stirling and their successors, of all and sundry the lands, tenements, houses, buildings, churches, chapels, gardens, orchards, crofts, annual rents, fruits, duties, emoluments, feu-farms, alms and monies called daill silver and obite silver, and others whatsoever which pertained or are known to pertain to whatsoever chaplainries, altarages, prebendaries, or to whatsoever church, chapel or college, founded

nostri de Stirling, et de quibus capellani et prebende perprius in usu et
possessione fuerunt, ubicunque hujusmodi domus, edificia, tenementa, horti,
pomaria, annui reditus, fructus, proventus et emolumenta respective jacent aut
perprius levata fuerunt; cum manerierum locis, pomariis, terris, annuis redditibus,
emolumentis et divoriis quibuscunque, que olim ad Fratres Dominicanos [sive]
Predicatores [et] Minores sive Franciscanos dicti burgi nostri de Stirling pertinuerunt; vnacum omnibus et singulis terris, domibus et tenementis, jacentibus
infra dictum burgum nostrum de Stirling et libertatem ejusdem, cum omnibus
annuis redditibus levandis de quibuscunque terris, domibus et tenementis, infra
dictum burgum nostrum de Stirling datis, dotatis et fundatis, quibuscunque
capellaniis, alteragiis, ecclesiis, funeritus, lie funerallis, et anniversariis quibuscunque, existentibus infra hoc regnum nostrum; et similiter de omnibus et
singulis annuis redditibus alijsque divorijs per quascunque ecclesias extra
dictum burgum nostrum de Stirling preposito et ballivis huiusmodi, de communi redditu dicti burgi, cum pertinentiis earundem levari usitatis et
consuetis; quequidem carta est de data decimo quinto die mensis Aprilis
anno Domini millesimo quingentesimo sexagesimo septimo,—in omnibus capitibus, articulis, clausulis, conditionibus et provisionibus earundem.   Unacum

by whatsoever patrons within the liberty of our said burgh of Stirling, and of which the
chaplains and prebendaries formerly were in use and possession, wherever such houses,
buildings, tenements, gardens, orchards, annual rents, fruits, produce, and emoluments respectively lie or formerly were levied; with manor-places, orchards, lands,
annual rents, emoluments and duties whatsoever which formerly belonged to the
Dominican or Preaching friars and to the Minorites or Franciscans of our said burgh
of Stirling; together with all and sundry the lands, houses and tenements, lying
within our said burgh of Stirling and liberty of same, with all annual rents leviable
from whatever lands, houses and tenements, within our said burgh of Stirling, given,
granted, and founded to whatsoever chaplainries, altarages, churches, funerals and
anniversaries whatsoever, existing within this our kingdom; and likewise of all and
sundry the annual rents and other duties used and accustomed to be levied by whatsoever churches outwith our said burgh of Stirling from the provost and baillies of
the same, out of the common rent of the said burgh, with their pertinents; which
charter is of date the fifteenth day of the month of April in the year of our Lord
one thousand five hundred and sixty-seven,—in the whole heads, articles, clauses,

omnibus et singulis alijs cartis, infeofamentis, confirmationibus, preceptis et
instrumentis sasinarum, concessionibus, donationibus, privilegijs, libertatibus et
immunitatibus in eisdem contentis, factis, datis et concessis et confirmatis, per
predictos nostros nobilissimos progenitores burgo nostro de Stirling, burgensibus et incolis hujusmodi, de quocunque tenore seu quibuscunque tenoribus,
contento sive contentis, data seu datis, eedem sint; unacum omnibus
zenodochiorum mortificationibus et fundationibus, presertim zenodochiorum
nuncupatis lie *Spittellis Hospitall* et *Cowanes Hospitall*, terris, tenementis et
redditibus eisdem spectantibus, cum omni jure patronatus dictorum zenodochiorum et membrorum ejusmodi, predictis preposito, ballivis, consulibus et communitati dicti burgi nostri, concessis; et presertim, absque prejudicio generalitatis
supraspecificate, unam literam mortificationis factam et concessam per quondam
Adamum, commendatarium pro tempore Abbacie de Cambuskenneth, in favorem
zenotrophitarum pro tempore zenodochii burgi nostri de Stirling nuncupati
Spittellis Hospitell eorumque successorum, pro meliori auxilio et sustentatione
decrepitorum pauperum dicti zenodochij, virtute cujusquidem dictus com-
mendatarius summam viginti trium mercarum monete iis mortificavit;
quequidem mortificatio est de data vigesimo tertio die mensis Novembris

conditions and provisions of the same. Together with all and sundry other charters,
infeftments, confirmations, precepts and instruments of sasine, gifts, donations,
privileges, liberties and immunities therein contained, made, given and granted and
confirmed by our foresaid most noble progenitors to our burgh of Stirling, burgesses
and inhabitants thereof, of whatever tenor or tenors, content or contents, date or
dates, the same may be; together with all mortifications and foundations of hospitals,
especially of the hospitals called Spittell's Hospital and Cowane's Hospital, lands,
tenements and rents belonging thereto, with all right of patronage of the said
hospitals and members of the same, granted to the foresaid provost, bailies, councillors and community of our said burgh; and especially, without prejudice to the
above specified generality, a letter of mortification made and granted by the late
Adam, commendator for the time of the Abbey of Cambuskenneth, in favor of the
hospitallers for the time of the hospital of our burgh of Stirling called Spittell's
Hospital and their successors, for the better help and support of the decrepit poor of
the said hospital, by virtue of which the said commendator mortified to them the
sum of twenty three merks of money; which mortification is of date the twenty

millesimo sexcentesimo secundo; unacum ratificatione dicte mortificationis per quondam Joannem comitem de Mar concessa, de data decimo tertio die mensis Augusti millesimo sexcentesimo quarto.   Et similiter contractum de data decimo tertio die mensis Februarij anno Domini millesimo sexcentesimo trigesimoseptimo,initum et confectum inter prepositum, ballivos et consules dicti burgi nostri pro tempore, et quondam Alexandrum Cowane de Wester Polmais, heredem et executorem quondam Joannis Cowane, mercatoris, burgensis dicti burgi nostri, ejus fratris, penes dispositionem, mortificationem, resignationem et assignationem, terrarum, tenementorum, annuorum reddituum, summarum moncte aliorumque,inibi contentorum,factum in favorem prepositi, ballivorum et consulum, in usum dicti zenodochii nuncupati lie Cowanes Hospitell, et penes jus patronatus hujusmodi, modo in dicto contractu latius specificato; unacum cartis et sasinis desuper sequentibus per dictum quondam Alexandrum Cowane in eorum favorem concessis, cum carta alienationis et mortificationis per prepositum, ballivos et consules dicti burgi nostri, zenotrophite, preceptori et pauperibus dicti zenodochij nuncupati lie Cowanes Hospitell super dicto contractu procedenti inter ipsos et dictum Alexandrum facta et concessa,

third day of the month of November one thousand six hundred and two ; together with a ratification of the said mortification granted by the late John earl of Mar, of date the thirteenth day of the month of August one thousand six hundred and four. And likewise a contract of date the thirteenth day of the month of February in the year of our Lord one thousand six hundred and thirty-seven, entered into and made between the provost, bailies and councillors of our said burgh for the time, and the late Alexander Cowane of Wester Polmaise, as heir and executor of the late John Cowane, merchant, burgess of our said burgh, his brother, regarding a disposition, mortification, resignation and assignation, of the lands, tenements, annual rents, sums of money and others therein contained, made in favour of the provost, baillies, and councillors, for the use of the said hospital called Cowane's Hospital, and regarding the right of patronage of the same, in the manner more fully set forth in the said contract ; together with the charters and sasines following thereon granted by the said late Alexander Cowane in their favour, with a charter of alienation and mortification made and granted by the provost, bailies, and councillors of our said burgh, to the master, preceptor, and poor of the said hospital called Cowane's Hospital proceeding upon the said contract between them and the said Alexander,

per quas vero mortificaverunt et disposuerunt preceptori et pauperibus dicti
zenodochii terras aliaque inibi contenta, tenendas de nobis, prout cedem de
data vigesimo secundo die mensis Februarij anno Domini millesimo sexcentesimo trigesimo septimo, cum instrumento sasine desuper sequenti, latius
proportant; vnacum omnibus et singulis aliis juribus et securitatibus quibuscunque dictum zenodochium concernentibus generaliter et particulariter supra
specificatis. Unacum omnibus actis parliamentorum et generalium consiliorum
aliisque actis, sententiis et decretis, dictum burgum nostrum, libertates hujusmodi aliaque supramentionata concernentibus. Ac volumus et concedimus, et
pro nobis et successoribus nostris decernimus et ordinamus quod generalis hec
presens carta nostra confirmationis predicte nullatenus prejudicabit specialitati
suprascripte, neque specialitas generalitati prejudicio fuerit, ita quod presens
hec nostra confirmatio et premissorum approbatio est et omni tempore afuturo
erit tanti valoris, roboris, officacie et effectus, in omnibus respectibus, prefatis
preposito, ballivis, consulibus et communitati dicti burgi nostri, burgensibus
et incolis hujusmodi corumque successoribus, ac si omnia et singula predicta
infeofamenta, carte, donationes, concessiones, mortificationes, jura, tituli et

by which they mortified and disponed to the preceptor and poor of the said
hospital the lands and others therein contained, to be holden of us, as the same
of date the twenty-second day of the month of February in the year of
our Lord one thousand six hundred and thirty-seven, with the instrument of
sasine following thereon, more fully bears; together with all and sundry other
rights and securities whatsoever that concern the said hospital generally and particularly above specified. Together with all acts of parliament and general councils,
and other acts, sentences and decrees, that concern our said burgh, liberties of the
same and others before mentioned. And we will and grant, and for us and our successors we decern and ordain that this our present general charter of confirmation
foresaid shall noways prejudice the specialty above written, nor shall the specialty be
a prejudice to the generality, so that this our present confirmation and approbation
of the premises is and in all time coming shall be of as much strength, force, efficacy
and effect, in all respects, to the foresaid provost, bailies, councillors and community
of our said burgh, burgesses and inhabitants of the same and their successors, as if
all and sundry the foresaid infeftments, charters, donations, grants, mortifications,
rights, titles and securities, and every one of them, were inserted and expressed word

securitates, et unaqueque earundum, de verbo in verbum in hac presenti carta
nostra insererentur et exprimerentur; quocirca, ac cum omnibus defectibus,
impedimentis, objectionibus et questionibus quibuscunque, que contra validita-
tem earundem aut hujus nostre presentis confirmationis ejusmodi proponi
seu allegari poterint, nos pro nobis et successoribus nostris, cum avisamento et
consensu predictis, dispensavimus, tenoreque presentis carte nostre dispen-
samus imperpetuum.   Preterea, nos, cum consensu predicto, absque damno aut
prejudicio predictarum cartarum, infeofamentorum, fundationum, donationum,
mortificationum, concessionum, jurium, scriptorum et privilegiorum in eisdem
contentorum, ac in ulteriorem corroborationem eorundem, [et] accumulando
jura juribus, cum avisamento et consensu predictis, de novo dedimus, concessimus, disposuimus, creximus, et hac presenti carta nostra confirmavimus,
tenoreque ejusdem de novo damus, concedimus, disponimus, erigimus, ac pro
nobis et successoribus nostris pro perpetuo confirmamus, prefatis preposito,
ballivis, consulibus et communitati dicti burgi nostri de Stirling, eorumque
successoribus, totum et integrum dictum burgum nostrum de Stirling in unum
liberum Burgum Regalem, cum integris communibus nundinis, diebus foralibus,
communibus domibus, locis foralibus, et toto territorio eiusdem, terris, tenementis, acris, rudis, meniis, portis, plateis et calcepediis, *lie calsayes*, pontibus, viis,

by word in this our present charter; whereanent, and with all defects, impediments,
objections and questions whatsoever, which against the validity of the same or of
this our present confirmation of the same can be proponed or alleged, we for us and
our successors, with advice and consent foresaid, have dispensed and by the tenor of
our present charter do dispense for ever.   Further, we, with consent foresaid, without hurt or prejudice of the foresaid charters, infeftments, foundations, donations,
mortifications, grants, rights, writings and privileges contained in the same, and in
further corroboration of the same, and heaping rights upon rights, with advice and
consent foresaid, of new have given, granted, disponed, erected, and by this our present charter confirmed, and by the tenor hereof of new give, grant, dispone, erect, and
for us and our successors for ever confirm to the foresaid provost, bailies, councillors
and community of our said burgh of Stirling, and their successors, all and whole
our said burgh of Stirling, in a free Royal Burgh, with the whole common fairs,
market days, common houses, market places, and the whole territory of the same, lands,
tenements, acres, roods, walls, streets, gates and causeways, bridges, ways, passages,

s

passagiis, piscationibus, communibus moris, portubus, naviumque receptaculis, *lie harbories*, annuis redditibus, prebendarijs, capellanijs, zenodochijs, patronatibus, integrisque pertinentiis earundem; unacum omnibus et singulis proficuis, privilegijs, tholonijs, custumis, libertatibus et immunitatibus quibuscunque ad dictum burgum pertinentibus, et de quibus predicti prepositus, ballivi, consules et communitas dicti burgi nostri, suique predecessores, perprius in usu et possessione fuerunt. Cum plena et speciali potestate et libertate ipsis habendi et eligendi, annuatim, prepositum, ballivos et consules, pro meliori gubernatione dicti burgi nostri; acta, statuta et ordinationes, faciendi et publicari et observari causandi infra dictum burgum nostrum, territorium et integram libertatem eiusdem, legibus et consuetudinibus dicti regni nostri minime repugnantes. Ac cum potestate dictis preposito, ballivis, consulibus et municipibus dicti burgi nostri, eorumque successoribus imperpetuum, habendi, vtendi et exercendi (prout huc vsque in vsu fuerunt) artem, *lie trad et traffik*, mercandi et emendi [et] vendendi, *lie blok et cop*,[1] omnia genera mercimoniorum, tam bonorum huius regni nostri quam alieno[2] allatorum, non solum infra dictum burgum nostrum, territorium et iurisdictionem eiusdem

fishings, common muirs, ports, harbours, annual rents, prebendaries, chaplainries, hospitals, patronages and whole pertinents of the same; together with all and sundry the profits, privileges, tolls, customs, liberties and immunities whatsoever belonging to the said burgh, and whereof the foresaid provost, bailies, councillors and community of our said burgh, and their predecessors, have been previously in use and possession. With full and special power and liberty to them of having and electing, yearly, a provost, bailies and councillors, for the better government of our said burgh; of making acts, statutes and ordinances, and causing them to be published and observed within our said burgh, territory and whole liberty of the same, not repugnant to the laws and customs of our said kingdom. And with power to the said provost, bailies, councillors and burgesses of our said burgh, and their successors for ever, of having, using and exercising (as hitherto they have been in use) the trade and traffic of merchandising and buying and selling (blok and cop) all sorts of merchandise, as well the goods of this our kingdom as those brought from abroad, not only within our said burgh, territory and jurisdiction of the same, but also within all other

<hr />

1 " mercandi et emendi et vendendi lie blok et top"—*C.*   2 "Aliunde"—*C.*

verum etiam infra omnes alias boudas situatas infra dictum vicecomitatum
nostrum de Stirling, tam regalitatis quam regalis, *lie regalitie et royalitie*, in
longitudine et latitudine ejusdem; ac eam speciali inhibitione omnibus personis
minime liberis quod nulli eorum audeant sive presumant vti et exercere dictam
artem mercandi infra aliquam partem ejusdem vicecomitatus de Stirling
(exceptis burgensibus dicti burgi nostri de Stirling).　Et presertim, absque
preiudicio generalitatis predicte, nos cum avisamento et consensu predictis,
damus, concedimus et disponimus, prefatis proposito, ballivis, consulibus et
communitati dicti burgi nostri de Stirling, eorumque successoribus, omnes et
singulas particulares terras aliaque subtusmentionatas que per ipsos eorumque
predecessores tanquam partes communis boni et patrimonii dicti burgi nostri
gavisi et possessi fuerunt, viz., terras nuncupatas *Eister Craiges*, cum *outsetts*
earundem et pertinentiis ad easdem spectantibus, jacentes inter murum
dicti burgi nostri et terrentem nuncupatum *lie Eister Burne, lie South
Braes* sub muro dicti burgi nostri et omnibus terris ex boreali latere
ciusmodi nuncupatis *lie Quhinnes et Gowanehillis*, terras nuncupatas
Parkfield, Gallowfield, Gallowfald, Justingflatis, Brighauche, et integras
moras nuncupatas novas et pristinas Moras Burgales dicti burgi nostri, terras

bounds situated within our said sheriffdom of Stirling, as well regality as royalty, in
the length and breadth of the same; and with special prohibition to all persons
not freemen that none of them dare or presume to use and exercise the said
trade of merchandising within any part of the said sheriffdom of Stirling (except
burgesses of our said burgh of Stirling).　And especially, without prejudice to the
generality foresaid, we, with advice and consent foresaid, give, grant, and dispone
to the foresaid provost, bailies, councillors and community of our said burgh of
Stirling, and their successors, all and sundry the particular lands and others under
mentioned which have been enjoyed and possessed by them and their predecessors as parts of the common good and patrimony of our said burgh, that
is to say, the lands called Easter Craigs, with the outsets of the same and
pertinents belonging to the same, lying between the wall of our said burgh
and the burn called the Easter Burn, the Southbraes under the wall of the said
burgh and all the lands on the north side of the same called the Whins and Gowane
hills, the lands called Parkfield, Gallowfield, Gallowfald, Justingflats, Brighaugh,
and the whole muirs called the new and old Burgh Muirs of our said burgh, the

nuncupatas Pratum Burgale, *lie Burrowmedow*, jacentem ex australi latere dicte aque de Forth iuxta Abbatiam de Cambuskenneth, croftas terrarum vocatas *Myretounis Croft, Lawsones Croft* et *Brownes Croft*; vnacum piscationibus tam salmonum quam aliorum piscium super dicta aqua de Forth ad dictum burgum nostrum pertinentibus; necnon, omnes et singulas terras nuncupatas *Spittelltoun, Spitelllandis, Spittellkerse*, et prata earundem, Spittellmyre cum omnibus huiusmodi pertinentiis tam ex australi quam boreali partibus dicte aque de Forth; cum omnibus et singulis domibus, edificiis, toftis, croftis, partibus, pendiculis et pertinentiis earundem quibuscunque; et cum crofta nuncupata crofta Sancti Laurentij, *lie St. Laurance Croft* jacente apud finem pontis de Stirling et *lie Lady Croft* et *Lady Rig* jacentibus ex boreali latere dicti burgi nostri cum croftis nuncupatis *Ruid Croft, Seiknainis Croft et Seikmanis hous* et horto eiusdem, jacentibus ex australi latere dicti burgi nostri inter eundem burgum et viridarium *lie Park de Stirling;* et similiter illam petiam fundi nuncupatam Vallem, *lie Valley*, prope cemiterium dicti burgi nostri; vnacum integris [domibus, terris, hortis et rupibus, in quorum possessione nunc existunt, jacentibus subtus castrum nostrum extra][1] precinctum et bondas castri et pallatij nostri de Stirling;

lands called the Burgh Meadow lying on the south side of the said water of Forth near to the abbey of Cambuskenneth, the crofts of land called Myretoune's Croft, Lawson's Croft and Brown's Croft; together with the fishings as well of salmon as of other fishes upon the said water of Forth belonging to our said burgh; likewise, all and sundry the lands called Spitteltown, Spittellands, Spittelkerse and meadows of the same, Spittelmyre and all the pertinents of the same as well on the south as on the north side of the said water of Forth; with all and sundry houses, buildings, tofts, crofts, parts, pendicles and pertinents of the same whatsoever; and with the croft called Saint Lawrence Croft, lying at the end of the Bridge of Stirling, and the Lady Croft and Lady Rig lying on the north side of our said burgh; with the crofts called Roodcroft, Seikman's Croft and Seikman's house and the yard of the same, lying on the south side of our said burgh between the said burgh and the Park of Stirling; and also that piece of ground called the Valley lying near the churchyard

---

[1] The words within brackets appear in the precept of sasine and in the copy charter made in 1714, but are omitted in the Great Seal register.

cum omnibus et singulis partibus, pendiculis, toftis, croftis, outsettis, domibus,
edificiis, integrisque pertinentiis quibuscunque omnium et singularum predictarum terrarum particulariter suprascriptarum. Prout etiam, cum
avisamento et consensu predictis, dedimus, concessimus et disposuimus et hac
presenti carta nostra confirmauimus tenoreque ejusdem damus, concedimus,
disponimus, ac pro nobis et successoribus nostris pro perpetuo confirmamus
predictis proposito, ballivis, consulibus et communitati dicti burgi nostri de
Stirling, eorumque successoribus quibuscunque, omnes et singulas terras,
tenementa, domos, edificia, ecclesias, capellas, hortos, pomaria, croftas, annuos
redditus, fructus, devorias, proficua, emolumenta, firmas, monetas, obitales, *lie
daill silver et obite silver*, quascunque, que ad aliquas capellanias, altaragia,
prebendarios, seu ad quamcunque ecclesiam, capellam vel collegium, infra
libertatem dicti burgi nostri de Stirling, per quemvis patronum fundatas
quomodocunque pertinuerunt aut pertinere dignoscuntur, et de quibus
prebende et capellani in possessione fuerunt, vbicunque huiusmodi domus,
edificia, tenementa, horti et pomaria iacent, seu dicti annui redditus, fructus,
proventus et emolumenta, perprius levata fuerunt ; cum maneriorum locis,

of our said burgh; together with all houses, lands, yards and crags, in the possession
of which they now are, lying under our castle beyond the precinct and bounds of our
castle and palace of Stirling; with all and sundry parts, pendicles, tofts, crofts, outsets, houses, buildings, and whole pertinents whatsoever of all and whole the foresaid
lands particularly before written. As also, with advice and consent foresaid, we
have given, granted, disponed, and by this our present charter confirmed, and by
the tenor of the same we give, grant, dispone, and for us and our successors
for ever confirm to the foresaid provost, bailies, councillors and community of
our said burgh of Stirling and their successors whatsoever, all and sundry the
lands, tenements, houses, buildings, churches, chapels, gardens, orchards, crofts,
annual rents, fruits, duties, profits, emoluments, fermes, daill silver and obit
silver, whatsoever, which have in any manner of way belonged or are known to
belong to any chaplainries, altarages, prebendaries, or to whatsoever church, chapel
or college, within the liberty of our said burgh of Stirling, by whatsoever patron
founded, and of which the prebendaries and chaplains have been in possession,
wheresoever such houses, buildings, tenements, gardens and orchards lie, or the said
annual rents, fruits, profits and emoluments have been previously levied ; with the

pomariis, terris, annuis redditibus, emolumentis et divoriis quibuscunque, que
perprius ad Fratres Dominicanos [sive] Predicatores [et] Minores sive
Franciscanos dicti burgi nostri de Stirling pertinuerunt; vnacum omnibus et
singulis terris, domibus et tenementis, jacentibus infra dictum burgum nostrum
de Stirling et libertatem eiusdem; cum omnibus annuis redditibus levandis de
quibuscunque terris, domibus et tenementis, jacentibus infra predictum burgum
nostrum de Stirling, datis, dotatis et fundatis quibuscunque capellaniis,
alteragiis, ecclesiis, funeralibus et aniversariis, vbicunque jacent infra hoc regnum
nostrum; ac etiam omnes et singulos annuos redditus aliasque devorias levari
vsitatas per quamcunque ecclesiam aut beneficium extra dictum burgum nostrum de Stirling, cum pertinentiis, a proposito, ballivis et consulibus eiusdem,
de communi redditu dicti burgi cum pertinentiis; vnacum iure patronatus,
advocatione et donatione, zenodochij Sancti Jacobi prope dictum burgum
nostrum de Stirling, cum integris terris, prediis, redditibns et possessionibus,
eidem spectantibus; cum advocatione, donatione et iure patronatus capellanie
altaris Sancti Laurentij fundate infra ecclesiam de Stirling, cum omnibus terris,
redditibus et privilegiis, ad eandem spectantibus; ac cum advocatione,
donatione et jure patronatus dictorum zenodochiorum nuncupatorum *lie
Spittellis Hospitell et Cowanes Hospitell;* omnibusque et singulis aliis terris

manor places, orchards, lands, annual rents, emoluments and duties whatsoever
which formerly belonged to the Dominican or Preaching friars and Minorites
or Franciscans of our said burgh of Stirling; together with all and sundry lands,
houses and tenements, lying within our said burgh of Stirling and liberty of the
same; with all annual rents leviable from whatsoever lands, houses and tenements,
lying within our foresaid burgh of Stirling, given, granted and founded to whatsoever chaplainries, altarages, churches, funerals and anniversaries, wheresoever they
lie within this our kingdom; and also all and sundry annual rents and other duties
accustomed to be levied by whatsoever church or benefice outwith our said burgh of
Stirling, with the pertinents, from the provost, bailies and councillors of the same
out of the common rent of the said burgh with the pertinents; together with the
right of patronage, advocation and donation, of the Hospital of Saint James beside
our said burgh of Stirling, with the whole lands, estates, rents and possessions
belonging thereto; with the advocation, donation and right of patronage of the
chaplainry of the altar of Saint Lawrence founded within the church of Stirling,

redditibus, tenementis et possessionibus quibuscunque eisdem spectantibus seu ad dictum burgum nostrum de Stirling quomodocunque spectare seu pertinere valentibus et de quibus prepositus, ballivi, consules et communitas dicti burgi nostri de Stirling, eorumque predecessores, in possessione nunc sunt aut temporibus retroactis fuerunt diem date presentis carte nostre precedentibus. Insuper nos, cum avisamento et consensu predictis[1] damus, concedimus et disponimus, predicto burgo nostro de Stirling libertatem habendi vnam mer-catorialem gildriam, *lie merchand gildrie*, in futurum, cum potestate vtendi et exercendi omnes libertates, privilega et immunitates quascunque, ad dictam mercatorialem gildriam spectantes simili modo et adeo libere in omnibus respectibus prout huevsque eandem exercuerunt. Prout etiam, damus, con-cedimus et disponimus, predictis preposito, ballivis et consulibus, communi-tati et burgensibus dicti burgi nostri de Stirling, eorumque successoribus, privilegium duorum dierum fordium, hepdomadatim, vnam earundem die Mercurij alteram vero die Saturni; cum quatuor liberis nundinis annuatim,

with all lands, rents and privileges belonging to the same ; and with the advocation, donation and right of patronage of the said hospitals called Spittellis Hospital and Cowanes Hospital ; and with all and sundry other lands, rents, tenements and possessions whatsoever belonging to the same or that may belong or pertain to our said burgh of Stirling in whatsoever way, and of which the provost, bailies, councillors and community of our said burgh of Stirling and their predecessors are now or have been in possession in times past preceding the date of our present charter. Moreover, we, with advice and consent foresaid, give, grant and dispone, to our foresaid burgh of Stirling, the liberty of having a merchant guildry in future, with power of using and exercising all liberties, privileges and immunities whatsoever belonging to the said merchant guildry in like manner and as freely in all respects as they have hitherto exercised the same. As also, we give, grant and dispone, to the foresaid provost, bailies and councillors and community of our said burgh of Stirling, and their suc-cessors, the privilege of two market days, weekly, one of them on Wednesday and the other on Saturday ; with four free fairs yearly, that is to say, the first

---

[1] In the copy the following words inserted here:—"dedimus, concessimus, et disposuimus, et hac presenti carta nostra confirmauimus, tenoreque eiusdem damus concedimus, disponi-mus proque nobis et nostris successoribus pro perpetuo confirmamus predicto burgo," etc.

prima scilicet earundem tenendi, inchoandi et existendi, super *lie Hallow Thursday* decem diebus precedentibus festum Pentecostes, annuatim, et deinde per spatium octo dierum duratura omni tempore affuturo primus nundinalis dies de Stirling nuncupanda; secunda vero predictarum liberarum nundinarum tenendi, existendi et incipiendi, vigesimo die mensis Julij annuatim et postea per spatium octo dierum duratura nuncupauda secundas dies nundinalis de Stirling in futurum; tertia vero dictarum nundinarum existendi et incipendi octavo die mensis Septembris annuatim et postea per spatium octo dierum duratura nuncupata *lie Latter Ladyes day* in autumno; quarta vero dictarum nundinarum tenendi vigesimo secundo die mensis Octobris annuatim et deinde [per] spatium octo dierum continuandi postremus dies nundinalis *lie Latter Fair day* de Stirling in futurum nuncupanda; cum potestate predictis preposito, ballivis, consulibus et communitati dicti burgi nostri de Stirling, corumque successoribus, factoribus, telonibus et servis suis, eorum nominibus, levandi omnes tollonias, custumas, feoda, impositiones et exactiones, omnesque alias libertates et divorias usitatas et consuetas, de et ab omnibus personis ad dictas nundinas reparantibus et frequentantibus durante predicto spatio; cum omnibus aliis libertatibus, privilegiis et immunitatibus ad predictas liberas nun-

of them to be held, begun and continued upon the Hallow Thursday ten days before the feast of Pentecost, yearly, and thereafter continuing for the space of eight days to be called in all time to come the First Fair day of Stirling; the second of the foresaid free fairs to be held, begun and continued, on the twentieth day of the month of July, yearly, and thereafter continuing for the space of eight days, to be called the second fair day of Stirling in future; the third of the said fairs to be held and begun on the eighth day of the month of September yearly and thereafter to continue for the space of eight days, to be called the Latter Lady's day in autumn; and the fourth of the said fairs to be held on the twenty-second day of the month of October yearly and thereafter to be continued for the space of eight days, to be called in future the Latter Fair day of Stirling; with power to the forsaid provost, bailies, councillors and community of our said burgh of Stirling and their successors, their factors, customers and servants, of levying in their names all tolls, customs, fees, impositions and exactions, and all other liberties and duties used and wont of and from all persons repairing to and frequenting the said fairs during the foresaid space; with all other liberties, privileges and immunities, belonging or that can justly belong to the

dinas spectantibus seu juste spectare valentibus, simili modo et adeo libere in
omnibus respectibus sicuti burgenses Edinburgi, Perthe, aut cujusvis alterius
burgi infra hoc regnum nostrum eorum foralibus diebus et nundinis utuntur et
fruuntur vel prout ipsi eorumve predecessores temporibus retroactis usi et
gavisi sunt.   Cum pleno etiam privilegio et libertate dictis preposito, ballivis,
consulibus et communitati dicti burgi nostri, et suis successoribus, habendi,
gaudendi et possidendi, officium vicecomitatus intra semetipsos in predicto
burgo et territoriis ejusmodi pro nunc et omni tempore futuro, et tenendi
vicecomitatus curias infra dictum burgum nostrum et territorium ejusdem
inter vicinos et incolas dicti burgi nostri et alios quoscunque que attachiari
contigerint et culpaverint infra eundem pro quacunque causa seu offensione,
super quibus predictus vicecomes judicare poterit toties quoties visum fuerit;
et utendi dicto officio vicecomitatus pro causa vel crimine quibuscunque que
pro tempore occurrere contigerint, et super omnibus personis que intra dictum
burgum et territorium ejusdem pro predictis culpis et transgressionibus [ita[1]]
committendis apprehense fuerunt; sectas vocandi, absentes amerchiandi, dictos
transgressores et delinquentes eorumque comburgenses transgredientes ut
dictum est accusandi, puniendi et vsque ad mortem iustificandi, secundum eorum

foresaid free fairs, in like manner and as freely in all respects as the burgesses of Edinburgh, Perth, or any other burgh within this our kingdom, use and enjoy their market
days and fairs, or as they themselves or their predecessors have in times past used
and enjoyed them.   With full privilege also and liberty to the said provost, councillors and community of our said burgh, and their successors, of holding, enjoying and
possessing, the office of sheriff within themselves in our foresaid burgh and territories
of the same for now and in all time to come, and of holding sheriff courts within our
said burgh and territory thereof betwixt the neighbours and inhabitants of our said
burgh and others whomsoever who shall happen to be attached and indicted within
the same for any cause or offence, on which the foresaid sheriff shall have power to
judge as often as seems expedient; and of using the said office of sheriffship for
whatsoever cause or crime which shall happen to occur for the time, and upon all
persons who have been apprehended within the said burgh and territory of the
same for committing the foresaid faults and transgressions; suits to call, absents to
amerciate, the said transgressors and delinquents and their co-burgesses transgressing

[1] C.

T

culpas legibus dicti regni nostri concordantibus; clericos, seriandos, officiarios, adiudicatores aliaque membra dictarum curiarum necessaria constituendi; ac omnia et singula alia quecunque agendi, exercendi et vtendi, intra semetipsos infra dictum burgum nostrum et territorium eiusdem, que ad officium vicecomitatus de iure et consuetudine huius regni nostri pertinere dignoscuntur, adeo libere ac cum tam amplis privilegiis prout dictus burgus noster de Edinburgh aut quivis alius burgus regalis [infra hoc regnum nostrum dictum officium vicecomitatus gaudet et possidet; ac etiam nos pro nobis et nostris successoribus dedi]mus[1] et concessimus, tenoreque presentis carte nostre damus et concedimus prenominatis preposito, ballivis, consulibus et communitati dicti burgi nostri, eorumque successoribus, ad eorum proprium vsum imperpetuum, omnes et singulas eschaetas, commoditates, amerciamenta et proficua, dicti officii vicecomitatus intra seipsos et infra dictum burgum et territorium eiusmodi, et que in quoscunque malefactores aliasque personas transgressores devenire seu contingere possint, et super huiusmodi escaetis et commoditatibus in com

as said is to accuse, punish and justify even unto death, according to their faults agreeable to the laws of our said kingdom; to appoint clerks, sergeants, officers, dempsters and other necessary members of the said courts; and of doing, exercising and using all and sundry other things whatsoever among themselves within our said burgh and territory of the same which to the office of sheriffship of law and custom of this our kingdom are known to belong, as freely and with as ample privileges as our said burgh of Edinburgh or any other royal burgh within this our said kingdom, possesses and enjoys the office of sheriff; and also we for us and our successors have given and granted and by the tenor of our present charter give and grant to the before-named provost, bailies, councillors and community of our said burgh and their successors, for their proper use for ever, all and sundry escheats, commodities, amerciaments and profits of the said office of sheriffship within themselves and within the said burgh and territory of the same, and which may happen or fall upon whatsoever malefactors and other persons transgressing, and upon such escheats and commodities to dispone at pleasure for the

[1] In the copy the following words inserted here:—" concessimus et disposnimus, et hac presenti carta nostra confirmauimus, tenoreque ejusdem damus, concedimus, disponimus, proque nobis et nostris successoribus pro perpetuo con- firmamus prenominatis preposito," etc. The register at this part is somewhat illegible, and there is a blank in the extract between the words " regalis" and " dedimus."

munem vsum dicti burgi nostri ad libitum disponendi. Insuper, nos¹ damus, concedimus et disponimus, ipsis eorumque successoribus, jus privilegium et libertatem omnium viarum, platearum, *lie lonyngis*, et passagiorum ducentum ab et ad dictum burgum [nostrum] terras, moras, piscationes, portus et navium receptacula, *lie harberies*, eiusdem; et observandi et defendendi easdem vias et passagia ne quovismodo per ipsos infringentur [aut] violentur seu minuantur, observata ommimodo in omnibus partibus dictorum passagiorun latitudine sex vluarum, vt subditi nostri facilius ad predictum burgum nostrum accedant et ab eodem discedant; et si huiusmodi passagia et pristina *lie loaningis* maiora et latiora fuerunt vllo tempore preterito, cum potestate iis tuendi ciusmodi passagia in pristinam eorum latitudinem et integritatem sicuti temporibus retronetis gavisi et possessi fuerunt. Et similiter, nos pro nobis et successoribus nostris, cum avisamento et consensu predictis, dedimus, concessimus et disposuimus,² tenoreque presentis carte nostre damus, concedimus et disponimus, preposito, ballivis, consulibus et communitati antedictis dicti

common use of our said burgh. Moreover, we give, grant and dispone, to them and their successors, the right, privilege and liberty of all ways, places, loanings and passages leading from and to the said burgh, lands, muirs, fishings, ports and harbours of the same; and of keeping and defending the said ways and passages lest in any way they should be infringed upon or broken up or lessened by them, there being always kept in all parts of the foresaid passages the breadth of six ells, that our subjects may the more easily come and depart to and from our said burgh; and if such passages and old loanings have been greater and broader at any former time, with power to them of maintaining such passages to their original breadth and entirety as in times past they have been enjoyed and possessed. And in like manner we for us and our successors, with advice and consent foresaid, have given, granted and disponed, and by the tenor of our present charter give, grant and dispone to the provost, bailies, councillors and community aforesaid of our said

¹ "dedimus, concessimus et disposuimus, et hac presenti carta nostra confirmauimus, tenorque ejusdem damus, concedimus et disponimus, proque nobis et nostris successoribus pro perpetuo confirmamus ipsis eorumque successoribus," etc.—*C*.

² "et hac presenti carta confirmauimus, tenorque ejusdem damus, concedimus et disponimus, proque nobis et nostris successoribus pro perpetuo confirmamus prenominatis preposito," etc.—*C*.

burgi nostri, eorumque successoribus, totas et integras parvas custumas infrascriptas, solvendas per personas libertate dicti burgi non donatas, minimeque
burgenses eiusdem, omnium bonorum accedentum et discedentum per portas
et pontem dicti burgi nostri, vnacum divoriis librandi et mensurandi, *lie
weighage et mettage*, in tabula et inventorio eiusmodi subsequentibus contentis,—videlicet, pro vnoquoque onere, *lie laid*, mercimoniorum, vt pote
pellium et coriorum, lane, linte, cannabi,[1] ac omnium aliorum huiusmodi
bonorum et mercimoniorum, octo denarios; et pro sarsina earundem, *lie
burdein*, quatuor denarios. Item, pro quovis onere equino carnium, piscium
frumenti aliorumque commoditatum quocunque,[2] quatuor denarios; et pro
sarsina earundem, duos denarios; item, pro quovis onere aratrorum, *lie pleuch
graith*, plaustrorum, vehiculorum, occarum et vectularum aliorumque eiusmodi,
et pro vnoquoque onere calcis, ollarum fictilium et vrnarum, importato et ex-
portato, quatuor denarios; et sarsina eorundem[3] duos denarios; et pro vnoquoque
equo, equa, aut equulo, *lie staige*, octo denarios; pro quovis bove aut vacca, octo
denarios; pro quovis ove mactili, duos denarios; pro quovis agne, vnum denar-

burgh, and their successors, all and whole the petty customs underwritten payable by persons not presented with the freedom of the said burgh, and not
burgesses of the same, of all goods entering and leaving through the ports and
bridge of our said burgh, together with the dues of weighing and measuring
(weighage and mettage) contained in the following table and inventory
thereof,—that is to say, for each load of merchandise, such as skins and hides, wool,
lint, hemp, and of all other such goods and merchandise, eight pennies; and for
a burden thereof, four pennies; item, for each horse-load of flesh, fishes, grain and
other provisions whatsoever, four pennies; and for a burden thereof, two pennies;
item, for each load of ploughgraith, carts, wains, harrows and barrows and other
suchlike gear, and for each load of lime, earthen pots and pitchers, imported and
exported, four pennies; and a burden thereof, two pennies; and for each horse, mare,
or staig, eight pennies; for each ox or cow, eight pennies; for each sheep fit for
slaughtering, two pennies; for each lamb, one penny; for each score of geese, twelve

---

[1] There is a blank here in the extract. In
the "Signature" [No. liv.] the articles are
described as "ilk laid of merchandice, sic as
skyn, hyde, claithe, woll, lint, hemp, irone,
ase, and all vther siclike sorte of wares."

[2] "commeatuum quorumcunque"—C.

[3] "lie burdein"—C.

ium; pro singulis viginti anscribus, duodecem denarios; pro sue, quatuor denarios; et pro quocunque stanco, *lie staine*, lane, butiri, casci, sevi et liutei Scotici, ponderato et vendito in dicto burgo nostro, per municipes eiusdem duos denarios, et per omnes alios quatuor denarios; item, pro quovis onere commeatuum importatorum infra menia seu loca foralia dicti burgi nostri, pro stationum locis et aularum censibus, lie *stand roume* et *hall muill*, et supportatione dictarum aularum et communium locorum foralium, solvendo duodecem denarios vnoquoque die forali, vna cum eschaetis dictorum commeatuum vendibilium infra dictum burgum nostrum allatorum in manibus mangonum et propolarum existentium sive penuariis impositorum, lie *houseit*, et ad macellas et fora minime presentatorum; item, pro mensuratione omnium generum commeatuum venditorum et mensuratorum infra dictum burgum nostrum, pro vnoquoque onere eorundem duodecem denarios.   Ac preterea, dicti prepositus, ballivi, consules et communitas eorumque successores, pro petuo, capient duplum dictarum custumarum tempore nundinarum annuatim dictis quatuor nundinis; et fruentur, gaudebunt et possidebunt, omnes et singulas huiusmodi custumas dicti burgi nostri infra et extra portas eiusdem et super stratis et plateis et intra loca foralia eiusdem nunc ad loca foralia appunctuata et destinata seu per ipsos eorumque successores appunctuanda

pennies; for each swine, four pennies; and for each stone of wool, butter, cheese, tallow and Scots lint, weighed and sold within our said burgh, by the freemen of the same two pennies, and by all others four pennies; item, for each load of victual imported within the walls or market places of our said burgh, for stand room and hall muill, and for the upholding of the said halls and common market places, twelve pennies to be paid every market day, together with the escheats of the said victuals brought within our said burgh for sale being in the hands of regraiters or forestallers or housed in girnels and not presented at the market places and markets; item, for the measuring of all kinds of victual sold and measured within our said burgh, for each load thereof twelve pennies.   And farther, the said provost, bailies, councillors and community and their successors, for ever, shall take double of the said customs in the time of the fairs yearly at the said four fairs; and they shall use, enjoy and possess, all and sundry such customs of our said burgh within and outwith the ports thereof and upon the streets and lanes and within the market places of the same now appointed and appropriated or to be appointed and

et destinanda impostorum, cum liberatione et mensuratione, lie *weyage et mettage*, stationum censibus, *lie stand maills*, dictorum fororum, cum custumis vulgo nuncupatis *laidell et gait dichtings*, omnibusque aliis divoriis, custumis, vicecomitis feodis, divoriis et exactionibus, in et circa dictum burgum, sicut dicti prepositus, consules et communitas dicti burgi nostri de Stirling eorumque predicessores, per semetipsos, servitores et firmarios suos, nunc in vsu et possessione levandi et recipiendi sunt aut ante hac fuerunt infra sive extra dictum burgum et apud loca predicta, simili modo et adeo libere et in eadem forma prout burgi nostri Ediuburgi aut Perthe, aut quivis alius burgus regalis infra hoc regnum nostrum Scotie virtute eorum iufeofamentorum levare possuut; et generalitas presentis carte nostre minime specialitati preiudicabit, neque specialitas generalitati preiudicio fuerit vllo respectu. Preterea nos, cum avisamento et consensu predictis, dedimus, concessimus et disposuimus, tenoreque presentis carte nostre damus, concedimus et disponimus[1], prefatis preposito, ballivis, consulibus et communitati dicti burgi nostri de Stirling, eorumque successoribus, totos et integros eorum portus et navium receptacula

appropriated for market places by them and their successors hereafter, with weighage and mettage, stand maills of the said markets, with the customs commonly called ladle and gait dichtings, and all other duties, customs, sheriff's fees, duties and exactions, in and about the said burgh, as the said provost, bailies, councillors and community of our said burgh of Stirling and their predecessors, by themselves, their servants, and farmers, are now or have been before this time in use and possession to levy and receive the same within or outwith the said burgh and at the places foresaid, in like manner and as freely and in the same form as our burghs of Edinburgh or Perth, or any other royal burgh within this our kingdom of Scotland, are empowered to levy in virtue of their infeftments; and the generality of our present charter shall not prejudice the speciality, nor shall the speciality be a prejudice to the generality in any respect. Moreover, we, with advice and consent foresaid, have given, granted and disponed, and by the tenor of our present charter give, grant and dispone to the foresaid provost, bailies, councillors and community of our said burgh of Stirling, and their successors, all and whole their ports and harbours upon the said water of Forth, together with

---

[1] "et hac presenti carta nostra confirmauimus, tenoreque eiusdem damus, concedimus, disponimus, proque nobis et nostris successoribus pro perpetuo confirmamus, prefatis," etc.—*C.*

super dicta aqua de Forth, vnacum littoribus, *lie landing places*, pristinis et
novis, huiusmodi, et integris domibus et hortis desuper edificatis et rudis
burgalibus eisdem adjacentibus: cum omnibus et singulis viis, semitis, passagiis,
stratis, plateis et calcipediis, ducentibus ab et ad dictos portus et navium
receptacula et littora, respectiue, tam pristina quam nova; cum omnibus et
singulis privilegiis, custumis, portus et textrine monetis, *lie heavin silver et
dock silver*, littorum, debitis, *lie schoir silver*, anchoragiis, custis, *lie cowstes*,
assise bollis, *lie assyse bollis*, redditibus, divoriis et casualitatibus, dictorum
portuum vsitatis et consuetis; ac presertim omnia et singula privilegia,
custumas, portuum monetas, anchoragia, textrine et littoris monetas, exactiones, redditus et casualitates, dictorum portuum de Stirling inframention-
atas, quas in hac presenti carta nostra inserendas ordinavimus, et observandas
et perimplendas per omnes nostros subditos et exteros reparantes et frequent-
antes ad et ab dictos portus, et quod huiusmodi ignorantiam nulli pretendant,
videlicet, monetam nuncupatam *heavin silver*, omnium personarum municipum,
minime municipum et extraneorum, auferentium seu habentium aliqua bona
in vel per dictos portus de Stirling aut per aliquam partem infra bondas predictas dicte aque de Forth:—item, omnium saccorum siue sarsinarum et
doliorum bonorum, municipes dict burgi nostri de Stirling solvent duos

landing places thereof, old and new, and whole houses and gardens built thereon,
and the burgh roods adjacent thereto; with all and sundry ways, paths, passages,
lanes, streets and causeways, leading from and to the said ports and harbours and
landing places, respectively, as well old as new; with all and sundry privileges,
customs, haven silver, dock silver, shore silver, anchorages, cowstes, assize bolls,
rents, duties and casualties of the said ports used and wont ; and especially all and
sundry privileges, customs, haven silver, anchorages, dock and shore silver,
exactions, rents and casualties of the said ports of Stirling undermentioned, which
in this our present charter we have ordained to be inserted, and to be observed and
implemented by all our subjects and strangers repairing and frequenting to
and from the said ports, and that none pretend ignorance of the same, that is to
say, the money called haven silver of all persons free men, unfreemen and
strangers, carrying away or having any goods in or through the foresaid ports of
Stirling or through any part within the bounds foresaid of the said water of Forth:—
item, of all sacks or burdens and casks of goods, freemen of our said burgh of Stirling

denarios, aliorum burgorum sex denarios, et illiberi et minime municipes octo
denarios; cujusvis *lie daker* coriorum municipes dicti burgi sex denarios,
aliorum burgorum duodecem denarios, minime municipes et peregrini quadraginta denarios; frumenti, farine, brasij, salis, in hoc regno nostro crescentium
et confectorum, cuiusvis bolle, ad incolas dicti burgi nostre attinentis duos
denarios, municipes aliorum burgorum quatuor denarios, et minime municipes
et extranei octo denarios; carbonum et calcis, *lie lyme*, importatorum, cuiusvis
celdre, ad dicti burgi incolas pertinentium vnum denarium, ad liberos burgenses alterius burgi duos denarios, illiberos vero octo denarios; exportatorum,
spectantium ad dictum burgum nostrum duos denarios, ad liberos burgos
quatuor denarios, minime liberos sedecim denarios; cuiusvis bolle frumenti,
salis et bonorum penuariorum, *lie girnell guides*, ab exteros allatorum, ad
incolas dicti burgi attinentium duos denarios, municipes aliorum burgorum
sex denarios, minime municipes et extraneos duodecim denarios; tabularum, *lie
buirdis et duillis*, tegularum simplicium, vectium et spiculorum arcuareorum,
lie single roof, soale¹ et bowstingis, pro centum eorundem ad dictum burgum
nostrum spectantium, vnum, ad liberos burgos vnum, minime liberos vuum et
alienigenas vnum; cuiusvis trabis, *lie corbell et wainscott*, ad incolas dicti burgi

shall pay two pennies, of other burghs six pennies, and unfreemen and non-burgesses
eight pennies ; of each daker of hides, burgesses of the said burgh six pennies, of
other burghs twelve pennies, non-burgesses and strangers forty pennies ; of corn,
meal, malt, salt, grown and made in this our kingdom, for each boll belonging to the
inhabitants of our said burgh two pennies, burgesses of other burghs four pennies,
and non-burgesses and strangers eight pennies; of coal and lime imported, for each
chalder belonging to the inhabitants of the foresaid burgh one penny, to the
free burgesses of another burgh two pennies, and to unfreemen eight pennies ;
exported, belonging to our said burgh two pennies, to free burghs four pennies,
unfree sixteen pennies; of each boll of victual, salt and girnel goods, brought from
other countries, belonging to the inhabitants of the said burgh two pennies, bur
gesses of other burghs six pennies, non-burgesses and strangers twelve pennies, of
boards and deals, single roof, spars and bowstings, for the hundred of the same belonging to our said burgh one, to free burghs one, unfree one, and strangers one; of
each corbel and wainscott, to the inhabitants of our said burgh of Stirling two

¹ "sparris"—C.

nostri de Stirling duos denarios, liberorum burgorum quatuor denarios, et ad
minime liberos spectantium octo denarios; pro centum *lie Dansick knappell*
ad dictum burgum nostrum de Stirling spectantis vnum, liberos burgos
vnum, et ad alieniginas et minime municipes vnum; et pro centum *lie Noroway
knappell*, ad burgum de Stirling spectantis vnum, liberos burgos vnum, et ad
alieniginas et minime municipes vnum, et duplum eorundem, *lie doubill
knappill*, duplum solvent de *lie Dansick knappell; pro quovis centum
vectium nuncupatarum *lie riccar sparis*, ad burgum nostrum de Stirling
pertinentium vnum, ad liberos burgos vnum, et ad alienigenas et illiberos
spectantium vnum; pro quovis scapha seu parva cymba manuali, *lie little
handling boat*, quatuor denarios, pro magna cymba calcarea, *lie lyme boat*
cymba carbonaria et navicula, nuncupata *lie crear*, absque carchesio, pro
dicta moneta portali et textrine, vulgo nuncupata *heavin silver et dock silver*,
tres solidos; et pro navigiolo, *lie bark et crear*, cum carchesio, pro dicta moneta
portus et textrine, quinque solidos; pro quovis nave in dicto portu fluctuante,
pro dicta moneta nuncupata *dock silver*, decem solidos.   Et similiter dicti
prepositus, ballivi et consules dict' burgi nostri, eorumque successores, gaudebunt, vtentur et fruentur, omnibus aliis custumis et privilegiis infra dictos
portus navium receptacula et littora eiusmodi prout ipsi eorumque predecessores

pennies, of free burghs four pennies, and belonging to unfreemen eight pennies;
for the hundred Dantzick knappill, belonging to our said burgh of Stirling one, to
free burghs one, and to strangers and non-burgesses one ; and for the hundred
Norway knappell, belonging to Stirling one, to free burghs one, and to strangers
and non-burgesses one; and the double knappel shall pay the double of Dantzick
knappill; for each hundred of wicker spars, belonging to our burgh of Stirling one :
to free burghs one, and belonging to strangers and unfreemen one; for each skiff
or little handling boat, four pennies ; for a large lime boat. a coal boat, and
small ship called a crear and without a top-mast, for the said haven silver
and dock silver, three shillings ; and for a bark and crear with a top-mast,
for the said haven and dock silver, five shillings ; for each ship floating in the
said port, for the said money called dock silver, ten shillings. And in like manner
the said provost, bailies and councillors of our said burgh, and their successors, shall
enjoy, use and possess, all other customs and privileges within the said ports,
harbours and landing places thereof, as they and their predecessors formerly enjoyed

huiusmodi perprius gavisi sunt.   Cum potestate ipsis constituendi, edificandi, reparandi, fortificandi, muniendi et augendi huiusmodi portus, in et super locis maritimis infra bondas predictas, in solidiori et substantiali modo et forma vt melius indurent figentur et stabilientur pro salute omnium navium, navicularum, *lie crearis, barkes*, et aliorum vasorum ad dictos portus applicandorum, et tempore pacis et belli.   Et, quoniam huiusmodi portus et littora non sine magnis sumptibus et expensis dicto burgo nostro sustinentur et supportantur et reparatione deinde annuatim egebunt, idcirco, dedimus, concessimus et disposuimus, tenoreque presentis carte nostre damus, concedimus et disponimus,[1] prefatis preposito, ballivis et consulibus dicti burgi nostri, corumque successoribus, integra anchoragia, littoris et textrine monetas, lie *shoir et dock silver*, custumas, aliasque commoditates ad eandem pertinentes, ad effectum prescriptum applicandas.   Et quia nos, considerantes pontem de Stirling super dicta aqua de Forth et longam plateam seu calcipedium ad dictum pontem ducentem et ab eodem deducentem magnis egere sumptibus et expensis pro supportatione eiusdem, et quod predicti prepositus, ballivi, consules et communitas dicti burgi nostri, multum etiam onerati sunt pro

the same.   With power to them to establish, build, repair, fortify, defend and enlarge such ports, in and upon the sea coasts within the foresaid bounds, in a more solid and substantial manner and form that they might the better endure and be more fixed and stable for the safety of all ships, crears, barques, and other vessels sailing to the said ports, both in time of peace and war.   And, since such ports and landing places are not maintained and upheld without great outlays and expense of our said burgh and will require reparation hereafter yearly, therefore we have given, granted and disponed, and by the tenor of our present charter give, grant and dispone, to the foresaid provost, bailies and councillors of our said burgh, and their successors, the whole anchorages, shore and dock silver, customs, and other commodities belonging to the same to be applied to the purpose foresaid.   And because we, taking into our consideration that the bridge of Stirling upon the said water of Forth and the long street or causeway leading to and from the said bridge requires great charges and expenses for the upholding of the same, and that the foresaid provost, bailies, councillors and community of our said burgh have also

[1] " et hac presenti carta nostra confirmavimus,   ponimus, ac pro nobis et nostris successoribus tenoreque eiusdem damus, concedimus et dis-   pro perpetuo confirmamus, prefatis," etc.—C.

supportatioue meniorum suorum, portarum et platearum, igitur nos, cum
consensu predicto, damus, concedimus et disponimus, prefatis preposito,
ballivis, consulibus et communitati dicti burgi nostri, corumque successoribus,
custumas dicti pontis infrascriptas, videlicet, pro quovis sacco seu sarsina, *lie
pack*, lane, panni, lintei et lanci, pellium, linte, cannabi et *lie plaidingis,*
minime municipes dicti burgi solvendo duos solidos, municipes vero eiusdem
duos[1] denarios; pro vnoquoque onere butiri, casei, sevi et ferri, minime
municipes duodecem denarios, municipes vero dicti burgi nostri sex denarios;
pro vnoquoque onere frumenti, carnis, piscium, aliorumque commeatuum,
minime municipes dicti burgi solvendo octo denarios, et municipes eiusdem
quatuor denarios; pro quovis onere salis plantarum, porrorum et fructuum,
illiberi dicti burgi nostri et libertate ejusdem minime donati solvendo pro
cisdem quatuor denarios, et libertate eiusdem donati et municipes eiusdem
burgi nostri duos denarios; ac pro sarsina, *lie burdlein*, dictarum mercuum
aliorumque venalium, dimidium precii dictorum onerum; pro vnoquoque
onere equino, *lie hors draught seu load*, lignorum, *lie timber*, minime municipes
quatuor denarios, municipes vero dicti burgi duos denarios; pro quovis onere
equino coriorum, minime municipes sedecim denarios, municipes vero dicti

been much burdened in upholding their walls, ports and causeways, therefore we,
with consent foresaid, have given, granted and disponed, to the foresaid provost,
bailies, councillors and community of our said burgh, and their successors, the
customs of the said bridge under written, that is to say, for each sack or pack of wool,
cloth, linen and woollen, skins, lint, hemp and plaidings, unfreemen of the said
burgh to pay two shillings, and burgesses thereof two pennies;[1] for each load of
butter, cheese, tallow, and iron, unfreemen twelve pennies, and freemen of our said
burgh six pennies; for each load of victual, flesh, fishes, and other provisions,
unfreemen of the said burgh to pay eight pennies, and freemen of the same four
pennies; for each load of salt, plants, leeks and fruits, unfreemen of our said burgh
and those not presented with its freedom to pay for these things four pennies, and
those presented with its freedom and burgesses of our burgh, two pennies; and for a
burden of the said wares and other wares for sale, one half the price of said loads;
for each horse draught or load of timber, unfreemen four pennies, and freemen of
the said burgh two pennies; for each horse load of hides, unfreemen sixteen pennies,

[1] In the "Signature" [No. liv.] the custom is stated to be twelve pennies.

burgi nostri quatuor denarios; pro vnoquoque equo seu equa vendibili ad
dictum forum accedenti, duodecem denarios; pro quovis bove seu vacca, octo
denarios; pro ove, minime municipes duos denarios;[1] pro sue, minime liberi octo
denarios, municipes vero quatuor denarios; pro vnoquoque dolio vini duos
solidos; pro dolio, *lie tun*, zithi sedecim denarios; et pro quovis onere cervisie octo
denarios; et pro onere carbonum vnum denarium. Mandando et precipiendo
omnibus et singulis legiis et subditis nostris et peregrinis omnibusque aliis
quorum interest quod denuo et indilate respondeant et gratuiter solvant prefatis preposito, ballivis, consulibus et communitati dicti burgi nostri de Stirling,
eorumque successoribus, factoribus, collectoribus, firmarijs et custumarijs suis,
omnes et singulas antedictas custumas, monetam portus et littoris, vulgo nuncupatas *heavin silver et shoir silver*, exactiones et custumas dicti burgi nostri et
pontis, aliasque custumas, redditus, devorias et casualitates, generaliter et particulariter suprascriptas, sub omni pena et damno inde sequituro. Prout etiam
nos, cum consensu predicto, damus et committimus nostram plenam potestatem
et commissionem prefatis preposito, ballivis et consulibus dicti burgi nostri de
Stirling, presentibus et futuris, infra integras bondas et libertates dicti burgi

and freemen of our said burgh four pennies; for each horse or mare coming to the
said market to be sold, twelve pennies; for each ox or cow, eight pennies; for a
sheep, unfreemen two pennies, [freemen one penny[1]]; for a swine, unfreemen eight
pennies, and freemen four pennies; for each tun of wine two shillings; for the tun
of beer sixteen pennies; and for each load of ale eight pennies; and for each load of
coals one penny. Charging and commanding all and sundry our lieges and subjects
and strangers and all others whom it concerns that forthwith and without delay
they answer and thankfully pay to the foresaid provost, bailies, councillors and
community of our said burgh of Stirling, and to their successors, their factors,
collectors, farmers and custumars, all and sundry the foresaid customs, money of the
port and shore, commonly called haven silver and shore silver, exactions, customs of
our said burgh and bridge, and other customs, rents, duties and casualties generally
and particularly before written, under all pain and loss that may follow thereupon.
As also we, with consent foresaid, give and commit our full power and commission
to the foresaid provost, bailies and councillors of our said burgh of Stirling, present
and to come, within the whole bounds and liberties of our said burgh, to put to due

---

[1] In Signature [No. liv.]:—"ilk sheip, ij d. of unfreemen and j d. of freemen."

nostri, debite executioni mandandi (quoties opus fuerit) acta et statuta parliamentorum nostrorum et generalium conciliorum que concernunt aut concernere possunt privilegium et libertatem dicti burgi nostri; cum potestate (si opus fuerit) vicinos, incolas et burgenses, convocandi, pro eorum auxilio et concursu in executioni dictarum legum nostrarum. Et nos, ex certa nostra scientia proprioque motu, cum avisamento et consensu predicto, vnivimus, annexavimus et incorporavimus, tenoreque presentis carte nostre, pro nobis et successoribus nostris, vnimus, annexamus et incorporamus, ad et cum dicto burgo nostro de Stirling, privilegiis et libertatibus antedictis eidem concessis, omnes et singulas predictas terras nuncupatas *lie Eister Craigis et outsettis* carundem, cum pertinentiis ad easdem spectantibus jacentibus, inter murum dicti burgi nostri et torrentem nuncupatum *Eisterburne, Southbraes* subtus murum dicti burgi nostri, cum integris terris ex boreali parte dicti burgi nostri vocatis *lie Whinnes* et *Gowanhillis*, terras nuncupatas *Parkfeild, Gallowfeild, Gallowfald, Justingflatis* et *Brighauche*, integras moras nuncupatas pristinas et novas Moras Burgales dicti burgi nostri, Pratum Burgale, *lie Borrow Medow*, ex australi latere dicte aque de Forth iuxta dictam abbatiam de Cambuskenneth, predictas croftas

execution the acts and statutes of our parliaments and general councils which concern or can concern the privileges and liberty of our said burgh (as often as there shall be need); with power (if there shall be need) to convocate the neighbouring inhabitants and burgesses for their assistance and concurrence in the execution of our said laws. And we of our certain knowledge and proper motive, with advice and consent foresaid, have united, annexed and incorporated, and by the tenor of our present charter, for us and our successors, do unite, annex and incorporate to and with our said burgh of Stirling, with the privileges and liberties foresaid granted to the same, all and sundry the foresaid lands called the Easter Craigs and outsets of the same, with the pertinents belonging to the same lying between the wall of our said burgh and the burn called the Easter Burn, the South Braes below the wall of our said burgh, with the whole lands on the north side of our said burgh called the Whins and Gowan Hills, the lands called Parkfield, Gallowfield, Gallowfald, Justingflats and Bridghauche, the whole muirs called the old and new Burghmuirs of our said burgh, the Borrowmeadow on the south side of the said water of Forth near the said abbey of Cambuskenneth, the foresaid crofts

terrarum nuncupatas *Myretoun Croft, Lawsonis Croft*, et *Brounes Croft*; ac
totas et integras predictas piscationes, tam salmonum quam aliorum piscium,
super dicta aqua de Forth infra predictas bondas ciusmodi particulariter
supramentionatas; vnacum omnibus et singulis predictis terris nuncupatis
Spittelltoun, Spittellandis, Brighauche, Spittellkerse, et pratum ciusdem,
Spittellmyre, integrisque earundem pertinentiis ex australi et boreali partibus
dicte aque de Forth; cum domibus, edificiis, toftis et pertineuciis earundem;
croftam terre nuncupatam croftam Sancti Laurentij apud finem pontis de
Stirling, Ladycroft, Ladyrig, jacentes ex boreali parte dicti burgi nostri, cum
croftis nuncupatis *lie Ruid Croft, Seikmanis Croft et Seikmanis Hous*, et
horto eiusdem jacentibus ex australi latere dicti burgi nostri inter dictum burgum nostrum et viridarium *lie Park de Stirling;* et similiter illam peciam
fundi nuncupatam Vallem, *lie Valley*, jacentem prope cemiterium dicti burgi
nostri; vna cum omnibus domibus, hortis, terris et rupibus, *lie craigis*, jaceu-
tibus subtus monticulum castri extra precinctum et bondas palatii et castri
nostri de Stirling; cum omnibus et singulis partibus, pendiculis, toftis, croftis,
outsettis, domibus, edificiis, cum omnibus earundem pertinentiis, particulariter
supra specificatis, jacentibus vt prefertur; predictos portus naviumque recep-

of lands called Myretoun croft, Lawson's croft, and Brouno's croft; and all and
whole the foresaid fishings, as well of salmon as of other fishings, on the said water
of Forth within the foresaid bounds of the same particularly above mentioned;
together with all and sundry the foresaid lands called Spitteltown, Spittellands,
Brighauche, Spittellerse and meadow of the same, Spittelmyre, and the whole
pertinents of the same on the south and north sides of the said water of
Forth; with the houses, buildings, tofts and pertinents of the same, the croft
of land called the croft of St. Lawrence at the end of the bridge of Stirling,
Lady Croft, Ladyrig, lying on the north side of our said burgh, with the crofts
called the Ruid Croft, Scikman's Croft, and Scikman's House, and garden of the
same, lying on the south side of our said burgh between our said burgh and the
Park of Stirling; and in like manner that piece of ground called the Valley lying
near the churchyard of our said burgh; together with all houses, gardens, lands and
crags lying under the Castlehill outwith the precinct and bounds of our palace and
castle of Stirling; with all and sundry parts, pendicles, tofts, crofts, outsets, houses,
buildings, with all the pertinents of the same particularly above specified lying as

tacula super dicta aque de Forth, cum littoribus, *lie landing places*, novis et
pristinis earundem, et integris domibus, edificijs et hortis desuper constructis,
et rudis burgalibus, lie *Borrow Ruidis*, eisdem adiacentibus; cum omnibus et
singulis vijs, passagijs, plateis, officio rececomitatus infra bondas et limites predictas; vna cum advocatione, donatione et jure patronatus dicti zenodochij Sancti
Jacobi prope dictum burgum nostrum de Stirling, cum advocatione, donatione
et jure patronatus, predicti capellanie Sancti Laurentij, omnibusque et
singulis alijs, terris, predijs, *lie roumes*, et possessionibus ad easdem spectantibus; vna cum duobus alijs zenodochijs antedictis, vno corundem Spitellis
Hospitall altero vero Cowanes Hospitell nuncupato, omnibusque alijs zenodochijs [et] rogatorijs, *lie almshoussis*, infra dictum burgum nostrum; et omnibus et singulis predictis ecclesijs, terris, molendinis, annuis redditibus, tenementis, hortis, terris, decimis reddizibus, alijsque particulariter et generaliter
supra expressis, infra et extra dictum burgum nostrum, eidem dotatis, fundatis
et annexatis; cum omnibus et singulis alijs patronatibus, terris, libertatibus,
alijsque respectiue particulariter et generaliter suprascriptis,—in vnum
integrum et liberum Burgum Regalem. Ac volumus et concedimus proque
nobis et nostris successoribus decernimus et ordinamus quod vnica sasina nunc

before written; the foresaid ports and harbours upon the said water of Forth, with
the landing places of the same, new and old; and the whole houses, buildings, and
gardens erected thereon and the burgh roads adjacent to the same; with all and sundry
ways, passages, streets, office of shariffship within the bounds and limits foresaid;
together with the advocation, donation and right of patronage, of the said Hospital of
Saint James near our said burgh of Stirling, with the advocation, donation and right of
patronage, of the foresaid chaplainry of St. Laurence, and all aud sundry other lands,
roumes and possessions belonging to the same; together with the two other hospitals
foresaid, the one of them called Spittell's Hospital and the other Cowanes Hospital,
and with all other hospitals and alms houses within our said burgh; and all and sundry
the foresaid churches, lands, mills, annual rents, tenements, gardens, lands, teinds,
rents and others particularly and generally above expressed, within and beyond our
said burgh, given, founded and annexed to the same; with all and sundry other
patronages, lands, liberties and others respectively, particularly and generally above
written,—into one whole and free Burgh Royal. And we will and grant and for us and
our successors decern and ordain that a single sasine now to be taken in virtue of this

virtute presentis hujus nostri infeofamenti, per deliberationem terre et lapidis
et vnius denarij argenti, per propositum vel aliquem vnum ballivorum dicti
burgi nostri de Stirling pro tempore, capienda apud crucem foralem dicti
burgi nostri, stabit valida et sufficiens erit sasina prefatis preposito, ballivis,
consulibus et communitati dicti nostri burgi de Stirling et eorum successoribus,
pro toto et integro dicto burgo nostro et integris terris, annexis, incorporationi-
bus, alijsque particulariter et generaliter supraexpressis, nunc eidem vnitis et
annexatis vt predicitur, non obstante quod dictus burgus, terre, portus, passagia,
custume, privilegia, libertates, iurisdictiones, ecclesie, decime fructus, redditus,
aliaque generaliter et particulariter supraspecificata ad eandem pertinentia,
discontigue jacent et indiversis partibus, absque vlla necessitate vllius alterius
sasine per successores suos imposterum sumende.   Tenendum et habendum,
totum et integrum predictum burgum nostrum de Stirling, cum integris terris
et domibus communibus, locis foralibus, et territorio ciusdem, terris, molendinis,
tenementis, acris, rudis, menijs, portis, plateis, pontibus, vijs, passagijs, portubus,
navium receptaculis, littoribus, annuis redditibus, prebendarijs, capellanijs,
zenodochijs, patronatibus, alijsque eorundem pertinentiis; vna cum omnibus
et singulis officijs, privilegijs, tolonijs, custumis, libertatibus et immunitatibus

our present infeftment, by delivery of earth and stone and of one silver penny, by the
provost, or any one of the bailies of our said burgh of Stirling for the time, at the
market cross of our said burgh, shall stand and be a valid and sufficient sasine to the
said provost, bailies, councillors and community of our said burgh of Stirling, and their
successors, for all and whole our said burgh and whole lands, annexes, incorporations,
and others particularly and generally above expressed, now united and annexed to the
same as said is, notwithstanding that the said burgh, lands, ports, passages, customs,
privileges, liberties, jurisdictions, churches, teinds, fruits, rents, and others generally
and particularly above specified belonging to the same, lie unconnected and in
different parts, without any necessity of any other sasine to be taken by their successors in time to come.   To hold and to have, all and whole our foresaid burgh of
Stirling, with the whole lands and common houses, market places, and territory of
the same, lands, mills, tenements, acres, roods, walls, ports, streets, bridges, ways,
passages, ports, harbours, landing places, annual rents, prebendaries, chaplainries,
hospitals, patronages, and other pertinents of the same ; together with all and sundry
offices, privileges, tolls, customs, liberties, and immunities whatsoever belonging to

quibuscunque ad dictum burgum nostrum de Stirling pertinentibus de quibus
prefati prepositus, ballivi, consules et communitas eiusdem eorumque predecessores perprius in vsu et possessione fuerunt; cum omnibus et singulis
prescriptis terris nuncupatis *lie Easter Craigis* et outsettis earundem et
pertinentiis ad easdem spectantibus, jacentibus inter murum dicti burgi
et torrentem nuncupatum *lie Eisterburne, Southbraes* subtus murum dicti
burgi nostri, et integris terris ex boreali parte dicti burgi nostri vocatis
lie Whines et Gowanhillis; terras nuncupatas *Parkfeild, Gallowfeild,
Gallowfald, Justingflatis,* et *Brighauche,* cum integris moris nuncupatis
novis et pristinis Moris Burgalibus dicti burgi nostri; terras nuncupatas *Burrowmedow* jacentes ex australi latere dicto aque de Forth iuxta abbatiam de
Cambuskenneth, croftas terrarum nuncupatas *Myretounis Croft, Lawsonis
Croft, Brounes Croft;* vna cum integris piscationibus tam salmonum quam
aliorum piscium super dicta aqua de Forth ad dictum burgum pertinentibus;
et similiter totas et integras predictas terras nuncupatas *Spittelltoun, Spittell-
landis, Spittellkerse* et pratum huiasmodi, *Spittellmyre,* et pertinentes earundem, jacentes tam ex australi quam boreali partibus dicto aque de Forth; cum
omnibus domibus, edificijs, toftis, croftis, partibus, pendiculis, et pertinertiis

our said burgh of Stirling of which the foresaid provost, bailies, councillors and
community of the same, and their predecessors, have been formerly in the use and
possession, with all and sundry the foresaid lauds called the Easter Craigs and outsets of the same and the pertinents belonging thereto, lying between the wall of
the said burgh and the burn called the Easter Burn, South Braes under the wall of our
said burgh, and the whole lands on the north side of our said burgh called the Whins
and Gowane Hills; the lands called Parkfield, Gallowfield, Gallowfald, Justingflats
and Brighauche, with the whole muirs called the new and old Burgh Muirs of our said
burgh; the lands called the Borrowmeadow lying on the south side of the said water
of Forth near the abbey of Cambuskenneth, the crofts of land called Myretouns
Croft, Lawson's Croft, Brownes Croft; together with the whole fishings as well of
salmon as of other fishings upon the said water of Forth belonging to the said burgh;
and likewise all and whole the foresaid lands called Spitteltoun, Spittellands,
Spittellkerse, and meadow of the same, Spittellmyre and pertinents of the same,
lying as well on the south as on the north side of the said water of Forth;
with all houses, buildings, tofts, crofts, parts, pendicles and pertinents of the

x

earundem; cum crofta terre crofta Sancti Laurentij nuncupata jacente apud
pontem de Stirling et lie *Lady Croft* et *Lady Rig* jacente ex boreali latere
dicti burgi nostri, cum croftis terre nuncupatis *Rude Croft, Seikmanis Croft,
SeikmanisHous,* et horto eiusdem,jacentibus ex australi latere dicti burgi nostri
inter dictum burgum et murum viridarij, *lie Park de Stirling;* necnon, illam
petiam fundi nuncupatam Vallem jacentem prope cemiterium dicti burgi
nostri; vna cum integris domibus, hortis, tenementis, terris et rupibus, jacentibus sub monticulo castri extra precinctum et bondas castri nostri et palatij
de Stirling; cum omnibus et singulis partibus, pendiculis, toftis, croftis, outsettis, domibus, edificijs et integris pertinentiis omnium et singularum terrarum
particulariter predictarum; ac cum omnibus et singulis predictis terris, tenementis, domibus edificijs, ecclesijs, capellanijs, zenodochijs, hortis, croftis,
annuis redditibus, fructibus, divoriis, proficuis, emolumentis, firmis, elimosinis,
lie dail silver, obitibus et anniversarijs, suprascriptis; cum manericrum locis,
pomarijs, terris, annuis redditibus, emolumentis et divorijs quibuscunque que
ad predictos. Fratres Dominicanos seu Predicatores [et] Minores [seu] Franciscanos, dicti burgi nostri perprius pertinuerunt; vna cum omnibus et singulis
predictis terris et tenementis iacentibus infra predictum burgum nostrum et

same; with the croft of land called the Croft of St. Lawrence lying at the bridge
of Stirling and the Lady Croft and Lady Rig lying on the north side of
the said burgh, with the crofts of land called the Rood Croft, Seikman's Croft
and Seikman's house and garden of the same, lying on the south side of our
said burgh between the said burgh and the wall of the Park of Stirling;
also, that piece of ground called the Valley lying near the churchyard of
our said burgh; together with the whole houses, yards, tenements, lands and
crags, lying beneath the Castlehill outwith the precinct and bounds of our
castle and palace of Stirling; with all and sundry parts, pendicles, tofts, crofts,
outsets, houses, buildings, and whole pertinents of all and sundry the lands
particularly before mentioned; and with all and sundry the foresaid lands, tenements,
houses, buildings, churches, chaplainries, hospitals, yards, crofts, annual rents,
fruits, duties, profits, emoluments, farms, alms, dail silver, obits and anniversaries,
above written; with the manor places, orchards, lands, annual rents, emoluments and
duties whatsoever which formerly pertained to the foresaid Dominican or 'Preaching
Friars and Minorites or Franciscans of our said burgh; together with all and sundry

libertatem ciusmodi, et cum omnibus annuis redditibus levandis ex quacunque
terra seu tenemento infra dictum burgum nostrum et libertatem ciusmodi,
ac cum omnibus redditibus levandis de quacunque domo, terra seu tenemento
infra dictum burgum nostrum, datis, donatis et fundatis, quibuscunque cap-
ellanuijis, altaragiis, ecclesijs et funeralibus et anniuersarijs, vbicunque eadem
existunt infra hoc regnun: nostrum; vna cum omnibus et singulis annuis
redditibus alijsque divorijs predictis, vsitatis seu de communi redditu dicti
burgi a preposito et balliuis eiusdem per quamcunque ecclesiam extra dictum
nostrum propter celebrationem suffrag.orum de mandari possunt; cum predictis
advocatione, donatione, et iure patronatus predicti zenodochij Sancti Jacobi
prope dictum burgum nostrum de Stirling, vna cum integris terris, predijs,
redditibus et possessionibus eidem spectantibus; cum advocatione, donatione
et iure patronatus dicte capellanie altaris Sancti Laurentij fundate infra dictum
ecclesiam de Stirling, cum omnibus terris, redditibus et privilegijs, ad eandem
spectantibus; cum advocatione, donatione etiure patronatus, dictorum zenodochiorum lie *Cowanes Hospitell et Spitells Hospitell* nuncupatorum; vna
cum predicta mercatoriali gildria omnibusque et singulis predictis terris, liberis

the foresaid lands and tenements lying within our foresaid burgh and liberty
thereof, and with all annual rents leviable from whatever land or tenement
within our said burgh and liberty of the same; and with all rents leviable from
whatever house, land or tenement within our said burgh, given, bestowed and
founded, to whatsoever chaplainries, altarages, churches and funerals and anniversaries wheresoever the same may be within this our kingdom; together with all and
sundry annual rents and other duties foresaid accustomed or that may be demanded
out of the common rent of the said burgh from the provost and bailies of the same
by whatsoever church outwith our said burgh on account of the celebration of
suffrages; with the foresaid advocation, donation and right of patronage, of the
foresaid Hospital of St. James near our said burgh of Stirling, together with the
whole lands, rooms, rents and possessions belonging to the same; with the advocation,
donation and right of patronage, of the said chaplainry of the altar of St. Lawrence
founded within the said church of Stirling, with all the lands, rents, and privileges,
belonging to the same; with the advocation, donation and right of patronage, of the
said hospitals called Cowanes Hospital and Spittells Hospital; together with the
foresaid merchant guildry; and with all and sundry the foresaid lands, free fairs

nundinis et fori hepdomadarijs, privilegijs et proficuis, que pertinuerunt aut ad eosdem pertinere possint; ac cum integris custumis dicti burgi nostri infra et extra portas et pontem et super plateis et infra forum et apud loca foralia dicti burgi nostri, cum stationum censibus, *lie standmaillis,* aliisque custumis, vicecomitis feodis, divorijs et exactionibus, prope dictum burgnm nostrum factis; vnacum dicto officio vicecomitis infra bondas predictas; cum omnibus libertatibus, privilegijs, escaetis, casualitatibus, penis, penalitatibus, amerciamentis, feodis et divorijs quibuscunque, generaliter et specialiter suprascriptis; ac totos et integros predictos portus etna vium receptacula super dicta aqua de Forth, vnacum littoribus pristinis et novis eiusmodi, cum omnibus domibus et hortis desuper constructis et udis burgalibus eisdem adjacentibus; vnacum omnibus et singulis vijs, semitis, passagijs, plateis, et calcipediis, ducentibus ad et ab dictos portus, navium receptacula et littora earundem, pristina et nova; cum omnibus et singulis privilegijs, custumis, moneta portali, moneta textrine, littoris debitis, anchoragijs, exactionibus, redditibus, devorijs, et casualitatibus dictorum portuum omnibusque eorundem pertinentiis suprascriptis, reliquisque privilegijs, libertatibus, commissionibus aliisque supraspecificatis,— prefatis preposito, ballivis, consulibus, communitati et burgensibus dicti

and weekly markets, privileges and profits which have belonged or can belong to the same; and with the whole customs of our said burgh within and outwith the ports and bridge and upon the streets and within the market and at the market places of our said burgh, with the standmaills and other customs, sheriff's fees, duties and exactions, made about our said burgh; together with the said office of sheriff within the foresaid bounds; with all the liberties, privileges, escheats, casualties, pains, penalties, fines, fees and duties whatsoever generally and specially above written; and all and whole the foresaid ports and harbours upon the said water of Forth, together with the landing places old and new of the same, with all houses and gardens built thereon, and the burgh roods adjacent thereto; together with all and sundry ways, roads, passages, streets and causeways leading to and from the said ports, harbours and landing places thereof, new and old; with all and sundry privileges, customs, haven silver, dock silver, shore silver, anchorages, exactions, rents, duties and casualties of the said ports, and all pertinents of the same above written, and other privileges, liberties, commissions and others above specified,—to the foresaid provost, bailies, councillors, community and burgesses of our said

burgi nostri de Stirling, eorumque successoribus, de nobis et successoribus
nostris, in feodo, hereditate, libero burgagio et libero vicecomitatu, infra
bondas predictas, imperpetuum, per omnes rectas metas suas antiquas et
divisas, prout jacent in longitudine et latitudine, in domibus, edificijs, boscis,
planis, moris, marresijs, vijs, semitis, aquis, stagnis, rivolis, aquis, pratis, pas-
cuis et pasturis, molendinis, multuris et eorum sequelis, aucupatiouibus, vena-
tiouibus, piscationibus, petarijs, turbarijs, carbonibus, carbonarijs, cuniculis,
cunicularijs, columbis, columbarijs, fabrilibus, brasinis, bruerijs et genistis,
silvis, nemoribus et virgultis, lignis, tignis, lapicidijs, lapide et calce; cum curijs
et earum exitibus, amerciamentis, Lerezeldis, bludewitis, et mulierum mer-
chetis; cum furca, fossa, sok, sak, thole, thame, wrake, wair, weth, wart,
vennysoun, infangthcif, outfaugthcif, pitt et gallous; cumque communi
pastura, liberoque introitu et exit.., ac cum omnibus aliis et singulis suis
libertatibus commoditatibus, profi..is, asiamentis ac justis suis pertinentiis
quibuscunque, tam non nominatis quam nominatis, tam subtus terra quam
supra terram, procul et prope, ad predictum burgum, terras, officium aliaque
predicta, cum pertinentiis spectantibus seu juste spectare valentibus quomodolibet in futurum, libere, quiete, plenarie, integre, honorifice, bene et in pace,

burgh of Stirling and their successors, of us and our successors, in fee, heritage,
free burgage and free sheriffship, within the bounds foresaid, for ever, by all their
right marches ancient and divided as they lie in length and breadth, in houses,
buildings, woods, plains, muirs, marches, ways, paths, waters, pools, rivulets,
meadows, grazings and pastures, mills, multures and their sequels, hawkings,
huntings, fishings, peat mosses, turf bogs, coals, coal heughs, rabbits, rabbit
warrens, doves, dovecots, smithies, brewhouses, heath and broom, woods, groves
and thickets, timbers, logs, quarries, stone and lime; with courts and their issues,
fines, hereyelds, bludewits, and merchets of women; with gallows, pit, sok, sak,
thole, thame, wrake, wair, weth, wart, vennysoun, infangtheif, outfangtheif, pit
and gallows; and with common pasture and free ish and entry, and with all others
and sundry their liberties, commodities, profits, easements and their just pertinents
whatsoever, as well not named as named, as well under the ground as above the
ground, far and near, belonging to the foresaid burgh, lands, office and others foresaid with their pertinents, or which may justly belong in any manner of way in time
coming, freely, quietly, fully, wholly, honorably, well and in peace, without any hind-

sine aliquo impedimento, revocatione, contradictione aut obstaculo quocunque.
Reddendo inde, annuatim, predicti prepositus, ballivi, consules et communitas
dicti burgi nostri, corumque successores, nobis et successoribus nostris, aliisque
a nobis jus habentibus, vt infra, videlicet, pro predicto burgo nostro de Stirling,
terris, molendinis, tenementis, acris, rudis, meniis, portubus, littoribus,
pontibus, vijs, passagijs, piscationibus, communibus moris, nundinis, foris
hepdomadariis, custumis, proficuis et privilegiis earundem, aliisque particulariter suprascriptis, divorias aliaque in antiquis infeofamentis earundem
contentis dicto burgo nostro concessis, extendentes ad summam sex librarum
tredecem solidorum et quatuor denariorum monete hujus regni nostri Scotie ;
et pro predicto officio vicecomitatus et jurisdictione eiusdem suprascripto,
justam et debitam administrationem justitie in dicto officio et jurisdictione;
ac pro omnibus et singulis predictis patronatibus, rogatoriis, zenodochijs,
capellanijs, ecclesijs, beneficijs, annuis redditibus, aliisque suprascriptis iisdem
spectantibus, dicti prepositus, ballivi, consules et communitas dicti burgi
nostri, et ministri apud dictas ecclesias, et eleemosynarij et pauperes dictorum
zenodochiorum, eorumque successores, invocande Deum Omnipotentem per pias
religiosas supplices et quotidianas preces suas pro nobis et successoribus nostris,

rance, revocation, contradiction, or obstruction whatsoever.   Paying therefor, yearly,
the said provost, bailies, councillors and community of our said burgh and their successors, to us and our successors, and to others having right from us, as aftermentioned,
that is to say, for our foresaid burgh of Stirling, lands, mills, tenements, acres, roods,
walls, ports, landing places, bridges, ways, passages, fishings, common muirs, fairs,
weekly markets, customs, profits and privileges of the same, and others particularly
above written, the duties and others contained in the old infeftments of the same
granted to our said burgh, amounting to the sum of six pounds thirteen shillings and
four pennies of the money of this our kingdom of Scotland; and for the foresaid office
of sheriff and jurisdiction of the same before written, the just and due administration of justice in the said office and jurisdiction ; and for all and sundry the foresaid patronages, almshouses, hospitals, chaplainrics, churches, benefices, annual
rents, and others above written belonging to the same, the said provost, bailies,
councillors and community of our said burgh, and the ministers at the said churches,
and the pensioners and the poor of the said hospitals, and their successors, calling
upon God Almighty by their pious devout supplications and daily prayers for us

ac perimplendo omnes alias divorias (si que sunt) in antiquis infeofamentis
eorundem contentis, tantum; vnacum servitio burgi debito et consueto pro
omnibus et singulis premissis. In cujus rei testimonium huic presenti carte
nostre[1] magnum sigillum nostrum apponi precepimus. Testibus : Predilectis
nostris consanguineis et consiliariis Joanne comite de Loudoun domino
Terrinzeane et Mauchline, nostro cancellario; Jacobo duce Hamiltoun
marchione Cliddisdalie comite Arranie et Cantabrigie domino Aven et
Innerdeall ; Willielmo Mariscalli comite domino Keith et Altrie, regni nostri
mariscallo; Roberto comite de Roxburgh domino Ker de Cesfuird et Cavertoun, nostri secreti sigilli custode; Willielmo comite de Lauerk domino
Mauchanschyre et Pomount, nostre secretario; dilectis nostris familiaribus
consiliariis, dominis Alexandro Gibsoun de Durie, nostrorum rotulorum registri
et consilij, clerico ; Joanne Hamiltoun de Orbestoun, nostre justiciarie clerico
et Joanne Scot de Scotstarvet, nostre cancellarie directore, militibus. Apud
Halyruidhous, decimo septimo die mensis Novembris anno Domini millesimo
sexcentesimo quadragesimo primo, et anno regni nostri decimo septimo.

and our successors, and fulfilling all other duties (if there are any) contained in the
old infeftments of the same, only; together with service of burgh used and wont for
all and sundry the premises. In witness whereof we have commanded our great
seal to be affixed to this our present charter. Witnesses : Our well beloved cousins
and counsellors, John earl of Loudoun lord Terrinzean and Mauchline, our chancellor,
James duke of Hamilton marquis of Clydesdale earl of Arran and Cambridge
lord Avon and Innerdale ; William earl of Marischall lord Keith and Altrie,
marischall of our kingdom ; Robert earl of Roxburgh lord Ker of Cesfurd and
Cavertoun, keeper of our privy seal ; William earl of Lanark lord Mauchanshyre
and Polmont, our secretary, our well beloved familiar counsellors ; sirs Alexander
Gibson of Durie, clerk of our rolls register and council ; John Hamilton of
Orbestoun, clerk of our justiciary ; and John Scott of Scotstarvet, director of our
chancery, knights. At Holyrood House, the seventeenth day of the month of
November in the year of our Lord one thousand six hundred and forty-one and in
the year of our reign the seventeenth.

[1] " carte nostre confirmationis."—C.

LVI.

EXCERPT from Minutes of Parliamentary Proceedings authorising Ratification of Charter by King Charles I. [No. LV.] to the Burgh of Stirling. Edinburgh, 16th March, 1649.

RATIFCATIOUN in favoures of the brught of Strivelcing of ane chairtour of coufirmatioun grantet be his Maiesties vnquhill Father, of happie memorie, to the said burgh, ratificing and approvcing the particular chairtoures, infeftmentis, giftis, donationes and vtheris thairin contenit. The dait of the foirsaid chairtour is 17th November, 1641.[1]

[Note on margin]:—Graunts ratificatioun, but deloits the clause of any receiviug the customes and what concernes the shirref.

LVII.

GRANT and Commission by the Commissioners of the Parliament of the Commouwealth of England for ordering and managing affairs in Scotland, authorising the inhabitants of Stirling to choose their Magistrates and Officers for the government of the Burgh. Dalkeith, 14th April, 1652.

BY the commissioners of the parliament of the Commonwealth of England for orderinge and managinge affaires in Scotland:—Whereas the Burgh of Sterling haue by theire deputy declared theire acceptauce of the tender of the parliament of the commonwealth of England to be incorporated into the commonwealth of England, and to be one therewith, and haue engaged themselues to liue peaceably vnder and yeild obedience vnto the authority of the Parliament of the commonwealth of England exercised in Scotland, who are therefore taken into the especiall protection of the

[1] It does not appear that any act of parliament containing a formal ratification of King Charles' charter was completed or followed upon the minute above printed.

parliament, and application hath bin since made to vs by the said deputy
prayinge our graunte and commission whereby the said burgh may be
authorised to elect officers to governe the said burgh; vppon serious consideration thereof, and beinge desireous to endeavour by all good waies and meanes
that the people of that towne may haue government and justice administred,
wee by virtue of the authority on that behalfe given vs by the parliament of
the commonwealth of England doe authorise and appoynte the neighbours
and inhabitants of the towne and burgh of Sterling, according to theire former rites and customes, from time to time to nominate and choose theire
magistrates and officers for the government of the said towne and burgh
and liberties thereof till further order; which magistrates and officers from
time to time chosen by them are neerby constituted in theire severall and
respectiue offices and are authorised to proceed in the execution of
theire severall trusts and places and in the execution of the government
within the said towne and burgh and liberties thereof accordinge as
hath bin vsuall and accustomed; provided that in all cases where formerly
the name or stile of Kinge hath bin vsed in the exercise of the aforesaid
governing of the said burgh the name of (the keepers of the libertye of
England by authority of Parliament) be inserted and vsed insteed thereof;
and that the persons from time to time elected and chosen as aforesaid
shall not proceed to the exercise of the said respectiue offices and places
vntill this oath ensuinge be administred to them by such as wee shall
appoynte to administer the same, expressinge at the administration of the
said oath to the said respectiue officers the name of the respectiue offices
they are chosen vnto.

THE OATH:—You shall sweare that you shall be true and faithfull to
the Commonwealth of England as it is now established without a
Kinge or House of Lords; you shall well and truly execute the office
of . . . within the towne and burgh of Sterling and the liberties
thereof accordinge to the best of your skill, knowledge and power.
(Soe help you God.)

And also that the oath heervnderwritten shall be administred to every burgess
or freeman of the said towne and burgh at the time of his admission by such

officer or officers as the oath to burgesses and freemen of the said burgh hath
bin heeretofore vsually administred, (that is to say,)

> You shall sweare that you shall be true and faithfull to the Common-
> wealth of England as it is now established without a King or House of
> Lords; and in order therevnto you shall be obedient to the iust and
> good government of this towne and burgh of Sterling; you shall to the
> best of your power mayntaine and preserve the peace and all the due
> franchises thereof; and accordinge to your knowledge and ability doe
> and performe all such other acts and thinges as doe belonge to a
> burgesse or freeman of the said towne.   (Soe help you God.)

And wee doe heerby declare that wee expect in such elections to be made as
aforesaid due care be taken that all persons chosen be men of integrity and
good affection to the peace and welfare of this Island and otherwyse fitly
qualified for theire trust.

And, lastly, wee appoynte that as well the electors as the persons elected doe
first subscribe the ensuinge declaration, beinge the effect of what the deputy
of the said burgh hath in theire name and on theire behalfe subscrived, (that is
is to say),

> We doe each of vs for himselfe declare our willinge and free acceptance
> of and consent vnto the tender made by the parliament of the Com-
> monwealth of England, that Scotland be incorporated into and made
> one commonwealth with England, that thereby the same government
> that is established in England, without a Kinge or House of Lords,
> vnder the free state and commonwealth of England, may be derived to
> the people of Scotland; and wee promise that wee will liue peaceably
> vnder and yeild obedience vnto the authority of the parliament of the
> Commonwealth of England exercised in Scotland.

Provided that the first election to be made in pursuance heereof be within
tenne daies after the date heereof.   Given vnder our hands, at Dalkeith, the
fourteenth day of April in the yeare of our Lord one thousand six hundred
fifty and two.

(Signed)	H. St. John.	Ri. Deane.
	Robert Tichborne.	R. Salwey.

LVIII.

CHARTER by King Charles the Second confirming to the Provost, Bailies, Council and Community of Stirling the Charter No. LV., and properties, rights and privileges therein contained; and also engaging not to erect burghs of barony or regality, or sanction markets or fairs, within two miles of the Burgh. Whitehall, 22d April, 1678.

CAROLUS, Dei gratia, Magne Britannie, Francie et Hibernie, Rex, fideique Defensor: Omnibus probis hominibus totius terre sue, clericis et laicis, salutem. Sciatis nos, cum avisamento et consensu predilectorum nostrorum consanguineorum et conciliariorum, Joannis comitis de Rothes, supremi cancellarii antiqui regni nostri Scotie; Joannis ducis de Lauderdale, solius secretarii status ejusdem regni; Joannis marchionis de Athole, Archibaldi comitis de Argyle, Alexandri comitis de Kincardine, Wilielmi comitis de Dundonald, et nostri confisi et predilecti consiliarii Caroli Maitland de Haltoun, nostri thesaurarii deputati dicti regni, commissionariorum nostri thesaurii et novarum augmentationum, ac etiam cum avisamento et consensu reliquorum dominorum nostri scaccarii nostrorum commissionariorum, ratificasse, approbasse, et hac presenti carta nostra confirmasse, tenoreque ejusdem ratificare, approbare, ac pro nobis et successoribus nostris pro perpetuo confirmare, ad et in favorem prepositi, balivorum consilii et communitatis burgi de Stirling, et

CHARLES, by the grace of God, King of Great Britain, France and Ireland, and Defender of the Faith: To all good men of his whole land, clerics and laics, greeting. Know ye that we, with advice and consent of our well-beloved cousins and councillors, John earl of Rothes, high chancellor of our ancient kingdom of Scotland; John duke of Lauderdale, sole secretary of state of the same kingdom; John marquis of Athole, Archibald earl of Argyle, Alexander earl of Kincardine, William earl of Dundonald, and our trusty and well-beloved councillor, Charles Maitland of Haltoun, our treasurer depute of the said kingdom, commissioners of our treasury and new augmentations, and also with advice and consent of the remanent lords of our exchequer, our commissioners, have ratified, approved, and by this our present charter confirmed, and by the tenor hereof ratify, approve, and for us and our successors for ever confirm, to and in favor of the provost, bailies, council and community of the

eorum successorum, pro perpetuo, cartam et infeofamentum illis concessas sub
nostro magno sigillo, dedata decimo septimo die mensis Novembris anno
Domini millesimo sexcentesimo quadragesimo primo, vna cum confirmatione
inibi contenta de illorum anterioribus cartis, juribus et infeofamentis, de et
circa erectionem dicti burgi in vno libero burgo regali et jurisdictiones et
privilegia ad prefatum burgum spectantes; de eorum terris, annnis redditibus,
superioritatibus, acris, croftis, toloniis, custumis, casualitatibus, libertatibus et
immunitatibus dicti burgi, et eorum hepdomodariis foris et annuis liberis
nundinis, cum toloniis, custumis [et] casualitatibus ad easdem spectantibus; ac
cum officio vicecomitis infra dictum burgum et territoria ejusdem; et cum
omnibus potestatibus, privilegiis et commoditatibus, ad dictum burgum pertinentibus; et eorum portubus et navium stationibus super aquam de Forth,
cum littoribus, *lie landing places*, antiquis, et novis; cum omnibus privilegiis,
custumis, littorum divoriis, *lie dock silver*, anchoragiis, et aliis casualitatibus
quibuscunque solitis et consuetis; et eorum piscatione super dictam aquam de
Forth et custumis pontis de Stirling solitis ac consuetis; ac de omnibus aliis
juribus et privilegiis qubiscunque sicuti eadem in dicta carta et infeofamento
enumerantur et collocantur,—in omnibus capitibus, articulis, clausulis, tenoribus,

burgh of Stirling, and their successors, for ever, a charter and infeftment granted to
them under our great seal, of date the seventeenth day of the month of November in
the year of our Lord one thousand six hundred and forty-one, together with the
confirmation therein contained of their previous charters, rights and infeftments,
of and concerning the erection of the said burgh into a free burgh royal and the
jurisdictions and privileges belonging to the foresaid burgh; of their lands, annual
rents, superiorities, acres, crofts, tolls, customs, casualties, liberties and immunities of
the said burgh, and their weekly markets and annual free fairs, with the tolls, customs
and casualties belonging to the same; and with the office of sheriff within the said
burgh and territory of the same; and with all powers, privileges and commodities
belonging to the said burgh; and with their ports and harbours upon the water of
Forth, with landing places, old and new; with all privileges, customs, dock silver,
anchorages, and other casualties whatsoever used and wont; and with their fishing
upon the said water of Forth and customs of the bridge of Stirling used and wont;
and of all other rights and privileges whatsoever as the same are enumerated and set
forth in the said charter and infeftment,—in all the heads, articles, clauses, tenors,

contentis et circumstantiis ejusdem, secundum formam et tenorem ejusmodi in omnibus punctis. Insuper, nos, in memoriam nostram revocantes quam fidele et obediens dictum burgum de Stirling est et fuit nobis et illustrissimis predicessoribus nostris temporibus nuper calamitosis, eorumque amicitia et bonum servitium exhibitum nobis quando nos in propria persona eis adfuimus annis Domini millesimo sexcentesimo quinquagesimo et millesimo sexcentesimo quinquagesimo primo, et magnum damnum et detrimentum quod burgenses dicti burgi tempore calamitoso pro eorum fidelitate erga nos perpessi sunt; et nos, etiam, perspicientes quantum prejudicium esset dicto burgo mercature negotiationi et jurisdictionibus ejusdem si aliqua vrbs vel villa intra duo millia passuum erigeretur et in burgo baronie vel regalitatis, vel si alique annue nundine vel fora hepdomodaria tenerentur vel observarentur intra duo millia passuum dicti burgi; et nos, firmiter statuentes opem adhibere et animum addere dicto burgo ac burgenses ejusdem securos reddere contra cuncta prejudicia et detrimenta istius generis: Igitur nos, pro nobismetipsis et successoribus nostris, in verbo principis, promittimus quod nunquam erigemus, nec patiemur erigi, quamvis vrbem vel villam intra duo millia passuum dicti burgi de Stirling in burgum baronie seu regalitatis, neque concedemus

contents and circumstances of the same, according to the form and tenor thereof in all points. Moreover, we, recalling to our remembrance how faithful and obedient the said burgh of Stirling is and has been to us and our most illustrious predecessors in the late troublous times, and their friendship and good services shown to us when we were present with them in proper person in the years of our Lord one thousand six hundred and fifty and one thousand six hundred and fifty-one, and the great damage and loss that the burgesses of the said burgh suffered for their fidelity towards us in the troublous time; and we, also, perceiving how great a prejudice it might be to the said burgh, trade, merchandise and jurisdictions of the same if any town or village within two miles should be erected into a burgh of barony or regality, or if any yearly fair or weekly markets should be held or observed within two miles of the said burgh; and we, firmly resolving to yield support and add encouragement to the said burgh, and to render the burgesses thereof secure against all prejudice and loss of that sort: Therefore we, for ourselves and our successors, promise to them, on the word of a prince, that we shall never erect, nor suffer to be erected, any town or village within two miles of the said burgh of Stirling into a burgh of

privilegium habendi seu tenendi hepdomodaria fora nec annuas nundinas
intra duo millia passuum dicti burgi; et si quevis talis donatio seu signatura
(per inadvertentiam) nostris manibus expedietur, nos stricte prohibemus et
inhibemus dominis nostri thesaurarii, et scaccarii, presentibus et futuris
eandem in scaccario expedire vel cartam desuper concedere; cum plena
potestate burgo nostro de Stirling declaratorias sententias desuper contra
cunctos interesse habentes prosequi.   Quinetiam ordinamus presentem cartam
nostram in proximo nostro parliamento ratificatum iri; et ad hunc effectum
status nostri parliamenti eandem conformiter ratificare authorizamus.   In
cujus rei testimonium huic presenti carte nostre confirmationis nagnum
sigillum nostrum appendi mandavimus.   Testibus: predilecto nostro familiari
consiliario, domino Thoma Wallace de Craigie, milite baronetto, nostre justiciarie clerico, et domini Wilielmo Ker, milite, nostre cancellarie directore.   Apud
aulam nostram de Whythall, vigesimo secundo die mensis Aprilis anno Domini
millesimo sexcentesimo septuagesimo octavo et anno regni nostri trigesimo.

[Indorsed thus]:—Written to the great scale and registrat the tuenty
day of September, 1678, (Signed) COKBURNE.   Scaled att Edinburghe the
tuentie sext day of September 1678.   xxiiij li. (Signed) Jo. CUNYNGHAME.

barony or regality, nor shall we grant the privilege to have or hold weekly markets
or annual fairs within two miles of the said burgh; and if any such gift or signature
(by inadvertence) is expede under our hands, we strictly prohibit and forbid the
lords of our treasury and exchequer, present and future, to expede the same in
exchequer or to grant a charter thereupon; with full power to our burgh of Stirling
to pursue declaratory sentences thereupon against all having interest.   Moreover,
we ordain that our present charter shall be ratified in our next parliament; and to
this effect we authorise the estates of our parliament to ratify the same accordingly.
In witness whereof, we have commanded our great seal to be appended to this our
present charter of confirmation.   Witnesses: our well-beloved familiar councillor,
Sir Thomas Wallace of Craigie, knight baronet, clerk of our justiciary; and Sir
William Ker, knight, director of our chancery.   At our court of Whythall, the
twenty-second day of the month of April in the year of our Lord one thousand six
hundred and seventy-eight and of our reign the thirtieth year.

LIX.

CHARTER by King Charles the Second confirming to the Preceptors of
Spittell's Hospital the lands o* Southfield with the teinds thereof.
Edinburgh, 15th February, 1684.

CAROLUS, Dei gratia, Magne Britannie, Francie et Hibernie, Rex, fideique
defensor: Omnibus probis hominibus totius terre sue, clericis et laicis,
salutem. Sciatis nos, cum avisamento et consensu [ut in alijs cartis consimilis
date] dedisse, concessisse, disposuisse, et hac presenti carta confirmasse,
tenoreque ejusdem dare, concedere, disponere, proque nobis et successoribus
nostris pro perpetuo confirmare, dilectis nostris Alexandro Edmonston,
mercatori, et Joanni Wallace, decano calciarium, burgensibus burgi de
Stirling, tanquam presentibus preceptoribus inferioris hospitij fundati in
burgo nuncupati *Spittells Hospitall*, eorumque successoribus preceptoribus
ejusdem, pro usu et utilitate pauperum ejusdem in perpetuum eorumque
assignatis, hereditarie et irredimabiliter, totas et integras illas quadraginta
acras terrarum vel eo circa nuncupatas *the Southfield*, cum decimis garbalibus
ejusdem inclusis, tenentibus, tenandriis et libere tenentium servitijs, alijsque
divorijs et servitijs, usitatis et consuetis, solvi de predictis acris et decimis
prescriptis, jacentes infra parochiam de Stirling et vicecomitatum ejusdem,

CHARLES, by the grace of God, King of Great Britain, France and Ireland,
and defender of the faith: To all good men of his whole land, clerics and laics,
greeting. Know ye that we, with advice and consent [as in other charters of the
same date] have given, granted, disposed, and by this present charter confirmed, and
by the tenor hereof give, grant, dispone and for us and our successors for ever confirm
to our well-beloved Alexander Edmonston, merchant, and John Wallace, deacon of
the shoemakers, burgesses of the burgh of Stirling, as present preceptors of the laigh
hospital founded in the burgh called Spittells Hospitall, and their successors, preceptors of the same, for the use and behoof of the poor thereof and their assignees
for ever, heritably and irredeemably, all and whole those forty acres of land or thereby
called the Southfield, with the teind sheaves thereof included, tenants, tenandries and
services of free tenants and other duties and services used and wont, to be paid of
the foresaid acres and teinds before written, lying within the parish of Stirling and
sheriffdom thereof, as the same are presently possessed by the vassals and tenants

prout eedem per vassallos et tenentes dictarum acrarum presenter possesse,
et bondate inter viam publicam ad burgum de Stirling ducentem ex
orientali, viam que ducit ad villam de Cambusbarron ex boreali, terras
de Torbrex et Whytehill ex [occidentali] et australi partibus. Quequidem
quadraginta acre terrarum et decime cum pertinentiis earundem Sic jacentes
et bondate ut supra, perprius hereditarie pertinuerunt ad dominum
Joannem Stirling de Keir per eum de nobis immediate tente, et per
ejus procuratores suo nomine specialiter et legitime constitutos, virtute
procuratorie resignationis in dispositione dictarum terrarum contente per
dictum dominum Joannem Stirling de Keir facta et concessa in favorem
Joannis Martine et Georgii Andersone, tunc preceptorum dicti hospitii,
corumque successorum preceptorum ejusdem, pro usu et utilitate pauperum
earundem, de data decimo quinto die mensis Novembris anno millesimo
sexcentessimo octogesimo secundo, debite et legitime resignate, sursum red-
dite et extradonate, erant in manibus dicti marchionis de Queensberry[1] et
reliquorum dominorum commissionariorum Scaccarij tanquam in manibus
nostris, in favorem proque novo infeofamento earundem dicto Joanni Martine
et Georgio Andersone, tunc preceptoribus dicti inferioris hospitii, eorumque

of the said acres and bounded between the public road leading to the burgh of
Stirling on the east, the road which leads to the town of Cambusbarron on the
north, the lands of Torbrex and Whytehill on the [west] and south parts. Which
forty acres of land and teinds with the pertinents thereof, lying and bounded
as above, formerly belonged heritably to Sir John Stirling of Keir, held by
him immediately of us, and by his procurators in his name specially and lawfully
constituted by virtue of procuratory of resignation contained in a disposition of the
said lands made and granted by the said Sir John Stirling of Keir in favor of
John Martine and George Andersone, then preceptors of the said hospital, and
their successors preceptors thereof for the use and behoof of the poor of the same,
of date of the fifteenth day of the month of November, in the year one thousand
six hundred and eighty-two, were duly and lawfully resigned, upgiven and over-
given, in the hands of the said marquis of Queensberry[1] and remanent lords
commissioners of exchequer as in our hands, in favor and for new infeftment of
the same to be made, given and granted, to the said John Martine and George

[1] One of the consenters to the charter.

successoribus preceptoribus ejusdem in perpetuum, ad usum et utilitatem
pauperum ejusmodi, eorumque assignatis, hereditarie et irredimabiliter, in
debita et competenti forma uti congruit, faciendo, dando et concedendo,
prout authentica instrumenta desuper suscepta in manibus Davidis Forrester, notarii publici, de data . . . latius proportant.   Tenendas et
habendas, totas et integras predictas quadraginta acras terrarum aut eo
circa nuncupatas *the Southfield*, cum decimis garbalibus earundem inclusis,
tenentibus, tenandriis et libere tenentium servitiis, jacentes et bondatas
ut dictum est, dicto Alexandro Edmanston et Joanni Wallace, presentibus
preceptoribus dicti inferioris hospitii, eorumque successoribus, preceptoribus
ejusdem, pro usu et utilitate pauperum ejusmodi, eorumque assignatis predictis in perpetuum, de nobis nostrisque successoribus in feodo et hereditate
in perpetuum, per omnes rectas metas suas, antiquas et divisas, prout jacent
in longitudine et latitudine, etc.   Reddendo inde, annuatim, preceptores
dicti hospitii eorumque successores, preceptores ejusdem, eorumque assignati
predicti, nobis nostrisque successoribus summam duodecim librarum monete
Scotie tanquam antiquam feudifirmam de predictis terris et decimis perprius solvi solitam et consuetam, et summam viginti sex solidorum et octo

Andersone then preceptors of the said laigh Hospital, and their successors preceptors thereof for ever, for the use and behoof of the poor of the same, and their
assignees, heritably and irredeemably, in due and competent form as accords, as
authentic instruments taken thereupon in the hands of David Forrester, notary
public, of date . . . more fully bear.   To hold and to have all and whole the
foresaid forty acres of lands or thereby, called the Southfield, with teind sheaves
of the same included, tenants, tenandries, and services of free tenants, lying and
bounded as said is, to the said Alexander Edmonston and John Wallace, present
preceptors of the said laigh hospital, and their successors, preceptors thereof, for
the use and behoof of the poor of the same and their assignees aforesaid for ever,
of us and our successors in fee and heritage for ever, by all their right marches, old
and divided, as they lie in length and breadth, etc.   Paying therefor, yearly, the
preceptors of the said hospital and their successors, preceptors thereof, and their
assignees aforesaid, to us and our successors, the sum of twelve pounds Scots money
as the ancient feu farm of the foresaid lands and teinds formerly used and wont
to be paid, and the sum of twenty-six shillings and eight pennies money foresaid, in

denariorum monete predicte in augmentationem rentalis, extendentes in
integro ad summam tredecim librarum sex solidorum et octo denariorum
monete predicte, ad duos anni terminos festa, videlicet, Pentecostes et Sancti
Martini in hieme per equales portiones nomine feudifirme ; et duplicando
dictam feudifirmam primo anno introitus cujuslibet heredis ad predictas terras
prout usus est feudifirme, et observando et perimplendo reliquas conditiones
(si que sint) in antiquis infeofamentis earundem contentas, pro omni alio
onere. . . . . [1] In cujus rei testimonium, huic presenti carte nostre
magnum sigillum nostrum appendi mandavimus. Testibus : . . . Apud
Edinburgum, decimo quinto die mensis Februarii anno Domini millesimo
sexcentesimo octogesimo quarto regnique nostri trigesimo sexto.

augmentation of rental, extending in whole to the sum of thirteen pounds six shillings
and eight pennies money foresaid, at two terms in the year, that is to say the feasts
of Whitsunday and Martinmas in winter by equal portions ; and doubling the said
feu farm the first year of the entry of each heir to the foresaid lands as use is in feu
farm, and observing and implementing the other conditions (if any be) contained in
the ancient infeftments of the same, for all other burden. . . . . [1] In witness
whereof we have commanded our great seal to be appended to this our present
charter. Witnesses : . . . . At Edinburgh, the fifteenth day of the month of
February in the year of our Lord one thousand six hundred and eighty-four, and of
our reign the thirty-sixth year.

LX.

ACT of Parliament appointing two Fairs, one in December and another in
    January, to be held in Stirling yearly.   Edinburgh, 14th September,
    1705.

OUR Sovereign Lady, with the special advice and consent of the estates of
parliament, ordains and appoints two fairs, one upon the first Tuesday of
December and the other on the last Tuesday of January, to be holden yearly
in all time comeing at and within the burgh of Stirling ; and gives and grants
to the magistrates and council of the said burgh, and their successors in office,

----
[1] Precept of sasine inserted here.

for the behoove of the community of the same, the right and priviledge of keeping the said fairs for all kinds of merchandice, with all the tolls, customes and casualities thereof, and all other liberties, priviledges and advantages used and wont to belong to any haveing the priviledge of keeping fairs and mercats within this kingdom.

XI.

ACT of Parliament appointing two yearly Fairs to be held upon the lands and barony of Balquidrock; with Protestation by the commissioner of Stirling against the same. Edinburgh, 14th September, 1705.

(1). ACT OF PARLIAMENT.

OUR Sovereign Lady and estates of parliament, considering that fairs and mercats in convenient places tend much to the good and advantage of the inhabitants thereof and of her Maiesties other leidges dwelling near thereto, and that it is very fit for these ends to authorize two fairs yearly on the dayes following upon the lands and barony of Balquidrock in the shire of Stirling and belonging to John Murray of Touchaddam, do therefore by thir presents appoint two fairs yearly, one upon the first Tuesday of July and the other on the second Thursday of November to be kept in all time comeing upon the lands and barony of Balquidrock, and have given and granted and hereby give and grant to the said John Murray, his heirs and successors, the right and priviledge of keeping the said yearly fairs for all kinds of merchandice, with all the tolls, customes and casualities thereof, and all liberties, priviledges and advantage used and wont to belong to any haveing the priviledge of keeping fairs and mercats within this kingdom.

(2). PROTESTATION.

There was a protestation against the said fair of Balquidrock, granted to the laird of Touchaddam, taken by the commissioner afternamed for the burgh of Stirling, who gave in the same in writing, to the tenor following:—I Colonell John Erskine, lieutenent governour of the Castle of Stirling, commissioner to the parliament for the burgh of Stirling, do in name of the said burgh protest against the fairs craved by John Murray of Touchaddam to be keeped within the barony of Balquidrock belonging to him, lying within two miles of the said burgh of Stirling, in respect the said burgh has an charter from King Charles the Second bearing that his Majesty nor his successors should not erect a burgh of barony or regality nor grant a priviledge of weekly mercats or yearly fairs within two miles of the said burgh, and upon the said charter the said toun has a decreet of declarator; and thereupon I ask and take instruments (that the said burgh may not be prejudged of their rights and priviledges) in the hands of Sir James Murray of Philiphaugh, one of the senatours of the colledge of justice and lord clerk register. In witness whereof I have written and subscribed thir presents, at Edinburgh, the fourteenth of September one thousand seven hundred and five years. *Sic Subscribitur:* Jo. Erskine. And thereupon took instruments.

APPENDIX.

APPENDIX.

1.—Charter by King Robert the Second, by which he gave, granted and confirmed to Richard of Wauflete that tenement lying in the town of Strivelyne which belonged to the late Hugh son of Thomas, and which belonged to the King on account that the said Hugh was a bastard, and died without heir of his body lawfully begotten. To be held by the said Richard and his heirs of the King and his heirs in fee and heritage, with all freedoms and easements, as freely as the said Hugh held it, for rendering to the King and other lords of the fee the services due and wont. In witness whereof the King commanded his seal to be appended. Witnesses : William, and John the chancellor, bishops of the churches of St. Andrews and Dunkeld; John the King's first-born son, earl of Carric, steward of Scotland; Robert earl of Fyf and of Menteth, the King's well-beloved son; William earl of Douglas and of Marr, the king's kinsman; Archibald of Douglas and Robert of Erskyne, the King's kinsmen, knights. At Edinburgh, 15th August, 13th year of the King's reign [1383].

[The charter is in the following terms]:—" Robertus, Dei gracia, Rex Scottorum: omnibus probis hominibus tocius terre, sue clericis et laycis, salutem. Sciatis nos dedisse, concessisse, et hac presenti carta nostra confirmasse Ricardo de Wauflete illud tenementum iacens in villa de Strivelyne quod fuit quondam Hugonis filii Thome et quod ad nos pertinet eo quod dictus Hugo fuit bastardus, et obiit sine herede de corpore suo legittime procreato. Tenendum et habendum eidem Ricardo et heredibus suis de nobis et heredibus nostris in feodo et hereditate, per omnes rectas metas et diuisas suas, cum omnibus et singulis libertatibus, commoditatibus, aysiamentis et iustis pertinenciis quibuscunque ad dictum tenementum cum pertinenciis spectantibus, seu quoquo modo iuste spectare valentibus in futurum, adeo libere et quiete, plenarie, integre et honorifice, in omnibus et per omnia, sicut illud tenuit dictus Hugo. Faciendo inde nobis et aliis dominis feodi dicti tenementi seruicia debita et consueta. In cuius rei testimonium presenti carte nostre nostrum precipimus apponi sigillum. Testibus: venerabilibus in Christo patribus, Willelmo et Johanne; cancellario nostro, Sanctiandree et Dunkeldensis ecclesiarum episcopis; Johanne primogenito nostro de Carric, senescallo Scocie; Roberto de Fyf et de Menteth filio nostro dilecto, Willelmo de Douglas et de Marre consanguineo nostro, comitibus; Archibaldo de Douglas et Roberto de Erskyne consanguineis nostro, militibus. Apud Edynburgh quintodecimo die Augusti anno regni nostri terciodecimo."

2.—Letters Patent by Robert, bishop of Dunblane, narrating that before him, sitting in judgment in his cathedral church of Dunblane, compeared a venerable man, Sir John of Acheray, treasurer of the said cathedral church, and John Brady, burgess of the burgh of Strivelynge, procurators and commissioners of honorable men, the provost, bailies and community of the said burgh, to the effect under-written, and presented a charter by King James the Second to the provost, bailies, burgesses and community of the burgh of Stirling of the patronage of St. James' Hospital dated at Strivelinge, 24th June, 1456 [No. xxiii., *antea* p. 36]; after examination and publication of which charter, the bishop, at the supplication of the said procurators, ordained the same to be transumed, and the transumpt to have the same force and validity as the original charter, and commanded the present letters patent containing the said transumpt to be written and published and confirmed with his seal. Done in the said church 21 November, 1457. Witnesses: John Cristini, Macolm Drummonde, canons of the church, and others. Certified by John of Spens and John Scot, priests of the diocese of Dunblane and notaries public. (Seal awanting.)

3.—Charter by William Bully, perpetual chaplain of the altar of the Holy Cross, founded and situated in the parish church of the burgh of Striviline, whereby for a certain sum of money paid to him in his urgent necessity he sold and granted to an honorable man, Macolm Flemyng, son and apparent heir of a noble and potent lord, Robert lord le Flemyng, the tenement with the pertinents described in charter No. xxiv. [*antea* p. 39]. To be held by him, his heirs and assignees, of the King for payment of the royal ferm and service of burgh used and wont; and paying to the altar of St. Ninian in the parish church and the perpetual chaplain thereof 6 s. 8 d., and to the altar of St. Thomas, the apostle, and perpetual chaplain thereof, 26 s. 8 d. In testimony whereof the seal of the granter, with the common seal of the burgh, solicited from the community assembled in the tolbooth, are appended. Witnesses: William Striveline of Ratherne, Macolme Forestar of Torwoud, George Striveline, John Striveline and Adam Mure, with sundry others. Dated at Striveline, 27th February 1471-2. (Seals awanting.)

4.—Charter by James III., King of Scots, under his great seal, confirming the foregoing charter by William Buly to Macolm Flemyng. Dated at Edinburgh 10th November, 1472. (Seal awanting.)

5.—Charter by Robert Gelis, elder, son and heir of the deceased Robert Gelis, burgess of the burgh of Striveline, and John Gelis, younger, son and apparent heir of the said Robert Gelis, whereby for a certain sum of money they sold and granted to a venerable man, Sir John Hastings, canon of the cathedral church of Dunblane, and his heirs and assignees, an annuulrent of six shillings payable furth of a tenement of master John Spaldyne, dean of Brechin, with the pertinents, lying within the said burgh on the north side of the High Street, between the land of John Kyrkwoud on the west, and the land of the deceased Robert Haket on the east. In witness whereof, because the granters had not seals, the said Robert Gelis senior procured to be appended the seal of a provident man John Bolat, burgess, and John Gelis procured the seal of a provident man John Gourlay, one of the bailies of the said burgh and giver of sasine of the said annual rent. Witnesses: John Lyntonn, John Glasgw, Thomas Fersithtson, John Fersithtson, Nicholas Taylyour, William Benny, John Auldcorn, Michael Taylyour, Alexander Brade, Alexander Kirkwoud and Sir James Darow, chaplain and notary public, with sundry others who were also present at the giving of sasine. Dated at Stirling 11th April, 1475.

6.—Instrument of sasine setting forth that in presence of the notary and witnesses, personally appeared a provident man, Gilbert Bechat, burgess of the burgh of Striveline, and resigned in the hands of David Murray, one of the bailies of the burgh, an annualrent of six shillings Scots upliftable furth of his tenement with the pertinents lying on the north side of the High Street, between the land of Robert Norton on the west and the land of Thomas Makfarlane on the east, by delivery of one penny; whereupon the bailie gave to a venerable man, Sir John Hastings, canon of the cathedral church of Dunblane, and his heirs and assignees, sasine of the annualrent, by exhibition of a penny as the custom of burghs is, conform to the tenor of a charter granted by the said Gilbert to him. Done on the ground of the said tenement, 18 April, 1478. Witnesses: Sirs Symone Joffrason, Robert Redehuch, John Malloch, Thomas Ason, chaplains; John Young, Thomas Makferlane, Robert Norton, John Murray, Thomas Smytht, John Robison,

2 A

John Huny, John Moden, John M'Kennyr, John Offeris and Patrick Gray ; with many others. James Darow, priest of St. Andrew's diocese, notary. (Seal awanting.)

7.—Charter by Adam Bully, burgess of the burgh of Striveline, whereby he, being in his legal power, moved with piety and meditation, prompted with the zeal of devotion and compunction, for the weal of his soul and of the souls of his progenitors and successors, for the honour and reverence of the holy and undivided Trinity and of the most blessed Virgin Mary and of all saints, gave, granted, assigned and confirmed for ever to the holy and undivided Trinity and altar of the same, founded and situated within the parish church of the Holy Cross of the said burgh by the deceased Sir Thomas Bully (of good memory) canon of the cathedral church of Glasgow, and to Sir Robert Symsone, perpetual chaplain of the said altar and his successors, perpetual chaplains thereof, celebrating divine service thereat, four merks Scots of annual rent to be uplifted furth of the granter's four merk lands of Ermore with the pertinents lying within the sheriffdom of Perth, wherein Donald Gilfulansone and Patrick Gilfulane dwelt and which they possessed in farm, for perpetual union and annexation to the said altar: To be held by the said altar of the Holy Trinity and Sir Robert Symsone, perpetual chaplain thereof, for his life, and by his successors after his decease celebrating divine service therein, from the granter and his heirs, of the holy and undivided Trinity and the blessed Virgin Mary, in fee and heritage, in pure alms forever, the said chaplains giving yearly at the said altar and daily when disposed a solemn divine service of masses and offering of prayers for the weal of the soul of the said Adam Bully and of the souls of his parents, progenitors and successors. Contains a clause of warrandice by the said Adam Bully and his heirs under obligation of all his lands and goods. Witnesses : master Duncan Bully, rector of Kynnel, Sirs David Robisone provost of the collegiate church of Maybole, John Hastingis canon of Dunblane, John Andrew rector of Mukart ; Mathew Forester, Duncan Forester, Herbert Murray, William Symsone, Alexander Muschet and James Redehuch, burgesses of the said burgh. Dated at the burgh of Stirling, 2 September, 1479. (Seal awanting.)

8.—Letters by the provost, bailies, councillors and community of the burgh of Striveline attesting that a discreet man Sir James Darow, perpetual chaplain of the altar of the Holy Cross founded and situated within the parish church of the said burgh, compeared before them sitting in judgment in their tolbooth in four of their chief courts successively and made process respecting a tenement with the pertinents commonly called Wardanis Land, lying within the said burgh between the land of the deceased Gilbert Legat on the north side and the parish church on the south side, on account of nonpayment for several years to him and his said altar of an annualrent of three shillings payable from the tenement, and that at the last diet of the courts he asked judgment that the possession of the tenement should, in default of payment of the amount, revert to him, and obtained pledge respecting this; after which the opposite party having been often called at the door of the court to compear and defend his cause, or satisfy the chaplain respecting the arrears of the annualrent, with damages and expenses of process, and not compearing, the court after consultation, by the mouth of Thomas Caithkyn, their judiciar or dempster, adjudged possession of the tenement to him; whereupon Charles Rede, one of the bailies of the burgh, give sasine to the chaplain and caused it to be publicly proclaimed that if any one having right or interest wished to reclaim the tenement they should come within the lawful time and satisfy as above and obtain peaceable possession of the tenement for ever as the order of law required. Sealed with the burgh seal and that of the bailie at Stirling, 20 November, 1481. Witnesses: Alexander Cunynghame of Auchinbowy; Duncan Forester, provost; Thomas Cragingelt, John Aisone, bailies; Richard Redehuch, James Redchuch, Alexander Muschet, John Abbircrummy, Sir Symon Joffrasone, James Cunynghame, Alexander Nortoun and Alexander Forester with sundry others. (Seals awanting.)

9.—Letters by the provost, bailies, councillors and community of the burgh of Striveline attesting that a discreet man, Sir Robert Symsone, perpetual chaplain of the altar of the Holy Trinity, founded and situated within the parish church of the burgh, compeared before them in four of their chief courts successively and made process [in the same form and with a similar result as narrated in No. 8] respecting a tenement of the deceased John Wourthy, with the pertinents, lying in the Castle Vennel, on account of nonpayment for several years to him and his said altar of an annualrent of fifteen shillings Scots payable from the tenement; also respecting a tenement of the deceased Bartholomew Skynnar with the pertinents lying within the said burgh between the land of John Galloway on the west side and the land of Sir James Darow on the east side on account of nonpayment of an annualrent of ten shillings Scots; and also respecting a tenement of the deceased David Baxster with the pertinents lying within the said burgh between the land of the deceased Thomas Tailyefer on the west side and the land of Adam Bulle on the east side, on account of nonpayment of an annualrent of ten shillings Scots. Mathew Gowane, dempster; David Murray, John Crag, John Aysone, bailie.

Sealed with the burgh seal and that of the bailies at Striveline, 2 December, 1489. (Seals awanting.)

10.—Instrument narrating that in presence of the notary and witnesses compeared a provident man Andrew Nortoun, burgess of the burgh of Striveling, and by overgiving of a penny resigned from himself and his heirs an annual rent of two shillings and fourpence to be uplifted yearly from a piece of land with the pertinents belonging to William Forsytht, burgess of the said burgh, lying within the said burgh in the vennel of the blessed and glorious Virgin Mary called *le Mary Wynde* on the west side of the High Street, between a waste land on the north side and the land of James Scot on the south side, in the hands of an honourable man, James Spettale, then one of the bailies of the said burgh, for the weal of his soul and the souls of his friends and in favour of the altar of the precious blood of our Lord Jesus Christ, founded and situated within the parish church of the Holy Rood of the said burgh. Which resignation being so made the said bailie gave sasine of the said annual rent to a discreet man, Sir John Clerk, alias Inglisman, chaplain of the said altar, in name and behalf of the said precious blood of our Lord Jesus Christ, and perpetual chaplains, his successors at the said altar, in pure and perpetual alms, by exhibition of a penny as the manner of burghs is and according to the tenor of the charter of foundation of the said altar. Done on the ground of the said piece of land, 30 August, 1502. Witnesses: John Aisoun, Alexander Aisoun, William Cosoure, William Haldane and others. Certified by Robert Cunynghame, clerk of the diocese of St. Andrews and notary public, and confirmed by the seal of the said bailie. (Seal awanting.)

11.—Instrument setting forth that in presence of the notary and witnesses personally appeared a provident man, Walter George, burgess of the burgh of Strivelin, and, not swayed by force or fear but of his pure and free will, moved with devout zeal and not unmindful of the salvation of his soul, conveyed and granted and perpetually confirmed to God Almighty and the blessed and glorious Virgin Mary and all saints, and to the perpetual chaplains of the parish church of the said burgh and their successors celebrating divine service there, an anvil, acquired by his own proper industry, standing in his workshop, with the stock thereof, for an exequy and anniversary to be celebrated yearly for ever on the day of the obit of the said Walter and Elene his spouse for the salvation of their souls, as the manner is. For effecting which the said Walter resigned the foresaid anvil and stock by delivery of earth and stone in the hands of an honorable man, Thomas Cragingelt, one of the bailies of the burgh, reserving freely the said stock and anvil to the granter for his life ; whereupon the bailie gave sasine of the same to a discreet man, Thomas Zoilay, chaplain, and bailie in name and on behalf of all and sundry the perpetual chaplains of the said parish church. Done in the workshop of the said Walter. 16 February, 1503-4. Witnesses: Walter Redehucht, John M'Kennare, John Caldare, George Alanson, Alexander Nychole, James Ranald, John Millar, John Ycuthstoun, John Loke, John Lange, John Peckone, John Quarroure and Sirs William Malux and Patrick Broun, chaplains, with sundry others. Thomas Kirkcaldy notary. (Seal awanting.)

12.—Charter by David Makilwane, son of the deceased Donald Makilwane, burgess of the burgh of Striveling, whereby for a sum of money paid to him in his urgent necessity, he sold and disponed to a discreet man, Sir John Aysoun, chaplain, his heirs and assignees, an annualrent of sixteen shillings yearly upliftable furth of a tenement of the deceased Andrew Murisoun, back and fore, with the pertinents, lying within the burgh between the land of the deceased John Patonsoun on the east and the land of David Greg on the west ; to be held of the King in fee and heritage. Sealed at Stirling, 26th March 1506. Witnesses : James Spetale, Edward Spetale, James Crom and John Lyell with sundry others. (Seal awanting.)

13.—Instrument narrating that, in presence of the notary and witnesses, compeared personally a provident man, Alexander Craig, burgess of the burgh of Striveling, and of his own free and spontaneous will, as was well known to the notary and as himself publicly acknowledged, resigned and quitclaimed an annual rent of seven shillings to be uplifted yearly from the tenement of Henry Neilsoun lying within the said burgh on the east side of the High Street, between the land of Andrew Camroun on the north and the land of James Mentetht, dwelling in the lordship of Mentetht, on the south side, with all right which he for himself or his heirs could claim in or to the same, by exhibition of one penny in the hands of an honorable man, James Spetall, then one of the bailies of the said burgh, for sasine thereof to be given to an honorable man, John Broune, then dean of gild, of the said burgh. Which resignation being so made the said James Spetall, bailie, in virtue of his office of bailliary, gave sasine of the said annual rent of seven shillings to the said John Broune by delivery of one penny in his hands as use was ; to be uplifted at the two usual terms of the year Whitsunday and Martinmas in winter by equal portions. Done on the ground of the said tenement, 18 February 1509-10, in presence of Henry Neilsoun, Thomas Drew, William Quhite, John Broune alias Swyne, John Myllare, Robert Stevnson and Sir David Nortoun, chaplain. Certified by Andrew Nortoun, clerk, of the diocese of St. Andrews, notary public, and confirmed by the seal of the said James Spetall, bailie. (Seal awanting.)

14.—Instrument setting forth that in presence of the notary and witnesses personally appeared an honorable man, George Crechtoun of Brethirtoun, burgess of the burgh of Strivoling, moved by zeal of devotion and holy motive, coming to the fore part of his tenement of land conveyed to him by John Douglas, burgess, between the land of William Danson on the east and the land of Richard Narne on the west, and there resigned in the hands of John Bully, one of the bailies, an annualrent of ten shillings Scots payable yearly furth of the fore part of the said tenement in favor of the perpetual chaplains of the parish church of the Holy Cross for ever; the said chaplains and their successors making therefor, for the salvation of the souls of the said George and of Alisone Mailvile, his spouse, and of their parents and successors and all friends and benefactors, and for the souls of all the faithful dead, pious offerings of funeral services and an anniversary once in the year, according to the form and tenor of the first foundation and rental of exequies and anniversaries founded and wont to be done in the said parish church. Whereupon the bailie gave sasine of the said annualrent to a discreet man, Sir Andrew Mortoun, chaplain and curate of the said parish church, and also procurator and bailie of the foresaid perpetual chaplains, in pure and perpetual alms according to the tenor of the foundation and rental foresaid. Witnesses : Sirs James Craig, elder, Walter Steward, William Aitoun, William Thomson, James Aikman, James Crechtoun, chaplains, David Bully, and sundry others. Andrew Nortoun, notary. Stirling, 4th August, 1511. (Seal awanting.)

15.—Instrument narrating that, in presence of the notary and witnesses, an honorable man, John Browne, burgess of the burgh of Strivoline, by overgiving of a penny, surrendered in the hands of an honorable man, John Bully, then one of the bailies of the said burgh, in favour of the altar of the precious and holy blood of our Lord Jesus Christ, founded and situated within the parish church of the Holy Rood of the said burgh, an annual rent of seven shillings yearly to be uplifted from a tenement of Henry Nelsone, weaver, lying within the said burgh in the vennel of the blessed and glorious Virgin Mary called le Mary Wynde, on the east side of the High Street, between the land of Adam Galloway on the south and the land of Nicholas Donaldsone on the north, and that for the weal of his own soul and the souls of his parents, predecessors, successors, friends, and all the faithful dead. Which resignation being so made the said John Bully delivered state and sasine of the said annual rent of seven shillings to a discreet man, Sir Patrick Clerk, chaplain of the said altar, on behalf of the said holy blood and to his successors, perpetual chaplains serving at the said altar, in free and perpetual alms, by exhibition of a penny as the use of burghs is, and according to the tenor of the charter of foundation of the said altar. Done on the ground of the said tenement, 4 December, 1515. Witness: Gilbert Fergussone, John Aliane, Robert Richartsone, John Michael, Robert Gervy, and others, burgesses of the said burgh. Certified by James Fresone, clerk, of the diocese of St. Andrews, notary public, with appending of the seal of the said bailie. (Seal awanting.)

16.—Instrument setting forth that, in presence of the notary and witnesses, personally appeared an honorable man, Duncan Forestar of Garden, knight, moved with devotion, not led, constrained or compelled by force or fear, but of his own free will, and passed to his two and a half rigs of land lying at the dovecot of John Bully next the High Street and there resigned an annualrent of thirteen shillings and fourpence upliftable therefrom yearly, and that in the hands of a worthy man John Aitkin, then one of the bailies of the burgh, for sasine to be given to the founded chaplains of the parish church of the Holy Cross. Whereupon the bailie gave sasine to a discreet man Sir James Aikman, chaplain, in name of the chaplains founded for the annual celebration of funeral services for the souls of Sir Duncan Margaret Forsith and Margaret Bothuele, his wives, and of all the faithful dead. Witnesses: Thomas Youngman, James Crag, chaplains; George Schaw of Knokhill, Alexander Murray, James Scot, Alexander Forestar, and sundry others. William Litstar, notary. Done on the ground of the said rigs, 12 April, 1518. (Seal awanting.)

17.—Instrument narrating that, in presence of the notary and witnesses, an honorable man David Greg, burgess of the burgh of Striveling, resigned and quitclaimed from him and his heirs in favour of the altar of the precious and holy blood of our Lord Jesus Christ, founded and situated within the parish church of the Holy Rood of the foresaid burgh of Striveling, an annual rent of five shillings yearly to be uplifted from the tenement and croft of Henry Ran, lying in the vennel of the blessed and glorious Virgin Mary, on the east side thereof, between the common vennel on the south side and the croft of the late Sir Robert Mure on the north side, in the hands of an honorable man, Richard Narne, then one of the bailies of the said burgh, by delivery of a penny as use is, for the weal of his soul, the soul of Jonet Wilyeamesoun, his spouse, his parents, predecessors, successors, and all the faithful dead. Which resignation being so made the foresaid Richard Narne, bailie, gave state and sasine of the said annual rent to a discreet man, Sir

Thomas Coling, chaplain of the said altar, in name and behalf of the said precious blood of our Lord Jesus Christ, and his successors, perpetual chaplains serving at the said altar, in pure and perpetual alms, by exhibition of a penny as the manner of burghs is and according to the tenor of the charter of foundation made thereupon. Done on the ground of the said tenement, 3 December 1518, in presence of John Broune, Robert Arnot, James Tennand, William Robisoun, William Wise, Nicholas Duncansoun, David Crag, David Aisoun, Alexander Crag, John Makky, serjeand, and sundry others. Certified by Robert Cunynghame, clerk of the diocese of St. Andrews, notary public, and corroborated by the bailie's seal. (Seal awanting.)

18.—Instrument narrating that, in presence of the notary and witnesses, a devoted father, Friar Vincent Litstare, prior of the place and convent of the Friars Preachers of the burgh of Striveling, with consent of the chapter, passed to the tenement of the late Donald Crum in the foresaid burgh, in the Myddill Raw on the south side of the High Street thereof, between the lands of Robert Duncansoune on the west, the land of Patrick Lawsone alias Litiljhone on the east and the common way which leads to the place of the Friars Minors on the south public High Street on the north, and, by exhibition of a penny, surrendered in the hands of Alexander Crag, then one of the bailies of the said burgh, an annual rent of 3s. 6d., Scots, from a greater annual rent pertaining to the said place and friars from the foresaid tenement, in favour of the founded chaplains of the parish church of the Holy Rood of the said burgh, as in warrant and clause of warrandice of an annual payment of 3s. 6d. for a certain garden let in feufarm by the foresaid founded chaplains to the above mentioned Friars Preachers and annexed to the south side of their orchard, lying contiguous to the croft of Gilbert Brady. After which resignation the said Alexander Crag, bailie, at the command of the said devoted friar, Vincent Litstare, prior as above, in name and behalf of the said place and convent, gave sasine of the said annual rent, as above, to Sir James Aikman, chaplain, procurator for the founded chaplains of the said church in warrandice as above, by delivery of one penny; and invested him therein as in warranty of payment of 3s. 6d. for the said garden and pertinents, to which in default of payment the said founded chaplains should have free entry and ingress. The seal of the said Alexander, bailie, was affixed in sign of his office. Done on the ground of the said tenement, 10 March, 1522-3. Witnesses: John Allan, John Cosland, John Alsunnour and William Forsitht, burgesses; and others. William Litstar, presbyter of the diocese of St. Andrews, notary. (Seal awanting.)

19.—Instrument narrating that, in presence of the notary and witnesses, Sir Alexander Stele, chaplain, moved with zeal of devotion, and not unmindful of the safety of his soul, granted, bestowed and for ever confirmed to God Almighty, the blessed Virgin Mary and all saints, and the perpetual founded chaplains of the parish church of the said burgh and their successors celebrating divine service therein, an annual rent of 10s. Scots to be uplifted yearly, first, from the tenement of the late John Stele his brother lying in the burgh of Striveline on the south side of the High Street six shillings, and from his back tenement with yard lying on the south side four shillings, at the two usual terms of the year, by equal portions, for exequies and an anniversary annually to be celebrated therein, for ever, on the day of the death of the said Sir Alexander, for the weal of his soul, the souls of his father, mother, brother, sister, parents, kindred, friends, and all the faithful dead ; and resigned the same in the hands of John Aitkin, then one of the bailies of the burgh, who thereupon gave sasine of the same to Sir James Aikman, chaplain and collector, in name and behalf of the perpetual founded chaplains of the said church. Done on the ground of the said lands 5 July 1525. Witnesses : George Stewart, Thomas Culper, Alexander Smytht, Andrew M'Kady, Andrew Stele, Walter Grahame, one of the ballies of the said burgh, John Stene, Robert Gillaspy and Mathew Fresar, and others. Certified by James Fresare, priest of St. Andrews diocese and notary. (Bailie's seal now awanting.)

20.—Charter by Archibald Redheacht, son of James Redheucht of Tulicht Heddill, lord of the fee of a croft of land called Muschettis Croft, with consent of his dearest and wellbeloved uncle, Alexander Redheucht of Megoure, whereby, considering that every one shall receive for his almsgifts a hundredfold, induced by zeal and piety, etc., for the weal of the souls of the said James and Margaret Symsoun, his father and mother, the soul of the said Alexander his uncle, and the souls of all the faithful dead, he granted and heritably confirmed for ever to God Almighty, the glorious Virgin Mary his mother, and all saints, and to the chaplains founded and to be founded of the parish church of the said burgh of Striveling and their successors, chaplains, all and whole the foresaid croft called Muschettis Croft, with the pertinents, lying within the liberty or territory of the said burgh, between the lands of Patrick Mentetht and Edward Forestar on the south side, the two riggis of the late David Gurlay, now of his heirs, on the north side, a narrow pool between the lands of Schippaucht and the said croft on the east side, and the common King's Highway which leads to the bridge on the west side ; which croft Alexander Murray, burgess of the said burgh, at command of the said Alexander, occupied; to be held by the said chaplains from the granter, his heirs and assignees, in pure and perpetual alms in fee and heritage for ever; paying therefor yearly the chaplains founded and to be founded of the church of the Holy Cross and their successors to the altar of Saint Peter and Saint Paul the Apostles situated in the parish church of the Holy Cross, and to the chaplains thereof who shall be for the time, an annual rent of six shillings Scots. Also the chaplains doing two anniversaries for the dead at the altar of St. James the Apostle situated within the said church [with various provisions regarding the celebration of the anniversaries, but the parchment at this part is somewhat mutilated, rendering what writing remains unintelligible]. Sealed with the seal of the granter and with the seal of the said Alexander, his uncle, in sign of his consent, and subscribed by them at the said burgh of Striveling, 7 February 1525-6. Witnesses: John Aitkin, David Greg, etc., burgesses and Sir William Litstar, chaplain and notary public. Subscribed 'Archibald Redeheuch wt. my hand' 'Alexr. Redhuch wt. my hand.' (Seals awanting and parts of parchment mutilated.)

21.—Instrument narrating that in presence of a notary and witnesses, the said Archibald Redeheucht, lord of the fee of the croft of land and others mentioned in the preceding charter, by delivery of earth and stone resigned the foresaid croft in the hands of Alexander Watson, bailie, in favour of the chaplains founded and to be founded of the parish church of the Holy Cross of the said burgh, for two anniversaries yearly to be made in all times to come, with all right he had to the same, from him his heirs and assignees. Which resignation being so made the said Alexander Watson, bailie, in virtue of his office of bailliary, at the special command of the said Archibald Redeheucht and Alexander Redehucht his uncle, delivered state and heritable sasine of the said croft called Muschettis croft with the pertinents to James Aikman, founded chaplain of the said church and procurator of the other founded chaplains of the same, by delivery of earth and stone, according to the tenor of the said charter and to their successors and invested the said James as procurator in real possession of the same. Paying therefor yearly, the said founded chaplains, to the altar of Saint Peter and Saint Paul the Apostles, situated within the aforesaid parish church, and to the chaplain thereof who should be for the time an annual rent of six shillings Scots; and also doing yearly two anniversaries for the dead at the altar of Saint James the Apostle situated within the said parish church, chanting and saying mass honorably in their vestments, as becomes, one of them for the souls of the said James Redeheucht and Margaret Symson, parents of the said Archibald, and the other for the soul of the foresaid Alexander Redeheucht, his uncle, and the souls of all the faithful dead, observing the restrictions of the said charter. Done on the soil of the said croft, 8 February, 1525-6. Witnesses: Hugh Hog, Nicholas Duncansoun, William Gethane burgess of the said burgh, and James Mukhart son of a burgess. Certified by William Litstar, priest of the diocese of St. Andrews and confirmed with the seal of the bailie. (Seal awanting.)

22.—Charter by King James the Fifth, under his great seal, whereby with advice and consent of the lords of secret council elected by the three estates in parliament, he ratified a charter, dated 8 April 1516, granted by his wellbeloved clerk, master David Abircrumby, subdean of the Chapel Royal of Striveling, whereby for augmentation of divine worship, to the praise and honour of God, the glorious Virgin Mary, and the honour and praise of Saint Michael the Archangel, and the whole court of heaven, and for the weal of the soul of the most serene Prince James the Fourth, most illustrious King of Scots, and of a venerable father in Christ, James Abircrumby, abbot of the monastery of Scone, and for the weal of his own soul, the souls of his parents and kinsmen and of all the faithful dead, he gave and granted to the altar of Saint Michael the Archangel, situated in the parish church of the Holy Cross of the burgh of Striveling. on the north side of the same church, and to the perpetual chaplain of the said altar who shall be for the time and his successors perpetual chaplains celebrating at the said altar and for ever to celebrate in divine offices to God at the same, in pure and perpetual alms, all and whole his tenement with the pertinents lying within the said burgh on the north side of the High Street thereof near the habitations of the butchers, between the land of the late Thomas Tailyefeir on the east and the land of the late John Cellie on the west as it lies in front and back. To be held by the said chaplain and his successors *(a me)* from the granter and his heirs for ever, for payment to the King and his successors of the royal maill and to the perpetual chaplain of the altar of our Lady situated in the said parish church on the south side thereof and his successors, chaplains of the said altar who shall be for the time, an annual rent of 20 s. 4 d. Scots. and to the altar of St. Anne, the mother of our Lady, situated within the said church and to the chaplain celebrating divine service thereat and his successors, chaplains, an annual rent of 20 s. Scots at the two usual terms. Further he willed that the provost, bailies, councillors and community of the said burgh, should be patrons of the said perpetual chaplainry of St. Michael and that they should be bound to provide a chaplain on a vacancy without simoniacal pravity and in the fear of God, by way of simple gift or grant, and such chaplain should not require collation or institution ordinary in any way. Willing further that none should be admitted to the said chaplainry unless he had been actually ordained a priest and was sufficiently instructed in chant and literature, made personal and continual residence within the burgh and should devoutly say mass daily at the said altar and not elsewhere, saving infirmity of body; possess no other benefice with cure or without; and at all vespers, compline, matins and high mass to be celebrated with chant within the said church be personally present in a clean and decent surplice with the other chaplains there serving God chanting and doing service, from beginning to end of divine worship; should keep no concubine, public or private, all on pain of deprivation. Further strictly charging the said perpetual chaplain once every year to make an anniversary to be celebrated by the whole choir of the foresaid parish church, at his expenses, for the soul of the granter. And the granter invoked the indignation of God against any of either sex who should presume to infringe his gift and will and beseeched all men to observe it. In witness whereof the granter subscribed, and his seal was appended, at the burgh of Striveling, 8 April, 1516, according to the computation of the Scottish Church. Witnesses : Duncan Forestare, knight of Carden ; Alexander Forestare, provost of the said burgh, Alan Stewart, Robert Farne, John Broune, Duncan Patonsoun, Robert Arnot, Alexander Watsoun, burgesses of the said burgh ; Sir Alexander Kowe, notary public ; James Crag and William Litstar. Which charter and gift, with the several rules and observances contained in it, the King, with consent aforesaid, ratified and in mortmain confirmed in all points, reserving the royal maill from the said tenement and the suffrages of devout prayers of the chaplain and his successors. Witnesses : most reverend and reverend fathers in Christ James archbishop of St. Andrews, chancellor, Gawin archbishop of Glasgow, Gawin bishop of Aberdeen; the King's well beloved cousins, Archibald earl of Angus lord Douglas, Colin earl of Ergyle lord Campbell and Lorne, John earl of Levenax lord Dernlie ; venerable fathers in Christ Patrick prior of the metropolitan church of St. Andrews, secretary, George abbot of the monastery of Holyrood, keeper of the privy seal ; the King's well beloved familiars John Campbell of Lundy, treasurer, and James Colvile of Vchiltre, comptroller and director of chancery. At Striveling, 16 November, 1525. (Seal awanting.)

23.—Charter by John Brady of Estir Kennet and burgess of the burgh of Striveling, by which, in his urgent necessity to relieve himself from the censures of Holy Mother Church, for certain sums of money for which he had been involved, he sold and confirmed to the founded chaplains of the parish church of the Holy Rood of the foresaid burgh and their successors, an annual rent of ten shillings

Scots to be uplifted yearly from his croft of land with the pertinents called the Berkhous Croft in the territory or liberty of the said burgh on the north side of the same, between the orchard and croft of the Preaching Friars of the said burgh on the north and east sides and the public street descending by the said friars and leading to the mill of the same on the west and south sides, at the two usual terms of the year, the feasts of Whitsunday and Martinmas in winter by equal portions, for a certain sum of money paid beforehand to him, in one whole and numerated sum, by an honorable man, Duncan Petersone, burgess of the said burgh, executor and sole intromitter with the testament and goods of the late David Greg, bequeathed by him for purchasing an anniversary for his soul and the soul of Jonet Williamsoun his spouse.   To be held by the chaplains and their successors, from the granter his heirs and assignees, of the king and his successors in fee and heritage; the said chaplains and their successors, for the soul of the said David Greg and Jonet Williamsoun and the souls of all the faithful dead, celebrating an anniversary on the day of his death, *viz.*, saying a *placebo* and *dirige* of nine lessons, with masses for the dead on the morrow in chant, honourably and decently as becomes; and that all the said chaplains be bound to be there present, and absent chaplains lose for that time their portion of the stipend.   Dated at the said burgh, 22 October, 1531.   Witnesses: Walter Cosland, bailie of the said burgh, Duncan Patersone, Sirs John Gray, Thomas Wilsoun, priests, and Sir William Litstar, priest and notary public.   (Signed) " Jhone Brade wt. my hand."   (Seal imperfect.)

24.—Charter by John Brady of Estir Kennet and burgess of the burgh of Striueling whereby he granted to the founded chaplains of the parish church of the Holy Cross of the foresaid burgh and their successors an annual rent of 20 s. Scots to be uplifted yearly from his croft of land with the pertinents called Hiltoun Croft, lying in the sheriffdom of Clakmannan on the north side of the bridge and water of Blak Dowan, between the lands of the lordship of Clakmannan on the west, south and east sides, and the common way on the north side, which James Redeheucht, burgess of the burgh of Clakmannan, then held in lease, in special warrandice and security of an annual rent of 10 s. Scots to be uplifted yearly from the tenement of land of the late John Offeris, butcher, lying in the said burgh of Striueling in the Myddill Raw on the south side of the High Street thereof, and of an annual rent of 10 s. Scots to be uplifted from his croft of land mentioned in the preceding charter; the said chaplains to have free regress to the said 20 s. of annual rent from Hiltoun Croft until they could peaceably possess the foresaid two annual rents according to the charters made thereupon.   Sealed and subscribed at the burgh of Striveling, 24 November, 1531. Witnesses: Duncan Paterson, Sir John Gray, Thomas Wilsoun, chaplains, and Duncan Forsitht. (Signed) "Jhone Brady wt. my hand." (Seal awanting.)

25.—Charter by Alexander lord Elphinstoun whereby he sold and confirmed to a respectable man, Sir John Patersoun, canon of the Chapel Royal of Striveling, his fore tenement of land, under and above, in the burgh of Striveling, on the north side of the High Street opposite the market cross which was formerly called Murisland, for a certain sum of money paid to him. To be held by the said John his heirs and assignees, from the granter and his heirs, of the King and his successors, in fee and heritage and free burgage for ever, for payment to the King of the royal maill and service within burgh, and all annual rents due from the said foretenement as half of the whole tenement. Further granting to the said Sir John Patersoun, his heirs and assignees, all his tenement of land back and fore with garden and pertinents in the burgh of Striveling in the Bakraw on the south of the High Street now inhabited by Isabella Rollok, widow, in special warrandice and security of the said fore tenement, by reason of life rent, etc. Dated at Elphinstoun, 6 May, 1533. Witnesses: Henry Huntar, canon of the Chapel Royal, William Johnstoun his lordship's own chaplain; James Rankin, his servitor; John Alschindir and William Alschindir, brothers german and burgesses of the said burgh; and Peter Rollok servitor to his lordship. (Signed) "Alexr. Lord Elphynstoun." (Seal remaining.)

26.—Instrument narrating that Sir James Nicholsoun, chaplain of the perpetual altar of St. Katherine, the virgin and martyr, founded in the parish church of the Holy Cross of the burgh of Striveling, passed to his fore tenement of land with the tofall tenement with the pertinents called the tenement of Saint Katherine lying in the said burgh on the south side of the High Street, and there, considering that the daily service at the said altar could not be sustained without supplement, to the praise of God Almighty, the most blessed Virgin Mary and all saints and St. Katherine the virgin, for the weal of his own soul and the souls of others, resigned his said fore tenement, viz., chambers upper and lower with the 'tofall' at the back with their pertinents, in the hands of Robert Arnot, then one of the bailies of the said burgh, from him his heirs and assignees in favour of the said altar for sasine to be given thereof in pure alms and mortmain reserving the franktenement to himself for his life. Whereupon the bailie gave sasine of the tenement to the said Sir James Nicholsoun, chaplain of the altar, in name and behalf thereof, for payment to Marion Bruce, her heirs or assignees, of 14 s. Scots yearly in name of annual rent. Done on the ground thereof, last of February, 1536-7. Witnesses: Alexander Forestare, provost of the said burgh; John Forestare, bailie thereof, etc. Certified by William Litstare, priest of the diocese of St. Andrews, notary, and confirmed with the bailie's seal. (Seal awanting.)

27.—Instrument whereby it is certified that in presence of the notary and witnesses an honorable man, John Forrester, one of the bailies of the burgh of Striveling, at command of the provost, other bailies, and councillors of the said burgh, passed to a certain waste tenement lying within the said burgh on the south side of the High Street of the same, between the land of James Yair and John Mentetht on the west side, the land of John Thomson on the east side, the King's highway on the north side and the Bakraw on the south side; and gave heritable sasine of the said waste tenement with the pertinents to a discreet man, Gilbert Maklellane alias Fergussoun, burgess of the said burgh, by delivery of earth and stone as use was, according to the tenor of the charter thereupon. Paying therefor, the said Gilbert and his heirs, yearly, from the said tenement to the prior and convent of the Preaching Friars of the burgh of Striveling the sum of four shillings of annual rent at the two usual terms of. the year, Whitsunday and Martinmas in winter, and king's mail and burgh service thence due and wont. Done on the ground of the said tenement, 20 December, 1541. Witnesses: William Forester, Duncan Forester of Ailmoir, Robert Tennand, Andrew Fergussoun, and others. Certified by John Grahame, notary public, and the seal of the bailie is attached. (Greater part of Seal remaining.)

28.—Tack and obligation, written on indented parchment, whereby "Schir William Alschindir, chaplane and servitour to my lord of Ergile, . . . settis and to male lattis to my louittis, Waltere Cosland, burges of Striueling, and Jonet Alschindir his spous, and to the langer levand of thaim twa, all and haill my land and tenement, bakside, foirside, vndir and abone, with the pertinentis, lyand within the said burgh on the northt part of the Quenis gait fornent the mercat croce of the samyn, betuix the land of Schir John Paterson and vmquhile Robert Paulie on the west part on that ane part, the land of Dauid Forester of Garden on the est, the yard of the said Dauid and John Ker on the north part and the commoun mercat gait on the southt parte, quhilk laitlie I haue optenit fra the said Walter and Jonet be conquest of alienatioun, redemable vndir reuersoun, for all the space, yeris and termes, that the alieratioun of the said tenement standis with me, my airis and assignais, vnredemit be thaim.   . . The saidis Waltere and Jonet

and thair subtenentis, gif ony thai mak thairin, sall yerelie vphald the said land
with the pertinentis durin the said space watterteicht and laifand the samyn in all
reparatioun and bigginis vndir and aboue in all thingis als sufficient as the said
tenement is presentlie now at thair entres in and thairto quhilk beginnand at the
day of the dait heirof. Payand yerelie thairfor, the said Waltere and Jonet his
spous and the langer levand of thaim twa or thair subtenentis, gif ony beis, to me,
my airis or assignais, the sovm of twenty merkis vsuall money of Scotland at twa
vsit termes in the yere, Witsonday and Martimes in wintir be evin portionns,
alanerlie : and the said Walter and Jonet sall yerelie durin the said space releif and
mak fre me my airis and assignais of the payment of all annuallis may be requirit of
the said tenement be quhatsumeuir personis, except the Quenis male and seruice
within burgh conforme to my charter alanerlie. And gif it sall happin the said
tenement ony tyme within the saidis takis, or yit afore the said redemptioun, till
cum ony maner of ruyne or skaith quhairthrow the samyn beis vnhabill till ansuere
me yerelie of the saidis tuenty merkis male, or nocht be redemyt be thaim be
wertu of my said reuersioun fra me my airis and assignais, in that cais the saidis
Walter and Jonet his spous bindis and oblyssis thaim faithfullie thair airis and
assignais be thir presentis to me my airis and assignais till mak the said land als
sufficient in all thingis to the effect forsaid as it is now presentlie at thair entres
thairto and ay and quhill the lauchfull redemptioun thairof without ony exceptioun
of the law or priuilege thairof to be allegiitin the contrar heirof, the saidis Walter
and Jonet, for thaim thair airis and assignais renunciand the samyn be thir presentis
for euir." To the part of "this endentit assedatioun and obligatioun" remaining
with the lessees Sir William "to hung" his seal and subscribed with his hand, and
Walter Cousland did similarly with the other part; and the two parts were inter-
changed at Stirling, 12th July, 1546. Witnesses: "Alexander Alschinder in
Menstre, James Robesoun, ballies of Strineling, George Vry, Gilbert Audirsoun,
Patrik Forsith, seriand, Duncan Andirsoun and Schir William Litstar, notary
public, witht vtheris diners." (Signed) "Sr. WILLIAM ALEXn. wyth my hand."
(Half of seal remaining.)

29.—Charter by James Nycholsone, vicar of the castle of Striveling,
whereby for the praise and honour of God Almighty, the glorious Virgin Mary,
St. Katherine the Virgin and all saints, for augmentation of divine worship,
and for the soul of a most illustrious Prince, James the fifth, King of Scots, and
Magdalene, his queen and daughter of the King of the French, and all the granter's
parents, benefactors, kinsmen and his predecessors founded at the altar of St.

Katherine, and of all the faithful dead, gave and granted to God Almighty, the blessed Virgin Mary and St. Katherine and to her altar founded within the parish church of the Holy Cross of Striveling and to a chaplain serving God and St. Katherine there, in divine service daily, h s tenement back and fore, high and low, with garden thereof lying in the said burgh, between the tenement of Sir John Crage, vicar pensioner of the said parish church on the north side, the said church on the south; also those two fore chambers with the waste piece of land behind between the tenement of John Brand on the west, of James Lang on the east, and of the late James Duncansone on the south; and the annual rents following, viz., from a tenement of the late Archibald Spettall in the said burgh in the Dirt Raw vj s., from the tenement of the late John Wilsone in the Dirt Raw iij s., from a tenement of the late James Cunynghame of Polmais iiij s., from a tenement of the late William Duncansone xiiij s., from a tenement of the late James Cunynghame of Polmais xxxii s., etc. Reserving certain annual rents, viz., from the two foresaid chambers lying on the south side of the said burgh, to the chaplains, choristers of the said parish church, for the anniversary of Merion Bruce, of good memory, xiiij s., and an annual rent of nine shillings to the chaplain of St. Michael, also an annual rent of 13 s. 4 d. to the chaplains, choristers of the said parish church, for an anniversary of the granter at St. Katherine's altar, etc. To be held by the said altar of St. Katherine the Virgin and a chaplain serving thereat, in pure and perpetual alms, etc. Sealed with the granter's seal and the common seal of the burgh, at Striviling, 5 February, 1555-6. (Notarial copy.)

30.—Instrument narrating that in presence of the notary and witnesses, John Donaldsone, grandson and heir of the deceased John Donaldsone, burgess of the burgh of Striueling, delivered to John Livingston, fiar of Kirkland, bailie in that part for Sir James Forrester of Torweidheid, knight, a precept of clare constat granted to him by Sir James, superior of the mill aftermentioned, with consent of Alexander Forrester, his son, and Sir John Murray of Touchadame, knight, and William Murray his son, for their interest, in favour of the said John Donaldsone as heir foresaid, in the mill of Gwnnerschaw, mill lands of the same, multures and sequels restricted thereto, and pertinents presently occupied by Walter Bayne, lying in the shire of Striviling, which were held of the said Sir James Forrester his heirs and successors in free blench for payment of one penny on the ground of the same at Whitsunday if asked. After the reading of which precept the said John Livingstonne, bailie in that part, delivered heritable state and sasine of the mill of Gwnnerschaw to John Donaldsone as grandson and

2 c

heir foresaid, personally present and accepting the same, by delivery of the clap of the said mill and earth and stone of the ground of the said lands. Done on the ground of the same, 4 August, 1624. Witnesses: Robert Levingstoune of Westir Greinyaird, younger; Walter Bayne, elder in Gwnuerschaw, Walter Bayne, younger his son, and John Robiesone in Littill Denovane. William Young, notary public. Registered at Sterling, 20th August, 1624. in "the third buik of my lord clerk register" conform to act of parliament.

31.—Instrument narrating that in presence of the notary and witnesses Andrew Sandis, one of the bailies of the burgh of Stirling, at the request of Alexander Cowane, physician, procurator and on behalf of William Crystesoun, at the Bridge of Stirling, and of Margaret Ker, his spouse, specially constituted by their letters patent to the effect underwritten, passed to their tenements of land or houses, yards, kiln, and garden then occupied by them within the liberty and territory of the said burgh at the bridge thereof, formerly belonging to John Ker, great grandfather of the said Margaret Ker, heritably; and there the said procurator, for fulfilling of letters of disposition made by William Crystesoun and his spouse to a noble lord Alexander lord Fenton, resigned the tenements or houses in the hands of the bailie as in the hands of the king, superior thereof, by delivery of earth and stone of the ground, for new infeftment to be made to Lord Fentoun his heirs and assignees whomsoever. Which resignation being so made the bailie by virtue of his office gave sasine of the tenements of houses to Donald Campbell, servitor and attorny and in behalf of Lord Fentoun by delivery of earth and stone of the ground thereof. Done on the ground of the same 21 January, 1626. Witnesses: Robert Forrester of Quenshauche; Edward Forrester, notary; William Crystesoun at the mill of Inneralloun; George Lapslie at the Bridge of Stirling; and John Forrester, serjeant of the burgh. John Williamsoun, notary.

II.—ABSTRACTS OF SOME OF THE DOCUMENTS CONTAINED IN FRAGMENTS OF PROTOCOL BOOKS.

1.—Instrument narrating that in presence of a notary and witnesses compeared an honorable man, Malcolm Makclery of Garten, attorney of the most excellent princess Queen Margaret, and presented to an honorable man James Schaw of Salchy, sheriff of Striveline, a brieve or precept of the King for sasine to be given to the Queen, or her certain attorney in her name, of all and whole the King's lordship of Tulycultre, with the pertinents; whereupon the sheriff gave to the attorney, in name of the Queen, sasine and possession of the lordship of Tulycultre, with the pertinents, by delivery of earth and stone of the lands, according to the tenor of the brieve or precept of the King. Done at the principal messuage of the said land, at the tenth hour forenoon, or thereabout, or the 29th day of October, 1473. Present: Sir Symone Gray, vicar of the parish church of Tulycultre, Thomas of Cragingelt, Thomas Morgan, and others.

2.—Instrument narrating that in presence of the notary and witnesses, personally compeared a discreet man master John Cant, chaplain, and nominated and ordained discreet men, masters Robert Cetis, Patrick Lange, Sir Robert Mure, chaplains, and James Allyrdes, clerk, his procurators and special deputies; giving to them and any of them his power and special mandate to accept in his name any ecclesiastical benefice or benefices, with cure or without, within the diocese of Glasgow, vacant or to be vacant, to be bestowed on him by a reverend father in Christ John bishop of Glasgow, even though it should be a canonry and prebend of the cathedral church or duty of a parsonage; and to require and crave collation, provision and investiture and real possession, and stall in choir and place in chapter in which such benefice might be; and to give for him the oath due and wont for observing the statutes, liberties and customs of the church, and any other oath which the order of law required. Done in the lodging of Adam Cosour in the burgh of Strivelin, 4th July, 1475. Witnesses: Adam Cosour, James Redhuch, John Gourlay, John Bolat, burgesses, and others.

3.—Fragment of instrument referring to marriage of William [lord Grahame?] and Annabella Drummond, that the said William and Annabella knew no hindrance to their marriage nor had made contract before, but saying they wished spontaneously to complete the said marriage and gave their corporal oaths thereon on the Holy Gospels, the said Sir Alexander put the right hand of the said William in the said Anabella's hand and, *per verba matr mon i de presenti*, as use is, fully conjoined the said William and Anabella in nuptial covenant and contract of marriage, who in name of matrimony kissed each other. Whereon all and sundry John Drummond of Cargil, father of the said Anabella, in her name craved instruments. Done in the parish church of Mothill at ten hours before noon or thereabout. Present, the said lord himself, and Thomas lord e Erskyn, Robert Douglas of Lochlevyn, David Grahame of Gargunnok, master Walter Drummond, Sir Andrew Drummond, vicar of Muthill, Robert Drummond of Ermer, Robert Grahame, Thomas Grahame, Mathew Forestar, Duncan Forestar, Walter Symson, William Chalmer and others. The beginning of the instrument containing the date is awanting, but the next consecutive entry in the protocol book is 26th November, 1479. [This fragment seems to relate to the marriage of William lord Graham, afterwards first Earl of Montrose, with Annabella Drummond, daughter of John Drummond of Cargill, first lord Drummond.]

4.—Instrument narrating that, in presence of the notary and witnesses, compeared a noble matron Eufame Levyngstoun, relict of a late honourable man, Malcom Flemyng, son and heir of a late noble lord Robert lord le Flemyng. and presented the following precept:—"Robert of Abircrummy of that ilk, knycht and schiroff of Pertht, to Johne Mackrone ane of the maris of the said scheroffdome, greting. Forsamekle as it is fund be a inquest that Malcome Flemyng, sone vmquhile to the lord Flemyng, deit vestit and saysit as of fe of the landis of Cammisdrany and that Eufame, his spous, aw to haue ane racionable terce thairof ; quharefor I charge you stratly and commandis that ye pas to the saidis landis, begynnyng at the southt, and gewe to the said Eufame and knaw the said Eufame to the terce of the saidis landis, and this be na way ye lefe vndone, vnder all charge that efftyr my folow; the quhilk to do I commit to you full pover be thir my letteris gevyn vnder the sele of office, at Pertht, the penult day of the monetht of Nouember the yer of God j^m cccc lxxix yeris." Which precept having been read the said John Mackrone, officer in that part, took it in his hands and personally past to the principal messuage of the said lands and by delivery to the said Eufeme of hesp and staple of the houses, and beginning at the south, gave and delivered to her her reasonable third part of the said lands, and recognosced her to the said third part and gave possession thereof as use is, in presence of Peter Cady, William Cochran and other witnesses. Done on the 1st of December, 1479, and 20th year of the reign of King James the Third.

5.—Instrument narrating that, in presence of a notary and witnesses, compeared a worthy matron, Marion Malvene, relict of the late Robert Malcomson, burgess of the burgh of Striveline, and resigned in the hands of Thomas Cragingelt, one of the bailies of the said burgh, by overgiving of earth and stone, her tenement lying in the said burgh between the lands of the late John Richardson on the west, the land of the late Patrick Warinok on the east, and her tenement in the said burgh between the land of the late Patrick Wrennok on the west and the common vennel of St. Mary leading to the bridge of the said burgh on the east; and other tenements in the burgh. Whereupon the said bailie delivered sasine of the foresaid tenements to an honourable man Dauid Forsytht as heir and grandson of the said late Robert Malcomson his grandfather. Done on the ground of the said tenements, 11th December, 1479. Witnesses: Alexander Cunynghame of [L]eky, James Nory of Torbert, William Mane, Sir Robert Muir, rector of Glendovane and others.

6.—Instrument narrating that James Schaw of Salchy resigned his half and second part of a croft and barn which he held from William Richardson by heritable right of the heirs of the late John Heyth in the territory of the burgh, between the land of Thomas Narne on the north and the land of the altar of St. Mary the Virgin founded within the parish church of the Holy Cross on the south, in the hands of Thomas Cragingelt of that ilk one of the bailies of the burgh, who gave sasine of the same to Adam Bully, burgess of the burgh. Done on the ground of the said croft, 18 December, 1479.

7.—Instrument narrating that in presence of a notary and witnesses an honourable man, William Symsone, one of the bailies of the burgh of Striveline, at command of the provost and other bailies, councillors and community of the said burgh, personally past to a tenement of the late John Patrick, baker, lying within the said burgh, in the Kirk Vennel of the said burgh, on the south side of the tenement of Henry Greg, and gave sasine of the same to a discreet man, Sir Richard Smythtson, perpetual chaplain of the altar of the blessed and glorious Virgin Mary, founded in the parish church of Striveline, in the north aisle of the same, in his own name and as procurator for Sir James Darow, perpetual chaplain of the altar of the Holy Cross of the said burgh, by virtue of a process led thereupon by the said chaplains in the four head courts of the burgh for default of payment of 15 s. due to the said chaplains and their altars for certain terms bypast and not paid, by delivery of earth and stone, according to the tenor of the said process. Present: Duncan Forestare, provost; Alexander Norton, one of the bailies of the said burgh; Alexander Cunyngahame, of Auchinbowy; Sir John Spens, chaplain and notary public; John Crag, James Redhucht, Adam Bully; Sir Robert Symsone, Sir Alexander Fresare, chaplains, and others.—17th January, 1479-80.

8.—Instrument narrating that Patrick of Mentetht, son and apparent heir of Elene Lochaw, relict of the late James of Mentetht, with his friends and prolocutor Alexander Muschet, then dean of gild of the burgh of Striveline, compeared personally before the provost, bailies, councillors and community of the said burgh, in the head court of the same held in the tolbooth thereof, and there set forth and declared that they and their friends were informed that the said Elene purposed to alienate and wadset certain annual rents and tenements lying in the burgh away from the said Patrick, her apparent heir, notwithstanding that the said annual rents and tenements [were granted] by the King to the lawful heirs of the said Elene, who had appeared elsewhere in a court of the burgh and declared that it behoved her, by real necessity to sustain her life, to wadset, and offering to wadset the same for that reason to her heirs and next friends; whereupon the prolocutor in name of the said Patrick offered there in judgment to sustain and find food and clothing to the said Elene honourably and daily as John Menteth of Rathow with his wife was able, and as his wife was clothed, in the dwelling-place of the said John with her heir, and in his name offering and affirming the same; and should the said Elen be unwilling to live with the said John and his spouse they offered to pay the said Elen for her sustenance yearly, during her life, ten marks in the burgh of Striveline, in consideration of the said rents and tenements not being alienated or wadset, and offered to find sufficient sureties in the burgh of Striveline; and if she refused or acted contrary thereto, the prolocutor protested that such alienation should be of no effect and should not prejudice the said Patrick and his heirs in time to come.[1] 17th January, 1479-80.

9.—Instrument narrating that Vmfrid Colquhoun of Lus, son and heir of the late John Colquhoun of Lus, knight, delivered a precept of sasine by John earl of Mar lord of Garcaucht and lord superior of the lands of Estyr and Westyr Sauling to William Marsar, brother german of Sir Laurence Marsar of Mckillour, his bailie in that part, for sasine giving of the lands of Mckle and Little Sauling and mill thereof in the barony of Sauling and shire of Fyfe, who gave sasine thereof to the said Vmfrid Colquhoun. Done at the principal messuage of Sauling, 31 January, 1479-80. And on 1st February following sasine is given to him of the Bordland Sauling on precept of sasine by Colin earl of Argyll lord Campbell and Lorne directed to Thomas Erskene, son of Thomas lord le Erskene, his bailie in that part, who gave sasine to John Erskene attorney of the said Vmfrid Colquhoun.

10.—Instrument narrating that in presence of a notary and witnesses compeared an honourable man Malcom Makelery of Garten, constable of the Castle of Striveline, in name and behalf of a noble lord Andrew lord Avandale, chancellor of the kingdom of Scotland and captain of the said castle, and, in terms of precept of the King contained in letters under his privy seal and subscription manual directed to the said lord chancellor, his captain of the said castle, and his constables deputes and keepers thereof, by overgiving of the keys of the said castle delivered the same with all apparatus and goods belonging thereto to noble and famous men, viz., master Alexander Inglis, provost of the collegiate church of Crichtoun, clerk register of the King, Sir Walter Davidson prior of Pettynveme, Alexander Lesly of Wardris, receiver general of the King and John Ros of Montgrenane, commissioners of the King in that

---

[1] For the old law regarding the sale of property in the circumstances narrated in this instrument, see *Leges Burgorum*, c. xlii. Ancient Laws and Customs of the Burghs of Scotland (Burgh Records Society), pp. 21-2.

part.   Which Castle, with the goods contained therein, the foresaid commissioners in name and behalf of the King received from the said Malcom Makelery, constable, in name of the said lord chancellor, by acceptation of the keys thereof, according to the tenor of the letters and mandate of the King; and being so delivered and received the lords commissioners delivered the keeping of the King's castle to an honourable man, Duncan Forestar, then provost of the burgh of Striveline, being sworn thereto, by delivery of the keys and goods of the same.   Present : William Edmonstoun of Duntretht, James Schaw of Salchy, Archibald Edmonstoun, James Nory of Terbert, William Stewart of Baldovane, John Cellar of Groneyardis and others — 23rd February, 1479-80.

11.—Instrument narrating that John Duncansone, burgess of the burgh of Strivelin, presented to the notary to be read an instrument taken by him in name of William Duncansone, his father, within the tolbooth of the burgh, on the grant of a certain annual pension of forty shillings to be paid to the said William by the provost, bailies, councillors and community of the said burgh yearly, out of their lands, in presence of William Symsone, then one of the bailies of the burgh, for audience of reading the said instrument and obtaining payment of one term of the said annual pension; the reading of which the said bailie will not wait to hear or pay the said sum ; which things being done the said John Duncansone set forth and declared how he with his wife and children had come sundry times from Lethe to the said burgh for payment of the said sum, and set forth the sum of five nobles six shillings and eight pence Scots in his labours for his expenses, and could not get payment thereof; for payment of which principal sum and expenses the said John solemnly protested in name of his said father.—Done in the Marketgait of the said burgh, 24th February, 1479-80.   Present : Sir John Cambus, chaplain, Henry Murray, John Bell, Fyllan Myll, Walter Hvny, and others.

12.—Instrument narrating that Adam Cosour, burgess of the burgh of Striveline, broke, cassed and annulled the sasine of a certain tenement in the said burgh between the lands of the late John Heth on the south and Jonet Gulde on the north, the sasine having been given, or more truly as he asserted, intruded by Malcom Forestar of Torwood, calling himself sheriff in that part, and taken by an honourable man Thomas Cocheran, by the breaking of a dish and casting the same with earth and stone beyond the bounds of the said tenement, protesting that the said sasine should not prejudice him or his heirs in time to come.   Present: Thomas Cragingelt, one of the bailies of the burgh, Hugh Lawson, John Hvny, Andrew Pully, chaplain, and others.   2nd March, 1479-80.

13.—Instrument narrating that the said Adam Cosour resigned an annual rent of 20s. out of a tenement in the burgh, between the lands of Gilbert Brady on the west, the lands of the late William Murray of Tulchadam on the east, an annual rent of 10s. from the tenement of Duncan Thomson in the said burgh, between the land of Richard Smethtson on the west, the common vennel to the place of the Friars of the said burgh on the east, an annual rent of 10s. from the tenement commonly called the *Trone land* on the west side of the High Street leading to the port of the said burgh, by overgiving of one penny in the hands of Thomas of Cragingelt, then one of the bailies of the burgh; and thereafter the said bailie gave sasino of the annual rent of 20s. to a discreet man Sir Andrew Bully, chaplain, in name and on behalf of God Almighty, St. Anne the mother of the glorious Virgin Mary and her altar founded by the said Adam in the parish church of the Holy Cross of Strivelin, and in name of the perpetual chaplain of the said altar; and of the annual rent of 10s. from the tenement of Duncan Thomson, and the annual rent of 10s. from the Trone to the said Sir Andrew, chaplain, in name and behalf of God Almighty and the glorious Virgin Mary and her altar founded by the said Adam, and situated within the said church, and perpetual chaplain of the same and of the said St. Anne and her altar and chaplain foresaid, by equal portions, to be expended for reparation of the same and maintaining the lights thereat. Witness, Thomas Stewart, Andrew Morys, John Glasgw, and others. 2nd March, 1479-80.

III.—Extracts from Fragmentary Council Records.

21*st October*, 1561.

Calsay, hevin.   The counsall ordanis the baillies to tak certane honest men with thame and visie the calsay to the hevin, and quhair it misteris to advis and ordane quhow it salbe reformit.

Mylnis.   The counsall approvis the act maid of befoir for defence of the mylnis.

4*th November*, 1561.

Wyne.   The consall ordanis that nane wyne be sauld derrar nor xiiij d. the pynt, vndir the paine of confiscing oft the pece; and that all tavernares sall all stamp thair stowpis vndir the said paines.

12*th December*, 1561.

Wyne.   The baillies and consall present for the tyme findis that the wyne is sauld furth of Johne Forester hous for xvj d. the point, nochtwithstanding the act befoir writtin, and thairfoir ordanis the said act to be put to executioun.

15th December, 1561.

Anent the propositioun of James Striueling of the Keir, prouest of Striueling, anent the vptenyng of the burrow mylnis, witht the croftis, yairdis and landis, pertenyng sumtyme to the Blakfreris in heretage, to the commone gude of this tovn to remane thairwitht perpetuallie, for sic ressonable caussis tobe done to the Quenis grace plessour as may be convenit with hir Maiestie, the haile consall hes thocht the samyn expedient to be laborit, and to tak vpon hand thairfoir the biging of the park dike with sic other thingis [as may] maist casellie be convenit, etc. ; and to that effect hes ordanit commissioun tobe gevin.

Mylnis, Blakfreris landis.

8th July, 1562.

The counsell being avisit with the charge and supplicatioune giffin be the Queenis grace vpon the complant of James G[. . . .], chapellin, ordinis the act maid and grantit be the counsell of befor to the said James to be fulfillit in all pointis; and gif the maltmen falyeis ordinis tham to be poindit for xij d., ilk day, for the said James sustentatioun.

Chapelliu, maltmen.

The counsall hes namit Johne Lecheman [and six others] to be auditouris of the townis comptis for this instant yeir.

Townis comptis.

16th July, 1562.

The haill counsall oblist tham and become cautioun and souerty to Johne Duncansoun, mynister of this brucht, to caus him to be payit yeirly of his stipend conform to the ordour tane and to be true, and to remane to him laute now inlikmaner as thai wer oblist off befor to releif the lard of Garden of the samyn stipend.

Mynister.

7th September, 1562.

The baillies and counsall being present for the tym, haiffand consideratioun of the silver pece tane fra Johne Forester as ane poind delyverit be him for breking of the actis and statutis befor writtin for selling of wyne by the ordinance, ordinis fyfe li. to be tane of the said siluer pece and the samyn applyit to the cleything of the pwr of the hospitall, and to mak tham clokis or gownis theirwith insafar as the samyn extendis to.

Pur of hospitall.

The baillies and counsall hes condiscendit that tua s. be gaderit of euery staig conforme to vs and wont thir xxty yeris bigan to be deliuerit to the thesaurare to mak compt to the tovn.

Staigs.

2 D

9th October, 1562.

Names of Council. Nomina Consulis:—James Stirling of Keir; Alexander Forester of Garden, provost; Robert Forester, younger, James Watsone, William Derrocht, baillies; Gawane Drummond, Alexander Watsone, Robert Forester of Boquhan, Johne Craigingelt of that ilk, William Mentetht of Randisurd, William Bell, Alexander Paterson, Robert Ramsay, Thomas Arnot, Duncan Forester of Arngibbon, John Forester of Logy; John Duncanson, mynister.

The merchandis:—Johne Lecheman, dene of gild, Robert Aleschunder, Alexander Duncansone, Johne Wallace, merchand, William Noruell, William Lowry, Johne Patersoun, James Gardinar, Alexander Ray.

The craftismen:—Johne Makalexander, Thomas Carnis, baxter, James Layng, maltman, Robert Scot, talyour, Alexander Gurle, skynnar, Johne Thomsoun, fleschour, Alexander Brown, wobstar, Robert Schort, cordinar, Johne Millar.

Waist land. The counsall has condiscendit and ordinit that the waist behind Thomas Carnis and William Gechtanis houssis in the Middill Raw be rowpit and sett in few to tham that will gif maist thairfor, and the samyn be rowpit thre syndry dayis.

Officers. Quo die, Johannes Duncan, Andreas Campbell, Willelmus Monocht et Dauid Robesoun, electi sunt in seriandos et jurarunt.

Halbartis. The counsall ordinis the thesaurer to caus mak four halbartis vpon the townis expens.

Puir barnis. The counsall havand consideratioun that thair is certane puir barnis greting and crying nychtlie vndir stairis for falt of lugeing, hes grantit that olklie ane laid of colis be laid in to the almous hous for lugeing of the saidis puris during this winter tyme.

Brew wyfiis. It is statut and ordinit that na maner of persoun brew or mak traffik within this brught bot allanerly honest menis wyfiis and widois, and thairfor ordinis the baillies to sers and seik the town and discharge the rest.

2nd November, 1562.

St. James Chepell. It is condiscendit be the counsall that all the stanis of Sant James Chepell be brocht to the vtility and proffit of the commoun werk, and that nane thairof be disponit to ony singular persoun except thai obtene licens; and gif ony dois in the contrar to pay for tham.

Settis. It is ordinit be the counsall that na settis be sett to ony persoun that hes takis of auld quhill thai pay fyrst the byrunnis.

The counsall hes condiscendit that Thomas Carnis and William Gichaine haif Waist land given for annual rent. the pece waist land in the Baikrow at the baksyd adiacent to their new foir lugeing for xl s. yeirlie of annuall to be payit to the thesawrar equaly betuix thame, and sall lewe the passage on the hie kingis gaitt lik as it is now in the baksyd equaly with the gavell of Dauid Bawegage and Andro Carnis.

10th November, 1562.

In presens of James Watsone and Williame Derroche, baillies, the settis rowpit within the burghe of Striuiling and sett them as followis :— Settis rowpit.

The small custumis sett to Gilbert Watsone for ane hundreth auchtene merkis and ane half.   Souerte, Alexander Gowrlaye

The geitt swoippingis sett to Alexander Gourlaye for fiftie twa merkis and half. Souirtie, Williame Derroche.

The Watter of Forthe sett to James Robertsone for xx li.   Souirte, Alexander Schortt.

Kingis maill, gyrs maill and stallachan, sett to James Thome for v li.   Souerte, Alexander Gourlaye.

The fische skemmyllis sett to Robert Scott for vij merkis.

The peckis sett to Johne Chalmer for xxv merkis and ane half.   Souirteis, Rechert Kidstoun and Johne Richartsone, baxster, coniunctlie.

The hevine silver remanis in the thesauraris handis.

18th November, 1562.

The prouest, baillies and counsall, being avisit anent the selling of wyne within this toun and anent the bill gevin in be the taverneris thairof, the saidis prouest, baillies and counsall, ordanis ney wyne with in this toun be sauld derrar nor xx d. the poynt of auld wyne, vndir the payne of confiscatioun and eschcitting of the pece of wyne that salhappin to be sauld. Taverneris, wyne.

22nd December, 1562.

The counsall hes ordinit that the mynister and William Noruell, thesaurar, pas to Edinburgh to the conventioun of the kyrk vpon the xxv day of December instant vpon the townis expenssis. Conventioun of kyrk.

9th January, 1562-3.

The prouest, baillies and counsall, except the dekinnis, hes condiscendit to len x li. to Robert Lakpreuik, prentair, for prenting of new bukis concludit be the kirk, takand souerte in Edinburgh for repayment. Prenting bukis.

26th February, 1562-3.

Comptis.

The persones chosin upon comptis :—Johne Lescheman, James Watsoun, Gawan
. Drummond, Robart Alexander, for merchandis ; James Laying, Thomas Carnis,
Robart Schort, John M'Alexander.

8th March, 1562-3.

Mylnis.

The quhilk day, counsall being avisit, ratifyit the act befor writtin anent the
defeus and persute of the mylnis, and sall pas with him to court or to courtis, and assist,
fortife and concur with him, and tak the burding vpoun thame of the said mater,
and quhat expens be maid thairupon to be allowit in the thesaureris comptis.

23rd April, 1563.

**John
Grahemes
buke of
instrumentis.**

Anent Johne Grahemes buke of instrumentis of the toun of Striueling and
certane euidentis and vtheris caussis concernyng the commoun wele of the toun,
and that the abstracting thairof fra the said Johne stayis and hinderis vther gude
actis and notable dedis and infeftmentis to be insert in the samyn wordy of memory
for the commoun wele and for the wele of minouris in sic causis as concernis thame;
thairfoir it is concludit be the counsall that the said Johne sall haiff his awin buke,
and he sall caus mak ane new buke and write and register thairin and draw furth
all things concernyug the toun and commoun welthe thairof apon the townis expens,
at the discretioun of the prouest and baillies, and siclik yeirlie in tyme cuming
quhen ony thing occurris that sall tueche the commoun wele; quhilk the said Johne
hes acceptit and to be collationate betuix and Mydsymmir nixtocum, vndir the
pane of ane hundreth li. In witnes heirof, the saidis prouest, baillies, and Johne
Graheme hes subscriuit this act with thair awin handis. (Signed) John Grahem.

2nd August, 1563.

Tolbuith.

The counsall ordanis the thesaurar to by tymmer and syllour the tolbuith, and
to allow the samyn thaukfully to him in his comptis.

27th August, 1563.

**Auchmowty,
gild fyne.**

The counsall, for certane motivis moving thame and for seruice done and to be
done, hes grantit to Johne Auchmowty to remett him the half of the gildis fyne for
the toun pairt ; and ordanis him to content and pay to the thesaurar ten poundis ;
and to aggre with the dene of gild and gild brethir for thair pairt.

Gild fynes.

And ordanis the remanent enterit for this yeir to pay conforme to the actis
maid thairupoun of before.

20th September, 1563.

The counsale of the burgh of Sterling being convenit in the counsalhous thairof, Thesaurer.
hes concludit to releif Williame Norwell, thesaurer of the said burgh, of the maillis
of the Ruid Croft insafar as he hes intromettit with and maid compt thairof to the
towneschip and auditouris of the comptis of the samin at the handis of Johne
Stoddert and all vtheris havand entres.

The prouest, baillies and counsale, present for the tyme, hes grantit to Alexander Patersoun,
Patersoun for his guid seruice done and tobe done to the towne the sowme of foure pensioun.
pundis money of yeirlie pensioun ; and ordanis the thesaurar present and tocum to
ansuer him of the samin termelie as effeiris.

8th November, 1563.

The prouest and baillies and counsall being present chesit the counsall of this Counsall
instant yeir :—   chesit.

James Striueling of Keir, provost ; Rouert Forester, Gawan Drummond,
Johne Leschman, bailies.

William Derroche, Alexander Forester of Garden, Johne Craigingelt of that
ilk, Robert Foster of Boquhan, William Menteith of Randisurde, Duncan Forester
of Arnegibbon ; Alexander Paterson, procuratour fiskaile.

Merchandis:—Alexander Ray, dene of gill, Robert Alexander, Andro Cowan,
Alexander Duncanson, Johne Wallace, merchand, William Norwell, Johne Paterson,
James Gardner, William Lowry.

The dekinnis:—Johne M'Alexander, William Geiching, James Leischman, Thomas
Lawsonn, Johne Hastie, Johne Robison, Johne Benny, Johne Hvtone, Archibald
Smyth.

The counsall ordinis the thesaurar to gif William Schang xl s. in almous and Almous.
other fowrty s. to Johne Henry.

10th November, 1563.

Small custumis sett to Gilbert Watsone for iiij{xx} iiij merkis ; gett dichtingis sett Common
to Alexander Gourlay for lij merkis ; pekis sett to John Huttoun for xiiij li. ; Kingis good sett.
maill sett to Andro Campbell for viij merkis ; Watter of Forth sett to the lard of
Poilmais for xxxiij merkis vj s. viij d.

20th November, 1563.

The counsall present for the tyme hes concludit to send cist Robert Forester, Susper sioun
younger, to purcheis suspensioun of hornyng purchest be the vicair, maister Alexander of hornyng.
Chalmer, and Johne Stoddart.

14th December, 1563.

Burgesses.   The counsall hes grantit that na burges be acceptit nor enterit in tyme cuming bot sall pay xl s. to the tovn.

Almous hous.   For the almous hous:—Johne Lescheman, Gawane Drummond, Johne M'Alexander, Johne Haistie.

Expenssis to Edinburgh.   The counsall ordanis Alexander Patersone to be ansuerit be the thesaurar of his expenssis to pas to Edinburghe for debaitting of the actioun intentit be Johne Stodhyrd and maister Robert Auchmowty, etc., and thairto stable procuratouris to answer for the toun.

8th April, 1564.

Price of wyne.   The counsell ordennes that James Far and James Hog sell the wyne now presently being amangis thair handis for xx d. the pynt, becaus it wes cleirly onderstand that the said wyne was coft for xlij li. the tovn ; and gif the said persounis disobeyis and will nocht sell the samin of the price aboune wrettin that the bailyeis sall pas and mak opene duris and caus nychtbouris and wther resortis to hef it of the samine price, and gif thai contend that thay salbe dischargit to sell wyne for yeir and daye.

8th August, 1564.

Brig of Tulibody.   The prouest, baillies and counsall, and gentill men present for this tyme, hes grantit all to contribut to the support of the brig of Tulibody, havand ane maister of werk to ressaue and gif compt and tobe taxt quarterlie to the sovm of ane hundreth merkis as the wark cumis fordwart and na vther way.

3rd November, 1564.

Hospitall, annual.   The provest, baillies and counsall, grantit tham to haif bocht fra Marioun Patersoun ane annuall rent of ten s., vsuall money of Scotland, yerly, to be vpliftit of all and haill the tenement of land pertening to Henry Cunynghame, quhilk is applyit to the hospitall of the said brucht ; therfor the saidis provest, baillies and counsall, oblissis thame and thair successouris to warrand the said Henry yeirly and ilk yeir of the said annuall and his airis at all handis quham it effeiris.

Common good.   The fische skemilis set to Thomas Norwell for 5 li. iij s. iiij d.; the hevin siluer set to James Ray for xxx s.; the gait dichting set to Alexander Gourlay for liiij merkis ; the peckis set to Johne Hutoun for xliiij li.; small custumis set to Gilbert Watson for iiij^{xx} vij merk vj s. viij d.; the Wattir of Forth set to James Robesoun

for xxxiiij merk ; the Kingis maile, gres maile and stallagin set to James Thom for
viij merkis ; the voltis occupeit be James Hog set to the said James Hog for xlij s.

The prouest, Johne Cragingelt of that ilk. The counsall.

Johne Leschman, Duncan Forester, and Gawain Drummond, Robert Forester,
baillies of this yeir.

James Striueling of Keir, Alexander Forster of Garden, Robert Forester of
Boquhan, William Mentetht of Randesurd, William Derroche.

Andro Cowan dene of gild, Alexander Ray, Johne Paterson, Robert Alexander,
James Watsoun, Johne Admowtie, William Norwell, Johne Wallace.

The dekinnis :—Johne M'Alexander for hammermen, Johne Millair for the
baxtaris, Alexander Kincaid for maltmen, Johne Benny for the skynnaris, Robert
Gvn for cordenaris, George Gardner for tailyeouris, Johne Thomsoun for the
fleschouris, Johne Hutoun for the wobstaris.

5th August, 1594.

The baillcis and counsale vnderstandand the necessetie of prouisioun of wynis
to the Baptisme of the Prince to be shawn, and the furnesaris of wynis hes bocht
the same vpone verray hie prices, thairfoir the counsale licentiattis thame to sell
thair Frenche wynis for vij s. the pynt fre. this furth, provyding that the wyne
sellaris within this burgh pers . . . . the euming of the embassadouris.[1] . . .

Baptisme of the Prince; price of wynis.

27th August, 1594.

It is statuite and ordanit be the prowest, balleis and counsale, for setting doun
of ane ordour for the pryce of chalmeris and bedding during the space of the
baptisme of the Prince, that is to say ane chalmer weill provydit in all necessaris,
honest in apparrell, everie bed being within the chalmer, fywe s. As alsua the
magistratis everie ane in thair awin quarter to pas throw the toun and to visie the
sufficiencie of chalmeris and bedding ; and [if thair be] fund chalmeris and bedding
in simple sort that the saidis chalmeris and [bedding] sall be sett at the discretioun
of the magistrat of the quarter ; and quha refuissis [and charges] mair nor it is
statuite be the magistrates to pay [. . . at the discre]tioun of the magistrat of the
quarter.[2]

Baptisme of the Prince; prices of chalmeris and bedding.

---

[1] The greater part of the leaf on which this is written has been torn off, and the remainder of the act is thus made unintelligible.

[2] This act being written on the other side of the same leaf as the preceding entry has also been partly destroyed.

21st October, 1594.

For the counsale.

It is concludit be the counsale and ordanit that na persone this yeir beand vpon counsale that compeiris not in counsale hous the hour quhairto he salbe warnit that they be poindit for ilk falt ij s. vnforgevin. And the absentis fra the honr, the balyeis dowbill and clerk dowbill wulaw vnforgewin. And quha beis within the toun and compeiris nocht he salbe poindit for iiij s.

28th March, 1595.

Brighauch.

The Brighauch being rowpit is sett for fyve yeirs to James Schorto with thir restrictionis following,[1] for the soume of fyftie thre pundis yeirlie.

21st July, 1595.

Lowrie, act; disobedience to bailie.

It is concludit be the counsall that Andro Lowrie sall remane in waird fra this day at xij houris to the morne at xij houris, and that for disobedience committit be him to Archibald Alschinder, baillie; and that he cume to that same place quhair he dissobeyit and thair crawe forgiwenes of the said baillie for the said offence; and incaice the said Andro commit the lyk in onie tyme to cume he sall pay ten pund.

29th July, 1595.

For Edinburgh, commissioner.

The counsale consentis and votis that Walter Cowane, burges of this burgh, salbe commissioner to convene at Edinburgh the first of August nixt, thair to treat vpon sic thingis as the haill commisioneris thair to be convenit sall think good.

6th September, 1595.

Staig syluer.

Staig syluer sett to Archibald Smythe for tuelff poundis money; pledge, James Ramsay.

Fair.

Reuineous of the fair sett to Stewine Aikmane and Jhone Watsoun for ten poundis monie; pledge, Willeame Gillespie, maltmane.

13th September, 1595.

For Forester, offens to minister.

The prouest, bailleis, and counsale ordanis, for the offens done be Jhone Forester, maltman, and his dochter to the minister of this burgh, first in respect the said Jhone misvsit the said minister be geving of him of evill language, and nixt, seing the said Jhonis dochter cuttit and destroyit the said ministeris staff, that the said Jhone and his dochter sall be put in waird in the tolbuyth and thair to remane for the space of xlviij houris and forder thairefter ay and quihill the said Johne find

---

[1] The restrictions referred to are not inserted in the record.

sufficient cautioun and souertie to satisfie sic actis and penalteis as the saidis prouest, bailleis and counsale, sall lay to thair charge, befoir thair cuming furth of the said waird. And the counsale dischargis the saidis bailleis of any taking of cautioun bot according to this act.

24th September, 1595.

In presens of the prouest, bailleis and counsale. The quhilk day, Jhone Allane, Laxster, become cautioun and souertie that Jhone Forester, his spous, and thair dochter, sall nather truble, molest, iniure nor challange the minister nor nain of his directlie nor indirectlye heirefter, ilk falt quhairin thai or ony of thame salhappin to be fylit of, the said cautioner to incur and pay the soume of ten li. to be distributit to the poor *toties quoties*. And the said Jhone Forester oblist him to releif his said cautioner of the act aboue writtin and panes specifeit in the same.

Forester, Allane, caution.

6th October, 1595.

Jhone Murray of Touchadame, prouest.   Provost.

Archibald Alexschunder, Walter Cowane, James Schorte, Jhone Miller, chosen in bailleis for this yeir.   Bailies.

The same day, Jhone Muschet, clark, resauit and suorne.   Clerk.

Counsale for this yeir of God j^m v^e four scoir fyftene:—   Council.

For merchantis : Duncane Paterson, dene of gild ; Walter Neische, Jhone Donaldson, Robert Alexschunder, Andro Cowane, Jhone Patersone, Jhone Scherar, James Gardner.

For craftismen : Robert Robertson, alias Tennent, convener ; Jhone Henderson, baxster; Alexander Dawson, tailycour; Thomas Reid, fleschcour; Jhone Gichane, cordiner ; Alexander Broun, wobster, skynner ; Jhone Layng, maltman, convener ; Jhone Cuthbert, skynner.

Omni gadderum : Robert Cragingelt of that ilk, Robert Forester of Boquhan ; Jhone Mersheall, Thomas Michell, litsteris.

10th October, 1595.

George Nicoll, cordiner, admittit in burges, hes sworne, hes payit iiij li ; comperit with his hagbut, steilbonet and sword. Nicoll, burgis.

13th October, 1595.

In presens of the prouest, bailleis and counsale, Thomas Cowper enterit in burges, hes sworn and payit iiij li. Dauid M'Ley, tailyeour, receavit in burges at the desyr of the prouest gratis. Burgesses.

21st October, 1595.

Council.   In presens of the counsall, being conuenit.

Burges.   Walter Mayne is enterit burges and gild, and suoirne *more solito* and sall pay xx li. Pledge, John Donoldsoun, and he to releiw his cawtioner; and armit with hagbit, steilbonett and suord.

Lopslie, burges.   Colein Lopslie, eldest soine of George Lopslie, is enterit burges, and sall pey xl s.; and hes hagbit and steilbonet, and is suoirne *more solito*. Pledge, Johne Layng.

Forester, burges.   Thomas Forester in Brigend, lawfull soine of vmquhile George Forester in Schiphawghe, is enterit burges and suorne *more solito*, and has payit xl s.

Fair.   Reuenowis of the last fair sett to Johne Cudbert for nyne poundis. Pledge George Norwell thesaurer.

27th October, 1595.

Waists feued, Stenesone.   The counsale agreis that James Stenesone sall haif seviu elnis east and west fra his warkhous end, and nyne elnis south and north at the west end of his hous, and that of the gait now lyand waist; for the quhilk he sall pay [*blank*].

Kynros.   The counsale condiscendis that Patrik Kynros haif the few of the pece waist betuix the twa pilleris nixt wast of Walter Hogis choip for payment of vj s. viij d. be yeir; and ane baillie to gif seising heirupone.

Schorte.   The counsale condiscendis that James Schorte haif the few of ane pece waist and chop quhilk was occupeit be the maister masoun for payment of viij s. be yeir; and ane baillie to gif seising heirupone.

10th November, 1595.

Sett of common good.   Peekis sett to Stenye Rytchie for xliiij merk, the ane half thairof payit and the wther half thairof at Witsounday. Pledge, Jhone Crawfuird, ilk fault ten pound at the counsallis discretioun. The said Stenye takand for ilk peck twa penneis, and gif it be within ane ferlet of aittis ane pennie. To be in nvmber fyftie peekis; and he and his cautioner obleisis thame to delyuer the saidis peckis at Mertymes nixtocume and to pay ten schillingis for ilk peck that inlaikis of the saidis fyftie peckis.

The watter of Fortht set to Alexander Young, baxster. Plaige Andro Cowane for xxxviij merkis.

Kingis Maill, gers maill and stallange, set to William Norie for viij li. x s. Plaige, Walter Watsone, tailyour.

Fesche skammellis set to James Wolsone for iiij li xl d.   Plaige Walter Sett of common good.
Cowane.

The burning irnes set to William Admune, baxster, for iiij merkis.

Gait dechtingis set to Arsbald Smyth for viij^xx iiij merkis; plaige, James Ramsay; with the lytill wolt.

Small customis set to Stene Akmane and Johne Craffurd for vj^xx vj merkis; plaige Arsbald Smyth.

24th November, 1595.

The counsall being convenit, efter sufficient tryall takin with the selleris of Candill. candill hes fundin the taweche bocht for xxxviij s., and thairfoir and in consideratioun of the derthe of victuall hes ordenit the candilmakeris to sell sufficient candill for xxxiiij d. the trois pound.

Efter resoning anent the officeris fies and thair inhabiliteis to serve as they Officers. wor wont, etc., thairfoir and for guid seruice heirefter, and that they sall beir thair halbertis dewle at all tymes and daylie, they hawe concludit the fowre officeris to hawe ten poundis yeirlie, to witt, ather of shame fyftie schillingis.

Archibald Allane, wreatter, enterit in burges and gild frelie gratis, hes suorne Allane enterit in burges and gild; minister. *more solito*, for the quhilk he sall trawell in the ministeris effairis vpoun the townis expenssis for the space of four yeiris nixt heirefter.   And failyeing of his diligence heirintill this act to be null.

11th December, 1595.

Ordanis the thesaurer to pay four pundis monie to the agent of burrowis for Agent of burrowis. persute the werkmen in clachannis and savorcoilis; and it salbe allowit be the counsale.

Jhone Donaldson, merchant, burges of this burgh, grantit him to haif ressauit Hospitale. fra the maisteris of the hospitale the scume of ane hundreth merkis, quhairwpon befoir Witsonday nixt he sall mak the hospitale sufficient securitye for ten merk the hundrethe.

26th January, 1595-6.

It is condiscendit be the haill counsall that the soume of ane hundreth merkis Minister. salbe tane for proffeit to the minister ay and qubill the ministeris stipend be gadderit in, quhilk the counsall ordanis to be done with diligence, and to pay the yeirlie proffeit thairof furth of the commonn guid; and failyeing of the said soume to be had for proffeit as said is to tak sua mekle of the commoun guid during the said space.

16th February, 1595-6.

Ordinance for the maltmen. The haill maltmen within this brucht is convict for the transgresing of the last ordinance and act maid anent the selling of malt, beiring that it sould not be licsume to thame to sell onie malt sen the last ordinance darrer nor ten pondis the boll quhill they sould haue meanit thame to the counsall, except Thomas Forrester and Jhone Scott and Alexander Thomsoun ; and thairfoir ordanit ilk ane of thame to be poyndit for four pondis to be vnforgewin, and to remane in waird quhill the samyne be payit ; and siclyk to sell the boll in tyme cuming for xvj merkis quhill thei meane thame selffis to the counsall wnder the paine foirsaid.

Anent the hychting of the pwpat. The haill counsall ordanes to tak sua mckle¹ of the commoun guid as will satisfie for the hychting of the pwpat.

8th March, 1595-6.

Council. At Sterling, the aucht day of Mercht 1595, in presens of the bailleis and counsall.

Thesaurar. George Noruell ressauit thesaurar for this present yeir.

19th March, 1595-6.

Council. At Sterling, the xix of Merche 1595, in presens of the prowest, bailleis and counsall.

Commissiouer, assemblie. Robert Alexander chosine for commissioner to the assemblie to be convenit in Edinburgh.

9th April, 1596.

At Sterling, the ix day of Apryill, 1596.

Baksteris. The prouest bailleis and counsale annullit and dischargit the act maid in the baxsteris fauouris in Nouember the yeir of God jᵐ vᶜ four scoir four yeiris, in respect it is notour to thame that they haif contrauenit the said act.

Minister. The counsale condiscendis that the minister haiff ane hundreth merkis of the reddeast of the commoun good of this burght for helping of him of this yeir in respect of the darth thairoff.

Wyne. The counsale ordanis that na wyne be sawld derrer nor vij s. iiij d. quhill the counsale be forder advysit, vnder the pane of x li.

¹ "xv pondis" deleted and "sua mckle" substituted.

30th April, 1596.

The haill counsale ordanis and decernis that in cais Andro Liddell, tailyeour, in ony tyme heirefter mak truble or dissobey the magistratis of this burgh, and beis ordourly convict thairfoir befoir the saidis prouest and bailleis, that he then and in that cais tyne his fredome and be banist this burgh during the will of the saidis prouest and bailleis ; becaus the said Andro is convict this day befoir William Henderson, constable depute, in his awin blood, throw trubling of Robert Robeson, *alias* Tennent, pewderar. *For Liddell, dissobeying magistratis.*

The prouest, bailleis, and haill counsale hes gevin the answer to the minister that they will tak sic ordour as in thaim lyis efter thair power agane the nixt yeir for ane helper to him in his doctrene as thair abeletie will permit, with the ministeris avyse. *For the minister.*

10th Maij, 1596.

Walter Cowane, bailyie, chosunc and electit be the counsall to be direct in commissioner to the conventioun presentlie appontit to be haldin at Edinburgh the xx day of Maij instant. *Commissioner to convention.*

The thrie woltis set to James Vre, Dauid Nicoll, and Mergrat Alexander, ilk wolt for sex pondis. *The woltis sett.*

14th May, 1596.

The counsale ordanis the thesaurer to get furth off Lynlythgw ane just forlett and ane pek, vpone the expensis of the burgh, with diligence. *Forlettis.*

14th June, 1596.

Walter Cowane ordanit to be commissioner at Abirdene ; and the thesaurer to pay his expensis accordinglie. *Commissioner for Abirdene.*

16th July, 1596.

James Bog, seruitour to his Maiestie, euterit in burges and gild, hes sworn, and that as ane that mareit Issobell Norvell, dochter eldest to vmquhill Johne Norvell, burges of this burch, hes payit xxvij d.; plege for wyne and wax, Alexander Cowsland. *Servitor to King, burges and gild.*

30th July, 1596.

The haill counsale condiscendis and decreis that na wyne be sauld derrer within this burgh nor viij s. iiij d. vnder the pane of v li. for ilk falt that contrauenis. *For wyne.*

Duncane Paterson, dene of gild and burges of this burgh, band and oblist him to satisfie to Jhone Tailyefeir, massoun, the somme of ij pundis money for beiting of the brig of Iunerallom within terme of law ; and the haile counsale ordanis the *Toun of Sterling, Tailyefeir, massoun.*

thesaurer of the said burgh to answer the soume of fyftie merkis for the said Duncanis releiff, lyik as they oblist thame to freyth, releif, and kepe skaythles the said Duncane of the act abone writtin and haill pointis, articlis and claussis thairof, at all handis haifand enteres. And forder sall seik the presbeterie, for releif of j^c merkis of the said first soum of ij^c li., and consentis that executoriallis pas as effeiris.

11th August, 1596.

For Falkland: repressing Islesmen.

The haill counsale condescendis that Jhone Patersoune pas to Falkland and thair to treat with his Maiestie and rest of burrowis anent the proclamatioun direct be his Hienes for raising of men of weir and paying of monie to that effect for repressing of the Ilismen. And ordanis the thesaurer to satisfie him his expenssis quhilk salbe allowit to him in his comptis.

7th September, 1596.

Staig Silver.

Staig siluer sett to James Ramsay for xij li. Plege, Archibald Smyth.

Fair.

Reuenewis of the fair sett to Stene Aikman for x li. Plege, James Ramsay.

24th September, 1596.

Commissioner

Jhone Patersoun and Archebald Alschunder, baillie, ordanit to serue for commissioners appointit to pas to the conventioun to be haldin at Dumfermbling the xxviij of this instant.

Kinross, Burges.

Malcome Kinros, saidler, enterit in burges, and hes suorne more solito, gratis, for sustentatioun of the barnis of vmquhill Dauid Kinros his father and guid mother.

4th October, 1596.

Provost.

Jhone Murray of Touchadame, prouest.

Bailies.

Bailleis:—Walter Cowane, Archebald Alexshunder, James Schorte, Jhone Miller.

Clerk.

Johne Mwscheit resauit clerk and sworne for this yeir, more solito.

Council.

Jhone Donaldsoun, deane of gild ; Duncane Patersoun, Robert Alexander, Androw Cowane, Walter Neische, Jhone Schearar, William Ayssoun, Jhone Patersoun.

For the craiftmen:—Robert Robertsone, convener; Jhone Henderson, baxster; James Allane, flescheour; Alexander Havin, skynner; Andro Thomeson, tailyeour; Robert Houstoun, cordiner; Moreis Ewyn, wobster; Duncan Patersoun, visitour of maltmen.

Malt.

Malt, ten pundis; aill, xviij d.

Wheat.

Quhyte, auchtene merks, and the pace accordinglie.

Tauche.

Tauche xxxvj s. the stane ; the pund of good and sufficient candill for xxx d.

21st October, 1596.

The counsall concluidis that the prowest, Archibald Alexander, and Walter Mylnis. Cowane, bailleis, and Robert Robesoun, alias Tennand, powdernr, pas to Thomas Erskeine of Gogar, and thair treat and commoun with him concerning his pretendit rycht of the mylnis and landis within this brught, vpoun sic conditiounes and restrictiounes as salbe set doun to thame be the counsall.

Rewynwies of the Latter Fair sett to Stewyne Aikmane for aucht pondis Latter fair. monie.   Pledge, Archibald Smyth.

25th October, 1596.

The counsale all in aue voce fand and ordanit that the malt mycht be sauld for Malt, aill. x li. the boll, with consent of the convener of the maltmen, and aill xviij d. tho pynt, vnder the pane of v li. for ilk contrauentioun.

10th November, 1596.

Peckis set to Stewin Richie for fyfte merkis; wattir of Forthe set to Duncan Common Patersone for twentie twa pundis; Kings maill, girs maill and stallage set to good. Johnne Hoge for viij li.; gait dichtingis sett to Archibald Smyth for twa hunderyit and ten merkis; fische skemmillis sett to Johnne Young for viij li.; small customes set to Stewin Aikman and Johnne Craufurd for sevin scoir merkis, with libertie to tak twa pennyeis of the laid and twa pennyois vecht; the carkage beif j peunye and the muttoun ane half pennye.

22nd November, 1596.

Duncane Patersone ressauit thesaurar for this yeir and hes sworn.   Thesaurer.

4th December, 1596.

The counsale ordanis Robert Alexschander to travell and treat with the maister Commissioner, of werk, William Schaw, anent the almoushous, and to obtene his rycht thairoff, gif almoushous. it in him lyis.

31st January, 1596-7.

The counsale hes ordanit Robert Alexschunder, Jhon Patersoun, Jhone Hender- Firlettis, jug. soun, baxster, and William Gillespy, maltman, to mett the firlettis with the jug the morne efter prayaris, and to report the sufficiency of the mesour.

4th February, 1596-7.

Firlettis.   The counsale ordanis Robert Alexschunder, Jhone Patersone, Jhone Hender-
sone, baxster, and William Gillespy, maltman, with advyse of James Stenesone,
maltman, to tak to Edinburgh with the firlettis, with ony vther quhom they pleas to
appoint, and that vpon Monunday nixt be x houris befoir nvne.

21st February, 1596-7.

Walter   The haill counsall hes condescendit and appointit Walter Cowane, baillie, com-
Cowane, com- missioner for the conventioun appointit to be haldin at Perth the last day of this
missioner.
instant, and ordanis the thesaurer to satisfie his expenssis.

Malcolme   Efter waird of court, Malcolme Burne in Gogar is enterit nychtbour and burges
Burne, burges within this brught, as immediat eldar brother to wmquhile George Burne; hes suorne
more solito and payit four pondis monie.

21st March, 1596-7.

Walter   Walter Cowane, baillie, is electit commissioner to convene with the rest of the
Cowane, com- commissioneris of burrowis at Edinburgh the first of Apryll nextocume, and als to
missioner ;
almoushous. treat and commoun with William Schaw, maister of werk, for the almoushous within
this brught.

2nd May, 1597.

Cowane, com-   Walter Cowane ordanit to be send in commissioner to Dundee, conforme to
missioner. the Kingis missive, and the thesaurer to satifie his expenssis.

Flescheours.   James Allane, deakon of the flescheouris, being accusit for abusing of the owtland
flescheouris in takyn of four penneis for ilk yong vaill enterand within this burgh
to be sauld [and thairby] contrauening the auld vse obseruit in sic cassis, confessit the
[breking] of the said auld vse and thairfoir becomo in the counsalis will for the same.
And in cais any contrauentioun salbe maid heirefter be ony of the deakonis that is
or salbe heirefter, the first falt to be xx li., and sua furth ilk falt xx li., to be payit
to the prouest and bailleis to the common vse of thame as they sall think gud.

Followis the ordinance:—Ane penny, twa scheip; ilk cow, ane penny; ilk twa
yeir auld and yeir auld vaill, ane penny; ane sowcand vaill, ane penny; twa lambis,
ane penny; twa kiddis, ane penny; the breking of ane cow, twa s.; the breking of
ane greit and small vaill, with oxin, ane sowyne, ilk pece ourheid, twa s.   And that
nane brek the premissis bot freemen, and that sufficientlie, equalie and justlie, [and
that at] the tyme the nychtbouris desyris thame, and that in cais the deakon failye
heirin he to be poindit for x li. for ilk falt, the same being tryit.   And that na

landwart flescheour sell nor brek ony flesche befoir aught houris in the morning vnder the pane of fourty s. for ilk falt.

James Allane convict in xl s. vnlaw.

The counsale ordanis the wapinschaw to be this day xx dayis and the toun to be in thair best array the xxiij day of Maij instant.

to Wappinschaw.

13th May, 1597.

In presens of the bailleis, James Wilsoun, swordslipper, is enterit in burges of this burgh, is sworne and payit four pund.

Sympsoun, burges.

25th July, 1597.

The counsall ordanis euerie day twa nychtbouris at the brig and twa at the port, and to abyd thairat euerie day fra fywe houris in the morning to aucht houris eftirnvne, daylic, during the space of the brutt of the pest, and that for outhalding of outland begeris.

Pest; outland beggaris.

2nd September, 1597.

The counsale ordanis that na persone within the toun, nather nychtbour nor vther, cum within the samyn bot at the porte or brig, vnder the pane of x li. ilk falt, and that thai bring sufficient testimoniall quhair they wer the day of befor and obtene the bailleis licence or thai cum in. And siclyik that nane within this burgh ressaue ony stranger within thair houssis bot first thai schaw the same to ane of the bailleis and get thair licence thairto.

Pest.

INDEX.

INDEX.

Horning purchased by vicar, 213.
Horses, stable for, belonging to convent of
Aberbrothock, 13; pasturage for, 14. (See
Staigs.)
Hospital, fines applied for clothing poor of,
209; annual rent applied to, 214; money
lent by masters of, 219. (See Almshouse.)
Hospital of St. James, sasine of, to be given
canons of Cambuskenneth, 26; life-rent of
lands of, reserved to John Palmer, 26; grant
by James II. to burgh of patronage and
lands of, 36-38, 184; annualrent from, to
St. James' altar, 49; confirmation of grant
by Charles I., 130, 142, 159, 163.
Hospitals, provision for, 93, 96; power to re-
pair ruinous places and apply same to. 95,
96. (See Ministry and Hospitality; also
Spittell's Hospital and Cowane's Hospital.
Hospitals of Stirling and Torphichen, duties
payable to, 16.
Hostilage in Stirling for abbot and convent of
Aberbrothoc, 12-14.
House of Lords, commonwealth established
without a, 169, 170.
Houston, Robert, cordiner, 222.
Hugh, John, son of, 20; son of Thomas, 133.
Hume, lord, (Alexander), 64, 66, 71.
Hunter, Henry, 198.
—— Maurice, bailie, 15.
Huntlie, carl of (George), 99.
Huntyngton, earl of, (John), 9.
Huny, John, 186, 207.
—— Walter, 207.
Hutone (Huttoun), John, 213, 214; webster,
215.

Inglis, Alexander, clerk register, 206.
Inglisman, Sir John Clerk alias, chaplain 188.
Inneralloun, bridge of, 221.
—— mill of, 202.
Innerdale, lord, 167.
Ireland, 124, 171, 175.
—— Thomas of, 20.

Island, grant of, to abbey of Cambuskenneth,
5.
Islesmen, repression of, 222.

James I., King, ordinance by, as to holding
parliament or four burghs, 34, 35.
James II., King, charter by, instituting a new
fair in Stirling, 30-32; charter by, freeing
burgesses of custom on salt and skins, 33-34;
letters by, appointing parliament of Four
Burghs to be held at Edinburgh yearly, 34-
36; charter by, to burgh of Stirling of
patronage of St. James Hospital, &c., 36-38,
184; act of parliament of, as to dyers selling
cloth, 80, 82; confirmation by Charles I. of
charters by, 119, 129, 130, 131.
James III., King, confirmation by, to Malcolm
Flemyng of site of Tolbooth. 41, 185; acts
of parliament of, against craftsmen using
merchandice, 81-83; grant by, to Queen
Margaret of lordship of Tulycultre, 202.
James IV., King, gift by, to burgh of sheriffship,
60-64, 113; grant by, to burgh of patronage of St. Laurence's altar, 64; charter by,
to burgh of Auld Park and patronage of St.
Michael's altar, 69-71; lands of Gallowhills
granted by burgh to, 69; act of parliament
of, as to privilege of using merchandice, 82;
grant by, to Robert Erskine, of sheriffship
of Stirling, 113; confirmation by Charles I.
of charters by, 119, 130, 131, 132; gift to
St. Michael's altar for weal of soul of, 195.
James V., King, charter by, ratifying acts as
to merchandice and charging enforcement
of laws against unfreemen, 80-85; confirmation by, of grant to the altar of St. Michael,
195; grant to St. Katherine's altar for weal
of soul of, and for soul of his Queen, 200.
James VI., King, remission by, to inhabitants
of Stirling for treasonable proceedings, 106-
8; baptism of Prince Henry, eldest son of,
215; servitor to, entered burgess, 221.
James, St., hospital of. (See Hospital.)

2 H